STUDIES I

Edited by

Robert Bernasconi
University of Memphis

A ROUTLEDGE SERIES

Studies in Philosophy

Robert Bernasconi, *General Editor*

HEIDEGGER ON EAST-WEST DIALOGUE

Anticipating the Event

Lin Ma

Routledge
Taylor & Francis Group

NEW YORK AND LONDON

First published 2008
by Routledge
270 Madison Ave, New York, NY 10016

Simultaneously published in the UK
by Routledge
2 Park Square, Milton Park, Abingdon, Oxon OX14 4RN

Routledge is an imprint of the Taylor & Francis Group, an informa business

Transferred to Digital Printing 2009

© 2008 Taylor & Francis

Typeset in Adobe Garamond by IBT Global

Library of Congress Cataloging-in-Publication Data
Ma, Lin, 1970–
   Heidegger on East-West dialogue : anticipating the event / by Lin Ma.
      p. cm. — (Studies in philosophy)
   Includes bibliographical references and index.
   ISBN 0-415-95719-2
   1. Heidegger, Martin, 1889–1976.   I. Title.

B3279.H49M23 2008
303.48'2182105— dc22   2007033734

ISBN10: 0-415-95719-2 (hbk)
ISBN10: 0-415-87214-6 (pbk)
ISBN10: 0-203-92778-8 (ebk)

ISBN13: 978-0-415-95719-9 (hbk)
ISBN13: 978-0-415-87214-0 (pbk)
ISBN13: 978-0-203-92778-6 (ebk)

Contents

Abbreviations of Heidegger's Works

GA	1975-	*Gesamtausgabe*
BT	[1927]	*Being and Time*
CP	[1936–38]	*Contributions to Philosophy (From Enowning)*; also referred to as "the *Contributions*"
DL	[1953/54]	"A Dialogue on Language: Between a Japanese and an Inquirer"; also referred to as "A Dialogue"
EHP	[2000a]	*Elucidations of Hölderlin's Poetry*
ET	[1930b]	"On the Essence of Truth"
HHI	[1942]	*Hölderlin's Hymn "The Ister"*
ID	[1955–57]	*Identity and Difference*
IM	[1935]	*Introduction to Metaphysics*
HJC	[2003c]	*The Heidegger-Jaspers Correspondence*
KD	[1958c]	"Die Kunst und das Denken"
LH	[1946b]	"Letter on Humanism"
M	[1952]	"Moira"

OM   [1936–46]   "Overcoming Metaphysics"

OWL   [1971]   *On the Way to Language*

TB   [1962–64]   *On Time and Being*

QT   [1953a]   "The Question concerning Technology"

WCT   [1951/52]   *What Is Called Thinking?*

WIM   [1929]   *What Is Metaphysics?*

WIP   [1956]   *What Is Philosophy?*

ZS   [2001]   *Zollikon Seminars*

The year(s) in square brackets conforms to the entry in the bibliography.

Note on Referencing

I have adopted the following conventions of reference. Secondary literature is referred to in the main text by author's last name, year of publication (in accordance with the bibliography) and page number in round brackets. If an author has only one publication mentioned in the bibliography, the year of publication is sometimes omitted. If the same source is cited several times in succession, only the page number is given in round brackets. The bibliographic details of a few works that are remote from the theme of this book are given in notes.

References to Heidegger's work are given either in square or round brackets without his name. Since it is rather important for my purpose to indicate the year when Heidegger expressed a certain view, I give the reference in square brackets according to the year/years when he made the statement. Often-cited works by Heidegger are referred to by abbreviations (without square brackets). When possible I cite from English versions of Heidegger's works (with "tr. m." indicating important modifications). Page numbers are given as [English edition]/[German edition]. In most cases the German edition cited is the *Gesamtausgabe*. When only the German version is available, the English translations are of my responsibility. When more than one edition or translation is mentioned in the bibliography, references are to the edition first mentioned in the bibliographic entry.

When giving the German original for a word or phrase in the main text, I place it in round brackets; when in a citation, I place it in square brackets. Unless otherwise noted, an omission sign in a citation indicates my own omission. When emphasis occurs in a citation (usually in the form of italics), I use "em. or." and "em. ad." to indicate "emphasis original" and "emphasis added" respectively.

Chinese text is usually given in both pinyin and characters. In citations or titles the original transliteration of Chinese words is often left unchanged. Chinese and Japanese names are given in the order of family name being followed by given names.

Acknowledgments

The support of Jaap van Brakel, the most conscientious reader of different versions of the draft, is indispensable to the research carried out in this book. He is one of the few philosophers who pay serious attention to the vexing issue of East-West dialogue that has remained excluded from the proper domain of philosophy. Robert Bernasconi ascribed considerable significance to this study, which, without his recommendation, would not have reached the readers in time. David Kolb generously provided me with valuable comments and suggestions after reading an earlier draft of this book, from which I benefited during the process of revision. Graham Parkes has also expressed positive opinions. I appreciate his broad-mindedness concerning my discussion of his writings.

When I was studying at Beijing University from 1987 to 1993, the image of *the* philosopher Heidegger was dominant in Chinese academic circles. My first attempt at a study under his influence was a Heideggerian elucidation of the poetry of Ruan Ji (210–263), whom I regarded as a "poet in an age of poverty." Without studying at Leuven, I may have been following the common practice of complacently relying on Heidegger or on any other philosopher. I am grateful to all my teachers at the Institute of Philosophy, K. U. Leuven for their stimulating lectures and for their other forms of presence. A special note is due to Karin de Boer, visiting lecturer during 2000–2001, who encouraged me to think for myself in philosophical studies.

K. U. Leuven has financially supported my study and research at Leuven, first in terms of an inter-faculty cooperation scholarship, then in terms of a grant from a research project and a "mandate" (research fellowship) awarded by K. U. Leuven Research Council. The Research Council has also offered me travel grants to present my work at a range of academic meetings in the United States, Europe, and China. I hereby express my gratitude for this continuous support.

An earlier exploration of "Heidegger's Comportment toward East-West Dialogue" (the title of the essay) written with J. van Brakel appeared in *Philosophy East and West* 56 (4), 2006. A version of Chapter six was published in *Asian Philosophy* 16 (3), 2006 under the title "Deciphering Heidegger's Connection with the *Daodejing*." Part of my reading of "A Dialogue on Language" appears in *Dao: A Journal of Comparative Philosophy* 4 (2), 2005. I am grateful to the editors of these journals, namely, Roger T. Ames, Brian Carr, Yong Huang, and to J. van Brakel for granting me permission to use these materials.

Introduction

This book traces a particular theme concealed in Heidegger's thinking and works, which has as of yet not been made the focus of a thorough and sustained investigation either because of the complexity of the subject or because of Heidegger's vacillation and evasiveness with respect to it. This theme is the emergence, course and intricacies of his reflection upon East-West dialogue. A systematic inquiry into this *Holzweg* in studies devoted to Heidegger is indispensable for thinking through his formidable legacy bequeathed to both Western and non-Western philosophers.

One cannot neglect the milieu in which Heidegger's philosophy was developed. In the earlier half of the twentieth century, the Western world was faced with grave crises. On the one hand, the "malaise of culture" predominated everyday human experience. As Safranski states, "The worldview essays of the period were marked by an uneasy sense of a declining, perverted, or alienated world" (1998, 152). Spengler's *The Decline of the West* was selling in huge numbers of copies.[1] Dadaism burst out against expressionism, conservatism, and hypocritical metaphysical hymns. Its declaration "rips to shreds all slogans of ethics, culture, and soulfulness" (152).

On the other hand, there was an acute sense of challenge by non-Western thought. Enlightenment thinkers commended and benefited from these "other" traditions in the seventeenth and eighteenth centuries.[2] Soon afterward, the defence of the Western tradition culminated in Hegel's grandiose speculative system wherein a variety of "cultures" were each meted out a place on the ladder of the development of the absolute spirit. When history enters into the twentieth century, Western philosophers are confronted with, in Husserl's words, "a plethora of works" about Indian philosophy, Chinese philosophy, etc,, which "are placed on a plane with Greek philosophy and are taken as merely different historical forms under one and the same idea of culture" (1935, 279).

My invocation of the historical background in the early twentieth century should not be taken to imply that my reading of Heidegger has been simplistically mediated through the lens of historical and cultural conditions. These brief references serve as a reminder that Heidegger has pursued his intellectual course in this milieu of the malaise of culture. In *Being and Time,* he describes the fallen state of *Dasein* as "confin[ing] its interest to the multiformity of possible types, directions, and standpoints of philosophical activity *in the most exotic and alien of cultures*" (*BT* 43/21; em. ad.). In *What Is Called Thinking?* [1951/52], with reference to the "lack of thought" in his age, Heidegger states,

> This tune [lack of thought] is familiar to us all *ad nauseam* from the standard appraisals of the present age. A generation ago it was "The Decline of the West." Today we speak of "loss of center." People everywhere trace and record the decay, the destruction, the imminent annihilation of the world. . . . The world, men find, is not just out of joint but tumbling away into the nothingness of absurdity. (*WCT* 29/30)

> Even in the decade from 1920 to 1930, the European world of ideas could not cope any longer with what was then looming on the horizon. What is to become of a Europe that wants to rebuild itself with the stage props of those years after World War I? A plaything for the powers and for the immense native strength of the Eastern peoples. (*WCT* 67/71)

Heidegger was not satisfied to remain a Hamlet in a world out of joint. One of his major concerns is to re-invigorate the impoverished spiritual strength of the Western world that is faced with the threat posed by nihilism and Eastern traditions. In the *Spiegel* interview, he famously claims that the transformation of the Western tradition cannot happen because of "any takeover [*Übernahme*] of Zen Buddhism or any other Eastern experiences of the world," and that "thinking itself can be transformed only by a thinking which has the same origin and calling."[3]

In spite of this central concern, Heidegger has manifested considerable interest in Eastern thinking, especially since the 1940s. In six of his essays and letters he cites from five chapters of the *Daodejing,* the most well-known ancient Chinese scripture. From time to time he makes inquiries about words or notions from Asian heritage, such as the Japanese words for art, language, appearance, and essence, and the Sanskrit words for Being, beings, unconcealedness, and forgetfulness. Furthermore, in the 1950s, he speaks of "the inevitable dialogue with the East Asian world" [1953b, 157f/41], and of "the realm of possible dialogue" between "the language of Europe and that of East Asia" [1955a, 321/424]. In the 1960s he makes such enigmatic remarks as, "The encounter with the Asiatic . . . is the verdict of what the fate of Europe will be" [1962a, 228], and "it has seemed urgent to me that a dialogue take place with the thinkers of what is to us the Eastern world" [1969b, 721].

The aim of this book is to provide a systematic and balanced treatment of Heidegger's reflection on the question of East-West dialogue against the background of his central philosophical concerns and orientations. I will sometimes use the phrase "Heidegger's comportment toward East-West dialogue." The word "comportment" translates the German word *Verhalten,* which originally denotes conscious or unconscious behavior in regard to individuals, animals and substances. It is also used when the behavior in question is the taking of an attitude or stance with respect to, for example, a country or government. The phrase "taking of an attitude" has the connotation that one's attitude does not always remain the same, that there are always changes and modifications in different situations. It also has the implication that, instead of indicating a static mental state, an attitude which is to be taken is more closely related to one's particular choices, for example, what one chooses to study and what not, where one prefers to travel and where not. One of the cognate words of *Verhalten* is *Verhältnis,* meaning "proportion, relationship." The correlated transitive verb *verhalten* means "to hold back, restrain"; hence *sich verhalten* suggests "to restrain oneself," as well as "to relate oneself to, to comport oneself."

What are involved in my investigation of how Heidegger is related to the issue of East-West dialogue are the remarks he makes, the action he takes, the modifications of the attitude he expressed, and the manner in which he often shies away from directly addressing the theme of East-West dialogue. I decipher many of his ambiguous and perplexing remarks or gestures by restoring them to their immediate and broad context. I delve into relevant presuppositions, emphases, and ambivalences when Heidegger confronts the issue of East-West dialogue and attempt to trace out a reasonable account of the place that a consideration of East-West dialogue occupies in the framework of his thinking.

A basic problematic with contributions devoted to Heidegger's Asian connection is the following. In quoting what they consider to be important evidence for their highly positive judgment on Heidegger's relation with Asian thought, some authors have taken insufficient care. Rather than checking the original reference or minding the context of the materials, they have relied on second-hand or third-hand citations. Proceeding from a few ambiguous or unreliable "facts," they have drawn highly speculative conclusions.

For instance, in his influential essay "West-East Dialogue: Heidegger and Lao-tzu," Otto Pöggeler writes, "Heidegger himself maintained, moreover, that from early on he had worked with Japanese scholars, 'but had learned more from Chinese.'"[4] For the citation "but had learned more from Chinese" Pöggeler gives the source as: page 102 of Hans Fischer-Barnicol's paper "Spiegelungen—Vermittlungen" that appeared in *Erinnerungen an Martin Heidegger* (Neske 1977). This remark, attributed to Heidegger, is quoted in many publications with exactly the same reference provided.[5] In fact, on reading Hans Fischer-Barnicol's text (1977), it transpires that there is no evidence that Heidegger has ever said such a thing. That from early on Heidegger had worked with Japanese scholars, but had learned more from Chinese, is in fact a passing remark made by the author of the article himself.[6] Since almost all of Heidegger's remarks bearing on East-West dialogue are sketchy or indirect, and occur on various complex occasions in an incidental or fleeting way, it demands careful investigation and critical evaluation before any assertion is made with respect to the meaning, intention, and implication of these articulations.

Some scholars have attempted to bring Heidegger's thinking to bear on the issue of intercultural dialogue or theory of comparative philosophy. I call this genre of writing Heidegger-inspired discourse. Certainly, such a discourse does not need to be concerned with whether Heidegger would find their theses acceptable, since the essence of a discourse that draws on a certain philosopher lies in application or expansion of a cue found in his writings. Yet the majority of contributors to such discourses have ascribed a highly positive stance toward a dialogue with the East to Heidegger *himself* without proper qualifications. Some of them take liberty with a few words by him and attribute to them implausible interpretations in isolation from both the immediate textual context and the broad embedment of the latter in his thinking. Some others, in acknowledging Heidegger's ambivalence on the East-West relation, have attempted to explain away the negative elements of his attitude toward a dialogue with Asian traditions. In my view, their understanding of Heidegger is not immune from the influence of Gadamer's neutralization of Heidegger's commitment to the Greek historic beginning.[7] While Heidegger is surely not Gadamer, the latter philosopher's thought, which has been most readily adopted by contributors to intercultural discourses, is not unquestionable.

The intention of this book is not to make an addition to either Heidegger-inspired discourses or comparative philosophy as commonly practiced. My primary concern is with the ways in which Heidegger *himself* has conceived the question of East-West dialogue and I base my examination on comprehensive studies of almost all of Heidegger's own texts relevant to the theme. One of my objectives is to present a Wittgensteinian "perspicuous representation" of those frequently cited observations by Heidegger. That is, to demonstrate what they do *not* mean and what they *do* or *could* mean by restoring them back to their proper contexts and by showing their place within the scaffold of his thinking. It is my belief that, when well-informed of Heidegger's own position and the relevant problematics involved in it, a Heidegger-inspired discourse will become more pertinent and effective.

Insofar as this book aims at approaching an adequate understanding of an important and yet complicated aspect of Heidegger's thinking: his comportment toward East-West dialogue, it is embedded in the scholarship under the rubric of "Heidegger studies." While noticing the widespread application of Heidegger's philosophy to Eastern thought, Sheehan suggests that his thought in these publications has often been "creatively" understood. This is perhaps why Sheehan hesitates including them into the mainstream of Heidegger studies (2001a, 185). The authors of a large percentage of publications comparing Heidegger and Eastern thought seem to have no intention of situating their writings in relation to the state of art of "Heidegger studies," to which belong predominantly professional philosophers working in the West.

I propose an approach that is internal and external at once. In terms of being internal, I probe Heidegger's writings carefully and attempt to discern and bring out the subtleties and nuances of his thought; I situate my interpretation of his corpus against the exegetical tradition of Heidegger studies. In terms of being external, I do not abide within the horizon of Heidegger's thinking by way of emulating his style of philosophizing, or of following up its lines of development. Rather, I examine his ideas and views in the broad milieu of the contemporary development of the philosophical enterprise, in which non-Western philosophy is receiving increasingly more attention, and continental philosophy is moving beyond Heidegger's legacy in which Western philosophy is claimed to be a tautology (*WIP* 31/30).

In concrete terms, I strive to inform this study of the tradition and new developments of the scholarship on Chinese philosophy. For example, in citing chapter 11 from the *Daodejing* in his essay "The Uniqueness of the Poet" [1943b], Heidegger changes the word *Wesen* and *Wesenheit* (which translates the word *yong*) in the German version he consults into *Sein*. Some scholars takes this modification to be the indubitable evidence for the great extent to which Heidegger has engaged in a dialogue with Laozi, since he has read his notions of "ontological difference" and "Being" into Laozi's thinking (see Chapter six). However, according to current scholarship on traditional Chinese thought, a concern with the question of Being, either in the sense of traditional Western metaphysics or as defined in Heidegger's own philosophy, is absent in ancient Chinese philosophy. Although in the past the Chinese words *you* and *wu* have in fact often been translated as Being and Nothing, there has been a consensus that they cannot be identified with Western philosophical notions. The word *you* overlaps with the sense of "having." It means "to be present" or "to be around," and has nothing to do with how the terms "Being" or "existence" are used in Western philosophy or in Heidegger's thought. Treating Heidegger's *reading* his notions *into* Laozi's thinking as incontestable evidence that he is a Daoist or intercultural thinker betrays the fact that those who subscribe to this theory are still adhering to the outdated practice of employing Western notions as the standard of philosophy.

One more remark is the following. Falling under expressions such as "Asian philosophy (thought, traditions)" and "Eastern thinking (thought, ideas)" are normally Indian, Chinese, and Japanese philosophical traditions.[8] One must be aware that within each of these philosophical traditions, there are numerous differentiations of schools and lineages. Therefore, it is almost impossible to provide a single set of neat characterizations of the "house" of "Chinese philosophy," let alone to proffer the "essential" features of "Eastern thinking." For instance, there is no consensus as to whether the Daoist privileging of "nothingness" should be taken to be the fundamental character of Chinese tradition. Furthermore, not only is it highly disputable whether Heidegger's nothing and the Eastern nothing are "the Same," it is also notable that the Buddhist nothing (*śūnyatā*) is not the same as the Daoist nothing (*kong* 空). Moreover, within each tradition, there have always been alterations and modifications of the nothing. Nagarjuna's nothing (*śūnyatā*) is not the same as Japanese Zen-Buddhist nothing; the nothing (*kū*) of the Kyoto School philosophers is again different from these two versions. In a word, one should guard against a monolithic way of understanding philosophy, thought, and tradition.

I now turn to an overview of the chapters in this book to give the reader an idea of the lines along which I carry out this investigation.

Chapter one delineates the contours of Heidegger's Asian connection. I give an account of the reception of Heidegger's work in Japan and comparative literature drawing on Heidegger and Daoism. I present a survey of the development of discourses bearing on Heidegger's relation to Asian thought, some of which argue for a direct influence of East Asian traditions on his thinking. Last, I introduce the background of Heidegger's essay "A Dialogue on Language" [1953/54], which is an important text for deciphering his view on East-West dialogue.

Reflections on the question of language and of Being have informed the entirety of Heidegger's philosophical life (Chapter two). Heidegger attempts to find a way of transforming Western language(s), the language of Being, by excavating the untapped resources of saying within the very language of Being. In my view, neither relativistic nor universalistic readings of Heidegger's thought are adequate.

Heidegger argues for an intimate relation between technology on the one hand, and Being, metaphysics, and philosophy on the other (Chapter three). According to him, the present world, which is in the grip of the *Ge-stell,* is a necessary unfolding of the history of Being. Heidegger insists that a reversal ("the other beginning") can only be achieved by self-transformation of Western-European thinking, because this is the *topos* where Being has shown itself in the beginning of history and has determined the destiny that unfolds in the *Ge-stell.* Almost all of Heidegger's oblique references to East-West dialogue appear in the context of a deep concern with the *Ge-stell,* and with the primary task of a dialogue with early Greek thinkers.

In the context of his elucidations on Hölderlin's poetry, Heidegger urges that the journey abroad to "the foreign" is a necessity for becoming-at-home (Chapter four). The stages in the process of not-being-at-home, passing-through-the-foreign, and becoming-at-home can easily be taken to be ontological terminology. However, the words "homeland" and "foreign" do not refer to randomly chosen geographical places. Heidegger ascribes to them both ontological significance and particular ontic references. Ontologically speaking, both "homeland" and the "foreign" are thought world-historically as "nearness to the source" (*LH* 257/338), that is, in terms of their essential connection with the unfolding of the history of Being. Ontically speaking, they are tied to the German and Greek Dasein, who share an "intimate" (*inniger*) relation. The tripartite delineation of homeland, the journey abroad, and homecoming is not intended by Heidegger to be an account for intercultural encounter, as some authors have suggested. In trying to bring Heidegger's writings to bear upon intercultural dialogue, one cannot completely ignore the original meaning of his terminology and relevant aspects of his thinking.

The misreading of the phrase "the few other great beginnings" in Heidegger's lecture "Hölderlin's Earth and Heaven" (1959) is one of the most prominent cases where a grand conclusion is drawn with respect to Heidegger's relation to Asian thought or his thinking on intercultural dialogue. A number of scholars have identified this phrase "the few other great beginnings" with non-Western, in particular East Asian traditions. Through a careful reading of this essay, I show that this phrase does not bear on East Asian traditions. Used as the plural form of the term "great beginning," the most plausible reference of "the few other great beginnings" is the four-fold

of heaven, earth, god and man, which belong in the sameness of the beginning of the in-finite relation. The four-fold is inseparably related to Greece,
which is the great beginning.

In the 1930s and again in 1962, Heidegger speaks of the "confrontation [*Auseinandersetzung*] with the Asiatic" of "the Greek Dasein" [1962a,
228] (Chapter five). The Asiatic under Heidegger's pen is the "greatest opposite" to Western philosophy, or "the most foreign and most difficult," which
held on to an incomprehensible and irrational notion of fate (*Fatum*). Furthermore, this confrontation is single-sidedly conceived. The West unilaterally overcomes the opposition of Asiatic mystic thinking. How the encounter
with the Greek affects the Asiatic side is left unthought. Heidegger may have
deliberately left the designation of the Asiatic vague so as to create room for
drawing implications for the contemporary world situation from that historical event of overcoming the Asiatic. When commenting on the early Greeks'
confrontation with the Asiatic in 1962, Heidegger has softened his militant
tone in the 1930s.

Although Heidegger exempts himself from a systematic and sustained
engagement with Asian thought, either on the basis of the belief that a true
encounter between East and West would only be possible after the West has
achieved a renewal of its own tradition, or for the reason of his ontic (which
is also ontological) ignorance of Asian languages, in actual practice Heidegger does engage with sources from Asian thought on various occasions.
Careful discernment is needed in ascertaining these encounters (Chapters
six and seven).

In 1946 Heidegger collaborates with Hsiao Shih-yi in translating several chapters from the *Daodejing*. Nevertheless, the actuality of such an event
alone cannot form the basis for exceedingly positive conclusion in relation to a
"dialogue" between Heidegger and Laozi. When his reference to the word *dao*
and his citations from the *Daodejing* are subject to intense contextual analyses (Chapter six), it can be seen that *dao* cannot be said to be the guideword
of Heidegger's thinking, and that he has carefully selected existing translations, and in some cases made modifications, in order to suit Laozi's verses to
his own philosophizing. He does not seem to concern himself with what this
scripture has to say, apart from its adaptability to his reflection on Being.

Chapter seven considers the complexity of Heidegger's connection with
Asian languages. Disparate strands of thoughts and considerations are entangled together in his relevant claims. On the one hand, he suggests that there
is a radical inaccessibility of these languages, and that it is impossible for him
to engage with Asian thought because of linguistic differences. On the other
hand, he makes inquires about words in these languages that might correspond

to some of his key notions important for his project of re-enacting the other beginning of Western philosophy. These signs and gestures apparently point to reverse directions and entail irreconcilable implications. I try to provide a balanced and convincing account so far as possible for Heidegger's reflection on Asian languages. In the process of my discussion I introduce quite some of Heidegger's little-known remarks in letters and conversations in the 1950s and 1960s, his inquiry about the Japanese word for art at a colloquium in May 1958 and his interest in Sanskrit words in the 1960s.

In his masterpiece "A Dialogue on Language," Heidegger has modified the Japanese notions *iki, shiki* and *kū,* and themes from the *Nō* play in order to suit them into his own writing (Chapter eight). He seems to be more interested in the service these themes can render to the composition of his essay than to know them in their Asian background. In the same fashion, he adapts the Japanese word *kotoba* to the overall structure of "A Dialogue," and to elaborate it in correspondence with his intonations on the nature of language, the nature of language as the house of Being, as monologue, as Saying, and as Ereignis.[9] These examinations constitute the basis of my *first reading* of "A Dialogue," which demonstrates that Heidegger has adroitly turned East-West dialogue, as broached in the opening part of his essay, into an architectonic monologue.

In the meantime, Heidegger seems to be considering whether his notion of dialogue, which in its true sense is Being's own Saying, and the idea of the Same, to be understood analogously with "*that* realm and abode about which they [the speakers in the dialogue] are speaking" (*WCT* 178/182; em. or.) and "the single source" (*DL* 8/94), could be applied to East-West "dialogue," and whether East and West could enter into a mode of belonging-together in the fashion of the belonging-together of Being and thinking (Chapter nine). In my *second reading* of this essay, I expose the strains and tensions that arise when Heidegger applies dialogue and the Same, two notions central to his thought, to East-West dialogue.

Chapter One
Heidegger's Asian Connection

Heidegger is one of the few Western philosophers whose thinking forms a sustaining source of attraction for Asian scholars and inspires numerous writings on comparative or intercultural themes. In view of the fact that Heidegger's remarks bearing on East-West dialogue are made mainly with respect to East Asian thought, I focus on East Asia in introducing his Asian connection.[1] First, I examine the reception of his philosophy in Japan, where his work has been disseminated, confronted, and canonized by important Japanese philosophers. This is followed by a brief overview of the literature on Heidegger and Daoism. Subsequently, I expose the general development of discourses under the rubric of Heidegger and Asian thought. An adequate understanding of Heidegger's essay "A Dialogue on Language" is requisite for ascertaining his comportment toward East-West dialogue. In the last part of this chapter, I introduce a few relevant issues surrounding this text.

HEIDEGGER IN JAPAN

Compared with situations in other Asian countries, the development of philosophy in Japan has been most intimately related with Heidegger. From as early as 1921 onward, Japanese scholars traveled to Germany to study with him and kept frequent and close contact with him until he passed away. The first substantive study of his philosophy in any language was contributed by Tanabe Hajime, one of his famous Japanese students, with the title "The New Turn in Phenomenology: Heidegger's phenomenology of life."[2] Appearing in 1924, this article written in Japanese pre-dated the publication of *Sein und Zeit*, Heidegger's *magnum opus*. The year 1933 saw the publication of the first monograph on Heidegger's thinking entitled *Haideggā no tetsugaku* (*The Philosophy of Heidegger*) written by Kuki Shūzō (1888–1941), another prominent Japanese student of Heidegger's.

Japanese scholars have been the forerunners in translating Heidegger's works since the first Japanese version of *Sein und Zeit* came out in 1939. This version is twenty-three years earlier than the first English translation published in 1962. In the next three decades, over five other Japanese translations of this masterpiece appeared.[3] This is extremely impressive in view of the fact that there are only two English versions, with the second one coming out as late as 1996. The publication of each piece of the *Gesamtausgabe* has been closely followed by its Japanese version. The earnestness with which Japanese intellectuals carried out the enterprise of translation is not seen in any other countries.

The reasons for the readiness with which Japanese philosophers received and responded to Heidegger's philosophy are complex. One of the crucial factors seems to be related with the need for modern academic rationales and systems in the process of Japan's modernization. After the Meiji Restoration in 1868, the country adopted Western culture and civilization and from that time forward entered the modern period. Around the turn of the nineteenth and twentieth century, numerous Europeans and Americans came to Japan to hold academic positions in various fields. From 1893 to 1914, Raphael von Köbel (1848–1923), who was born in Russia and educated in Germany, was teaching philosophy at Tokyo University at the invitation of the Japanese government. His students included Nishida Kitarō, Tanabe Hajime, Kuki Shūzō, Watsuji Tetsurō, and many others.[4] At that time, the Southwest German neo-Kantian school as represented by Rickert and Windelband, among other Western philosophical trends,were the best known in Japan. Germany was regarded as the "Mecca of philosophy."[5]

Before the late 1920s, Heidegger was not yet well known. It was primarily because they went to Freiburg to study with Husserl that Japanese scholars came to know Heidegger. In 1921, while working as Husserl's assistant, Heidegger met Yamanouchi Tokuryū, the first Japanese scholar with whom he made acquaintance.[6] During that time, as Heidegger himself recollected in "A Dialogue on Language," he read Husserl's *Logical Investigations* "with the gentleman from Japan" (*DL* 5/90). After returning to Japan, Yamanouchi founded the department of Greek philosophy at Kyoto University and introduced phenomenology. Most of the Japanese students who studied with Heidegger were intellectually related to Nishida Kitarō (1870–1945), who is considered as the first greatest Japanese philosopher in the modern era. His book *Zen no kenkyū* (*An Inquiry into the Good*), published in 1911, was considered to be the most important masterpiece in the new phase of Japanese philosophy. Yamanouchi, a younger colleague of Nishida, was one of the few thinkers who later on challenged his philosophical system.

In 1922, Tanabe Hajime (1885–1962) went to Freiburg to study under Husserl. He was later regarded as the second greatest Japanese philosopher. Soon afterward, Tanabe politely bowed out of Husserl's classes so as to attend the lecture course conducted by Heidegger in the summer semester of 1923, which was later published as *GA 63* under the title *Ontology: Hermeneutics of Facticity*. The concluding section of Tanabe's article "The New Turn in Phenomenology," already mentioned, contains an account of the last part of this course. Because the transcript published in Heidegger's *Gesamtausgabe* lacks the last one or two pages, Tanabe's material fills this breach.

Heidegger's philosophy formed the central reference of Tanabe's writings throughout his career. Nevertheless, there is duplicity involved in this intellectual bond. In a long essay published in Japanese in 1958, entitled "Ontology of Life or Dialectics of Death? A Polemical Engagement with Heideggerian Ontology,"[7] Tanabe puts forth a rather severe criticism of Heidegger's philosophy. When only the second part of this essay was translated into German as a contribution to the Heidegger *Festschrift* on the occasion of his seventieth birthday, the original criticism had disappeared (Tanabe 1959). What was left was mainly a positive evaluation of Heidegger's influence. For example, Tanabe stated that in Heidegger he seemed to find the philosophy he had been seeking (1959, 94).

Now I come to Kuki Shūzō (1888–1941), who plays an indispensable role in Heidegger's essay "A Dialogue on Language." He was actually Baron Kuki, not Count Kuki as Heidegger writes. Okakura Tenshin (Kakuzō, 1862–1913), who is known for such works in English as *The Ideals of the East* (1903) and *The Book of Tea* (1906) had an enduring influence on Kuki.[8] Kuki became a Catholic at the age of 23. From 1921 to the end of 1928, he spent almost eight years in Europe, studying under Rickert, Husserl, and Heidegger in Germany, and under Bergson in France. While polishing his French under the tutorship of Jean-Paul Sartre, who was then a young student, Kuki introduced Sartre to Heidegger's philosophy.[9] In 1927, he moved to Marburg in order to attend Heidegger's lectures. In August 1928, Kuki delivered two lectures in French, one on the notion of time and repetition in the Orient at a colloquium at Pontigny, and the other on the expression of the infinite in Japanese art.[10] Another representative work by Kuki is *Gūzensei no mondai* (*The Problem of Contingency*).[11] As mentioned in the foregoing, Kuki contributed the first book-length study of Heidegger's thought (published in 1933).

One of the major threads in "A Dialogue" is the meaning of the Japanese notion *iki* and Heidegger's discussions with Kuki on this matter (in 1927 or 1928). Kuki's first draft of *Iki no kōzō* (*The Structure of Iki*) was completed in Paris in 1926 and then published in 1930, one year after Kuki's return from

Europe.[12] In the view of some Japanese scholars, this book is a characterization of a distinctive Japanese *ethnos* from "a Westernized perspective."[13]

Heidegger's other renowned students include Miki Kiyoshi (1897–1945), who worked in social and political philosophy, Watsuji Tetsurō (1889–1960), who worked in ethics, and Nishitani Keiji (1900–1990). Miki contends that Heidegger's philosophy cannot be "contemporary" because his Dasein is confined to the standpoint of individual subjective life without social aspect. Watsuji Tetsuro studied Kierkegaard and Nietzsche in his early years and was the first to introduce existential philosophy to Japan. He also did research on ancient Japanese culture and early Buddhism and took it as his goal to represent Japan in his philosophy. Coming to Europe in 1927 and reading *Sein und Zeit* in the summer of 1927 while in Berlin, Watsuji was not completely captivated by Heidegger's work, as many of his Japanese compatriots were. This was probably due to his intellectual maturity at the time he went to Europe. He developed his own philosophy of being-in-the-world in conversation with Heidegger's thinking.[14] In his well-known work *Climates and Cultures: A Philosophical Study* (in Japanese, 1935), Watsuji claims that histories and cultures develop with multifaceted directions and modes and that it is wrong to judge the essence of culture for all peoples by the single type of European civilization. Watsuji criticizes Heidegger of paying little attention to space, which, in his view, prevents Heidegger from presenting a picture of human existence that allows for a true depiction of history.[15]

Nishitani is considered to be the third greatest Japanese philosopher. His most representative and influential treatises are his *Religion and Nothingness,* and *The Self-Overcoming of Nihilism.* He studied with Heidegger from 1938 to 1940 in Freiburg. A guest professorship at the University of Hamburg in 1964 and an award of the Goethe medal in 1972 took him to Germany twice again and created opportunities for long discussions with Heidegger. At Heidegger's death, Nishitani composed a haiku,[16]

At the death of the teacher Heidegger:
In the depth of the night shines
the bright moon lonely.

In an obituary in the evening edition of the Japanese newspaper *Yomiuri* on 25 May 1976, Nishitani states that, in wanting to question the grounding principles of metaphysics, Heidegger touches on Eastern thought, for example the thought of Laozi, of Zhuangzi or Zen-Buddhism (Nishitani 1976, 193).

There is a substantial body of literature discussing similarities or/and dissimilarities between Zen Buddhism and Heidegger's thought.[17] In their comparisons authors draw not only on ancient figures such as Dōgen, but also on contemporary philosophers such as Nishida and Nishitani. In the special issue of *Philosophy East and West* (1970) on "Heidegger and Asian Thought," among the five major pieces, three are centered on comparisons with Zen Buddhism.[18] On a few occasions, Heidegger himself comments on the alleged similarities between his thinking and Zen Buddhism, sometimes in a positive, sometimes in a negative direction. I will discuss these facets in Chapter eight.

Most of the Japanese philosophers who are connected with Heidegger are identified as Kyoto school scholars. Undeniably, Heidegger's philosophy has offered them an abundance of conceptual resources and inspiration.[19] Nevertheless, the Kyoto school philosophers formed their own original and distinctive thoughts, and posed "a disciplined and well-informed challenge to the definition of the history of philosophy itself" (Heisig 2001, 3). At the same time, confrontation with Heidegger's work constitutes an essential element in the development of modern Japanese philosophy. We can see the critical engagement with Heidegger's philosophy in the work of, among others, Tanabe, Watsuji, Nishitani, and Tsujimura.[20]

Already during his lifetime Heidegger's Japanese connection was obvious at several festive events. Tanabe Hajime's essay on the dialectics of death, already mentioned, was published in the *Festschrift* for Heidegger's seventieth birthday (Neske 1959). Another Japanese philosopher who played an important role in Heidegger's later years was Tsujimura Kōichi. Initially, Tsujimura knew his philosophy through Kuki's commentary on *Sein und Zeit*, which was his bedside reading. On the recommendation of his teachers Hisamatsu and Tanabe, he was able to study with Heidegger from 1956 to 1958. This information is from a transcript of a brief "Spoken Message" by Tsujimura, which was published in one of the *Festschriften* dedicated to Heidegger for his eightieth year in 1969.[21] In addition, Heidegger's hometown Messkirch organized a *Feierstunde* in 1969. Here Tsujimura delivered the keynote speech (*Festvortrag*) with the title "Martin Heidegger and Japanese Philosophy."[22]

Quite a few Japanese philosophers, most of them being Zen Buddhism specialists, regard Heidegger's thought as the type of Western philosophy that is most congenial to their tradition, and take his phenomenological methodology to be the "necessary detour" for any future development of Japanese philosophy whose original source is Zen Buddhism. Tsujimura remarks,[23]

> For me Heidegger is a kind of signpost . . . that can lead from Zen Buddhism to philosophy. More precisely, the way proceeds from Zen and

passes over a reflection on Heidegger's thought to a possible Japanese philosophy. It is a necessary detour. (1970, 27)

Oshima Yoshiko points to the relevance of Heidegger's philosophy to achieving her own "homecoming" in Zen Buddhism. She states that, without the help of Heidegger's work, she would not have found the right entrance (*Zugang*) to Zen (1985, 16). One of the Japanese scholars who have been instrumental in Heidegger's engagement with Zen Buddhist ideas is Hisamatsu Hōseke Shin-ichi (1889–1980), a well-known Zen Buddhist and university professor.[24] A colloquium on the theme "Art and Thinking" which Hisamatsu co-held with Heidegger on 18 May 1958 will be discussed in Chapter seven.

Heidegger is often cited as having said, "if I understand this man [Suzuki] right, this is what I have been trying to say in all my writings."[25] This hearsay is reported by William Barrett in the preface of his edition of Suzuki's essays without giving a specific reference. Authors who quote this remark have ignored Barrett's comment in the same place that there is much in Heidegger's thinking that cannot be found in Zen-Buddhism, and there is much more in Zen-Buddhism that cannot be found in Heidegger's thinking (Barrett 1956, xi). Petzet correctly observes, "In any case, it would be a mistake to want (as some have) to conduct, overzealously though with good intentions, a kind of thought-harmony that would span the peoples and to attempt a direct equa-tion of Zen with Heidegger's many paths of thinking" (167).[26]

HEIDEGGER AND DAOISM

From the 1970s onward, there has been a considerable interest in the affin-ity of Heidegger's writings with Daoism. I will discuss his encounter with the *Daodejing* in chapters six and seven. Here I provide a brief discussion of relevant comparative studies.

The term Daoism can refer to both *daojia* (the school of the *dao*) and *daojiao* (the religion of the *dao*). *Daojia* takes its basis from the central ideas embodied in the *Laozi* and the *Zhuangzi*. It is often called philosophical Daoism, as distinguished from *daojiao,* a type of religion that emerged with the deification of Laozi, whose revelation is said to be received by the *tianshi* (celestial masters). There seems to be a competition between scholars who ascribe greater similarities between Zen Buddhism and Heidegger and those who find more similarities between Daoism and Heidegger. In recent years, the latter have come to dominate.

In a number of works, Chang Chung-yuan attempts to interpret the *Daodejing* in light of Heidegger's philosophy.[27] According to him, "Heidegger is the only Western philosopher who not only intellectually understands *dao,* but has intuitively experienced the essence of it as well" (1975, ix). Furthermore, Chang considers his philosophy significant for promoting the East-West encounter. He maintains that Heidegger's "step back on the way of thinking" is comparable with Laozi's verse "To learn, one accumulates day by day. To study *dao,* one reduces day by day."[28] Through this way, East and West will encounter each other (1977b, 69).

In the view of Stambaugh (1984), *Weg* (way) and *Gelassenheit* (releasement) are the two central notions of Heidegger that definitely possess a Daoist flavour. They are far apart from traditional Western metaphysics. However, it seems that Stambaugh has unquestioningly identified the notion *Weg* of Heidegger with the *dao* of Daoism. This is particularly evident when she writes "Way (*Weg, Tao*)" (79).

May (1996 [1989]) has provided a detailed demonstration of striking similarities between Heidegger and Daoist thinking. Using the method of textual juxtaposition, he aims to show that Heidegger's text "corresponds almost verbatim" (29) to German translations of Daoist scriptures available to him. Here is an example of his method of juxtaposition, a line from the *Zhuangzi,* followed by a citation from Heidegger,[29]

> What gives things their thingness is not itself a thing.
> [The] thingness of the thing . . . cannot itself be a thing again.

May argues that Heidegger's idea that the thingly nature of the container consists in emptiness (*Leere*), as elaborated in his essay "The Thing" [1950b], comes from chapter 11 of the *Daodejing.*[30] A few other authors have noted and commented on the similarity between passages in Heidegger's essay "The Thing" and Laozi's chapter 11.[31] What is innovative about May's work is that he attributes this similarity to deliberate, albeit unacknowledged, borrowing by Heidegger. Wohlfart's article clearly follows up May's method and line of argument. On the basis of a careful comparative textual analysis of chapter 11 of the *Daodejing* and Heidegger's thematization of the "nothing," he concludes that Laozi was "one of the decisive sources of the later Heidegger" (2003, 52). These studies are made without the awareness that Heidegger actually cites the whole text of chapter 11 in an essay of 1943 [1943b]. I will discuss this episode in Chapter six.

Most of these authors have attempted to establish a special bond of Heidegger's philosophy with Daoist thinking, either in terms of undeniable resonances or in terms of direct influence. Two scholars have assumed

a critical stance in the late 1970s. One claims that Heidegger does not realize the freedom and creativity that is characteristic of Chinese *dao;* therefore, he should become a student of Zhuangzi or Laozi in order to learn a
new language (Cheng 1978). Another argues that both the human being
and (Western) history remain central in Heidegger's thinking. One could
integrate Heidegger's thought into Daoism without difficulty, but not vice
versa; it is absolutely necessary for Heidegger to abandon his *Seinsdenken*
and replace it with a Daoist naturalistic transformation (Fu 1978).[32] More
recently, Cheung observes that the relation between Heidegger and Daoism has been "over-interpreted and exaggerated" (1998, 156).

In my view, one can certainly find a large number of phrases and ideas
in Heidegger's writings that are strikingly similar to verses in the *Daodejing*.
However, while it surely sounds absurd to reason on this basis that it is actually Heidegger who has exerted influence on Laozi, *contemporary* understanding and interpretations of Laozi's *Daodejing* has been under the sway of
Heidegger's formidable presence as *the* philosopher.

DISCOURSES ON HEIDEGGER AND ASIAN THOUGHT

On 17–21 November 1969, an international symposium "Heidegger and
Eastern Thought" was held at Manoa in Hawai'i in celebration of Heidegger's eightieth year. This conference was the first one to have concentrated on the philosophy of a single Western philosopher in comparison
with various aspects of Eastern philosophical traditions. In addition to
Heidegger specialists of Western origin such as J. Glenn Gray, Calvin O.
Schrag, and Joan Stambaugh (the contributions of the latter two deal with
similarities or/and differences between Heidegger's thinking and Zen Buddhism), among the participants there were quite a number of established
scholars of Asian origin, including Chang Chung-yuan (who focuses on
Heidegger and Daoism), and Jarava Lal Mehta (on Heidegger and Indian
philosophy). The contributions to this symposium, consisting of five articles and comments on each, were published in the journal *Philosophy East
& West* (20:3) in 1970.

The collection *Heidegger and Asian Thought* edited by Graham Parkes
appeared in 1987 (paperback 1990). Consisting of thirteen contributions,
it has served as a major sourcebook for comparative studies of Heidegger
and Asian intellectual traditions. Yet it has not gone without criticisms. In a
review written in 1997, Carman and van Norden observe that the contributors either try to avoid or simply ignore the pervasively Western orientation of
Heidegger's philosophy, and his evident skepticism regarding the prospect of

any synthesis of Eastern and Western thought. Thus, the difficulties involved in the comparative enterprise are under-estimated from the outset.[33]

In this collection, Otto Pöggeler's essay "West-East Dialogue: Heidegger and Lao-tzu" (1987a) is the most influential and most often quoted essay from this collection.[34] It provides numerous records of Heidegger's encounters with Daoist texts, which is interspersed with accounts of his engagement with Hölderlin, Trakl, Rilke, Klee and Cézanne, and a commentary on the essay "Principles of thinking" (in which Heidegger cites Laozi). More importantly, Pöggeler puts forward a number of subtle questions concerning the prevalent positive judgment on Heidegger's Asian connection: Are Heidegger's Heraclitus and Laozi constructs for making his own point? Does he find in them only what he is seeking? Is the multiplicity of traditions ignored? Pöggeler also points to the diversity within both the Eastern and Western traditions, and interrogates Heidegger's idea of a single way to forgotten origins and Being and of the experience of stillness at the center of a new thinking (1987a, 72). It is a pity that these questions and subtle points have not yet been sufficiently appreciated by relevant scholars.

In 1989, in celebration of Heidegger's one-hundredth year, several events took place. They led to publications that form the indispensable basis for the German language literature on Heidegger and East Asia.[35] First of all is the collection *Japan und Heidegger: Gedenkschrift der Stadt Messkirch zum hundertsten Geburtstag Martin Heideggers* (Buchner 1989).[36] Except for Elmar Weinmayr and the editor Hartmut Buchner, all the authors are Japanese philosophers and scholars, such as Nishitani, Tanabe, Kuki, Suzuki, and Tsujimura. In addition, it contains several previously unpublished letters and short pieces of Heidegger from the period 1955–1980 relevant to his connection with Asian thought, which only appeared in the *Gesamtausgabe* much later.[37]

A centennial conference took place in München in January 1989; the proceedings were published with the title *Destruktion und Übersetzung: Zu den Aufgaben von Philosophiegeschichte nach Martin Heidegger* (Buchheim 1989). In April 1989, another centennial meeting took place in Bonn-Bad Godesberg on the "philosophical actuality of Heidegger," the contributions to which were published in three volumes (Papenfuß and Pöggeler 1992). Both proceedings contain a number of articles which will be referred to in subsequent chapters. Such renowned Heidegger specialists as Pöggeler and Biemel have contributed to the former publication and commented on Heidegger's "Asian connection."

In German-language publications of the 1990s a group of scholars have ascribed to Heidegger's thinking a unique significance for the foundation, initiation, and orientation of intercultural philosophy.[38] For example Eckard Wolz-Gottwald argues that Heidegger has presented the "beginning of a 'creative' intercultural philosophy as a third way" (1997, 99).[39] The most fully worked out view is that of Florian Vetsch, who ascribes to Heidegger an account of planetary unification by means of different traditions going back to their roots and contributing in various capacities to thwarting the danger of modern technology (1992, 85). His view will be discussed in Chapter four.

In 1996, the English translation of Reinhard May's work *Ex Oriente Lux: Heideggers Werk unter ostasiatischen Einfluß* came out, which was originally published in 1989.[40] May carefully compares Heidegger's sentence-construction, choice of words, and word fields in his writings, and compares them with relevant passages from German translations of East Asian classics. Taking these as convincing evidence, May argues that Heidegger's work was significantly influenced by East Asian sources and that, in some cases, "Heidegger even appropriated wholesale and almost verbatim" from the German translations of Daoist and Zen Buddhist classics (xviii). An example of his method of juxtaposition was already given in the section on Daoism.

May's in-depth study has brought about a new wave of interest in Heidegger's connection with East Asian thought and created a considerable impact on the general orientation of comparative studies of Heidegger. Convinced of May's findings, Parkes withdraws his statement in the Introduction to *Heidegger and Asian Thought* that studies of independent congruence of ideas are of the first primacy as compared with concentrating on the question of direct influence (1987, 2). Instead, he claims that May's discovery shows that "a chapter of the history of modern Western ideas may have to be rewritten" (1996, x).

It is worth mentioning that, while Parkes and May attempt to cast positive light on Heidegger's silence about his indebtedness toward ancient Asian thought, others sense that this may give rise to a second "Heidegger case." As a reviewer comments, "May's case threatens to damage Heidegger's standing as a philosopher more seriously than the familiar, and now substantiated, allegations of political involvement" (Cooper 1997, 243).

TEZUKA TOMIO AND "A DIALOGUE ON LANGUAGE"

"A Dialogue on Language: Between a Japanese and an Inquirer" (which I often refer to as "A Dialogue") is a peculiar essay in which Heidegger's quasi-autobiographical account of the basic orientation and sustained concerns of his philosophical life is interspersed with an abundance of Japanese notions and themes such as *iki, shiki* and *kū*, the *Nō* drama and the film

Rashōmon. In the beginning of "A Dialogue," Heidegger raises the question whether a dialogue between East Asian and European languages is possible (*DL* 8/93). Prominent in this essay is also Heidegger's familiarity with Japanese philosophers such as Kuki, Nishida and Tanabe. This is the only text where Heidegger consigns to writing his knowledge about Japanese intellectual heritage.

The year 1959 when "A Dialogue" was published in the collection *Unterwegs zur Sprache* [1959b] was the year when Heidegger turned seventy years old. Confucius, an ancient Chinese philosopher, states that the age seventy is an age when he came to "follow [his] heart's feelings without overstepping the bounds of propriety."[41] It is not implausible that Heidegger saw his seventy's year as an occasion to reveal some of the major concerns that have set the path of his thinking. That this revelation is accompanied by his memories of his contacts with the East Asian world is not without significance. It suggests the possibility that a reflection on East-West dialogue plays a role in Heidegger's philosophical exploration.

Jean-Luc Nancy (1990) and Robert Mugerauer (1988) each have contributed a substantial study of "A Dialogue." However, their analyses focus on the issue of hermeneutics, which is a standard topic of philosophical inquiry. The suggestiveness and ambiguities that infuse the presence and absence of Japanese themes, as well as the proximity and distance that are both reflected in the relation between the Inquirer and the Japanese, seem to have made the question of East-West dialogue so much a minefield that these two authors deem it wise to stay away from it.

As early as 1963, Pöggeler comments that "A Dialogue" "clearly demonstrate[s] the difficulty of [East-West] dialogue" (1987b, 3). George Pattison articulates a similar view in stating that "A Dialogue" is "very preoccupied with the extent to which transcultural understanding is at all possible" (2000, 201). Both these two scholars are more closely affiliated with the area called "Heidegger studies." They seem to have less interest in presenting Heidegger as the prototypical philosopher who has provided crucial *Wegmarken* for East-West dialogue. However, they have not yet spelled out in detail where the difficulties reside.

The majority of scholars tend to interpret Heidegger's position as favorable as possible. Mehta claims that in "A Dialogue" Heidegger evidently perceives in the Orient "possibilities which may prove valuable for the first steps towards the 'planetary' thinking of the future" (1970, 313). Vetsch sees in this essay a true intercultural dialogue, with the style of the text itself bearing kinship with ancient Chinese art and philosophy (1992, 116–129). Prins discerns in it "a praxis of an intercultural dialogue" as well (1996, 97). In the eyes of May, the whole piece is a deliberately "encoded" confession of Heidegger's debts to East Asian thought (1996, 49–50).[42]

The background of this essay is crucial for its proper understanding. Heidegger himself provides a somewhat misleading hint at the genesis of the dialogue: "The heretofore unpublished text originated in 1953/54, on the occasion of a visit by Professor Tezuka of the Imperial University, Tokyo" (*OWL* 199/269). This note easily misleads readers into considering "A Dialogue" as more or less a record of Heidegger's actual conversation with Tezuka, which is not the case.[43] Tezuka Tomio (1903–1983) was Professor of German literature at Tokyo University, member of the Japanese Academy, and translator of a number of German philosophers and poets.[44] At the end of March 1954, Tezuka paid a visit to Heidegger in Freiburg. Around the same period, he visited two other European scholars, namely, Werner Bergengruen and Eduard Spranger, and inquired about the significance of Christianity for Europe. Toward the end of January 1955, he published a report on these conversations in a column for the newspaper *Tokyo Shinbun*. When his Japanese translation of "A Dialogue" was published, Tezuka appended an explanatory afterword, as well as a detailed account of his conversation with Heidegger under the title "Haideggā to no ichi jikan" ("An Hour with Heidegger").[45] A reprint of the earlier report published in the newspaper was included as well.

As an accomplished scholar, Tezuka is seriously concerned about the spiritual and psychological state of the Japanese people after the end of the Second World War. That is actually the purpose and the intended topic for his visit on Heidegger. However, in the first half of their conversation, Tezuka was subjected to Heidegger's various questions about Japanese art and language. Only in the second half of their meeting was Tezuka given the opportunity to ask questions of his own concern. In the explanatory note appended to his translation of "A Dialogue," Tezuka unequivocally claims,

> Heidegger's work "A dialogue on language" is not an unchanged record of the conversation between him and me, but it was written out of the interest that arose in Heidegger's mind through our conversation. . . . That the visitor from Japan is a keen reader of Heidegger and is familiar with his thinking and ways of expression has nothing to do with me; but rather comes, it seems to me, partly from Heidegger's own motives and his need to write down this text. Not only is such specialist knowledge and terminology alien to me, but there are also in the text certain expressions and styles which—though not bearing on a specific idea—I could never have uttered if the visitor from Japan had been me.[46]

The fictional character of "A Dialogue" cannot be made clearer in any other evidence than in these frank clarifications.[47] Alertness to this aspect plays a crucial role in my investigation into the question of Heidegger's view of East-West dialogue. Another extreme is to assume that "the Japanese" in Heidegger's text has nothing to do with any Japanese individual. For example, Nancy describes the Japanese interlocutor as "at the same time the Western other and the representative of a former Japanese disciple of Heidegger" (226). However, the first fold of this characterization soon disappears in Nancy's text, whereas the Japanese visitor is only referred to as a disciple of the master's thought.

Tezuka's reports of his meeting with Heidegger are an important source for a proper appreciation of "A Dialogue." Since Parkes has translated "An Hour with Heidegger" into English, in the following I review the contents of the Heidegger-part of "Three Answers," and then make a few comments on their exchange when Heidegger makes the inquiries. Tezuka held a high respect for Christianity, which was often considered to embody profound spiritual strength and sublimity by East Asian intellectuals. In his view, the unconsciousness of everyday life in Europe was still deeply embedded in Christianity. He wanted to hear Heidegger's comments in this connection. Tezuka thus phrased his question, "Do you think this bourgeois version of Christianity has the power to move European culture toward a new development?" In response, Heidegger raised his eyebrows, shook his head vehemently, and said,

> It does not have this power. In the false conviction that it has lies a big danger for the German and European culture. This conventional religiosity and self-satisfaction . . . [unfinished sentence]. The force of a living faith is well present in the Italian people. (Buchner 1989, 179)

Tezuka proceeded to explain the background of his question. In his own country, there was nothing comparable to Christianity that could provide spiritual support. The Japanese people were suffering from a state of great confusion. They could only find, at most, false support in what was nothing but slogans. At these remarks, Heidegger responded, "You know, it is better to realize that there is no such support."[48] In the last paragraph of the Heidegger-part of the "Three Answers," Tezuka confesses that he has often ruminated over his inquiries with Heidegger, but could not find anything positive in his answers, which is consistent with Heidegger's assertion that the gods have fled. Tezuka concludes that the Japanese people often take the question of spiritual support as a general problem, and thus forget that it is an individual question.

Heidegger's inquiries with Tezuka are concerned with Japanese language and art. Their talk starts with Kuki's memory and a mention of Suzuki. After requesting Tezuka to write down in both Romanization and Japanese, a haiku by Bashō and a word-by-word explanation of it, Heidegger asked about the Japanese word for language. Then they discussed the special nature of Japanese art. After that, Heidegger asked about Japanese words for appearance [*Erscheinung*] and essence [*Wesen*], and about the film *Rashōmon*. Then, Tezuka was allowed to put forward his questions about the German poets Heidegger discussed. From their conversation, Tezuka could not resist the sense that Heidegger's inquiries were proceeding from pre-determined ideas. On three occasions in his account Tezuka gave explicit expression to such a sense.

The first occasion was when Heidegger hastily surmised that the Japanese word *kotoba* could mean *das Ding* (the thing). Tezuka found in this surmise an element of "forcing the word into a preconceived idea" (May 1996, 60). The second occasion occurred when Heidegger described the term "spiritual," which had been used by Tezuka, as metaphysical. Tezuka felt that "one would have to append an explanation of the Japanese understanding of metaphysics" (61). The third occasion was when Tezuka cited "the open" (*das Offene*) as a possible interpretation of *kū*. In doing this, he already had "a premonition that this would sit well with [Heidegger] as an interpreter of Hölderlin and Rilke" (62). Heidegger was indeed pleased with this interpretation.

From Tezuka's questions and reflections, it can be seen that he is an independent thinker and serious scholar in his own right. Notably, he was not a passive listener and answer-provider. He did not readily accept whatever Heidegger said. For instance, he did not agree with Heidegger's practice of presenting Rilke as a "poet in a destitute time." Neither did Tezuka over-interpret Heidegger's remarks in light of an idolized image of "the great philosopher," as some other people have done. All these features of Tezuka's scholarly integrity and personal character had disappeared when Heidegger described him as an uncritical admirer in "A Dialogue."

HEIDEGGER IN DIALOGUE WITH LAOZI?

Most scholars have taken the presence of the Japanese interlocutor in "A Dialogue" at face value (whether as a "real" or as a "fictional" Japanese). Kah Kyung Cho is perhaps the only author who has made a strong case against this reading (1992, 1993).[49] He argues that although Heidegger presents a Japanese visitor as one of the protagonists, judged by the essence of the East-West engagement in this essay, this dialogue is not one with Zen Buddhist thought or concerning the Japanese notion *iki;* nor is it one with

Baron Kuki, Tezuka Tomio, or with any other Japanese scholar. According to Cho, this essay is actually an intercultural dialogue with Laozi, the ancient Chinese philosopher; and *dao* acts as the *Leitwort* (guiding word) in this process of East-West encounter.

Cho maintains that, for Heidegger, the terms East and West do not refer to empirical geographical entities. Rather, they are endowed with ontological significance, and thus should be understood from the perspective of the history of Being (*Seinsgeschichte*), or in terms of "the nearness to the source" (*der Nähe zum Ursprung*) (*LH* 257/338). Cho explains that the term "source" means "the initial founding occurrence of truth itself," and that East and West are differentiated from each other on the basis of proximity to or distance from the source (1993, 151). Cho claims that the regional distinction between China and Japan is "unimportant" (151). The references to China or to Japan cannot be taken literally, but should be subjected to judgment from the ontological standpoint. This point is the basis on which Cho argues that the identity of the Japanese interlocutor in "A Dialogue" should not be taken at face value, and that one should not take it for granted that Heidegger attaches more importance to Japanese thinking than to Chinese thinking or any other East Asian tradition. These arguments open the way for Cho to contend that, in "A Dialogue," Heidegger is actually conducting an intercultural dialogue with Laozi.

In my view, Cho's primary thesis that the differentiation between East and West should be understood from the ontological instead of the ontic standpoint is quite problematic. It is unclear whether and how the ontological East and West have anything to do with the ontic East and West. If, as Cho insists, the referents of East and West in Heidegger's usage cannot be determined according to the ontic East and West in their respective internal complexity and varied modes of mutual relations, then on what basis can one differentiate the ontological East from the ontological West? This question becomes more relevant in view of the fact that Cho did not address the question which ontological side he deems to be nearer to the source, East or West. If they are near to the source in the same degree, if, ontologically speaking, they are "the same," then in what way can one sensibly speak of the East and West as two parties with genuine and meaningful differences, rather than two labels whose actual (ontic) contents have already been hollowed out in the name of the sublimity of the ontological? Furthermore, absent a meaningful distinction between the ontological East and the ontological West, in what ways can the talk of East-West encounter have any substantial meaning? On the other hand, how are we to make sense of Cho's insistence upon the ontological priority of Chinese thinking to Japanese thinking? If the ontic regional distinction between China and Japan, for this matter, is really trivial to Heidegger (and to Cho himself), why should not the ontological distinction be trivial as well?

Cho's thesis of ontological significance presupposes another thesis: compared with Japanese tradition, Chinese tradition is nearer to the source, or, alternatively speaking, occupies a more important place in the scheme of the history of Being. This thesis does not seem to be self-evident. If what Cho has in mind is no more than the empirical fact that the pre-modern history of Japanese tradition has been complexly intertwined with classical Chinese thought, then his thesis could be philosophically impartial. However, by analogy with Heidegger's idea that the West is ontologically the place where Being shows itself in response to which humankind comes to self-consciousness, Cho ascribes to Heidegger the view that Chinese tradition is ontologically nearer to Being than its sister tradition.

In making his case for the special significance of Chinese tradition, Cho places weight upon Heidegger's short-lived collaboration with Hisao in 1946, and draws attention to his alleged remark that he "had learned more from Chinese" (than from Japanese scholars). He also points to Heidegger's brief discussion and mention of *dao* in "The Nature of Language" (*OWL* 92/198) and "The Principle of Identity" (*ID* 36/101) respectively.[50]

Cho stresses that it is misleading to attempt to pin down the various "Eastern" stimulations on Heidegger's thinking and order them as a linear developmental process. This practice can only account for his Asian connection in terms of a simplistic borrowing or assimilation. According to Cho, Heidegger has integrated what he has learned from all those contradistinctive sources into one simple thought of his own, while retaining such distinctions as the "own" (*Eigenes*) and the "foreign" (*Fremdes*), the "before" (*vorher*) and the "after" (*nachher*), "Eastern" (*östlich*) and "Western" (*westlich*). This thinking does not abide by a logical order; rather, it keeps on moving backward and forward. Therefore, it does not make sense to trace out particular elements of influence on Heidegger's thinking.

It seems that Cho's pleading against an "empirical" account is made for the purpose of pre-empting criticisms of his claim (of the ontological priority of Chinese tradition) on the basis of evidence of Heidegger's bond with traditions other than Chinese Daoist thinking. For example, in an article from the same collection where Fischer-Barnicol's piece appears, Carl Friedrich von Weizcäcker recounts Heidegger's description of the deep impression Japanese Zen-Buddhism made on him in the 1960s: "it was as if a door were opened to/for him [Heidegger]" (Neske 1977, 247). If von Weizcäcker's record is reliable, and if we treat different sorts of anecdotal evidence with equal seriousness, then this statement is strong counter-evidence against Cho's ascription of a special status of Chinese thinking to Heidegger. Most probably, it is out of awareness of such possible confrontations that Cho urges for a non-chronological, "ontological" understanding, in the sense of his own usage of the word, of the manner in which Heidegger has integrated East Asian thinking into his path. However, in relying on the alleged confession cited from Fischer-Barnicol's article, in inducing the translation collaboration with Hsiao, and in attaching overdue importance to Heidegger's brief discussion and mention of *dao,* is not Cho exactly doing what he pleads against: that is, trying to trace out particular elements of influence on Heidegger's thinking?

Granted that Heidegger is somehow aware of the variations within East Asian traditions, so far there has not been discovered any piece of indisputable evidence that he assigns a hierarchy of ontological significance to these traditions. Therefore, it may smack of partisanship to insist without solid basis and sound reasoning that "A Dialogue" bears only on Laozi and the notion of *dao,* and has nothing to do with the Japanese notion *iki,* Japanese tradition in general, and Japanese scholars mentioned in it. In stating this, I do not mean that Heidegger's reading of the *Daodejing* and his reflection on the word *dao* have never played a role in his composition of "A Dialogue." Nor is it my intention to advocate making a Japanese Zen-Buddhist out of Heidegger. My point is to show that such an argument is philosophically pointless and is not helpful for promoting scholarly advancement with respect to the question of Heidegger's intricate connection with Asian thought.

Chapter Two

Language and Being: Central Themes

Heidegger is a prolific writer and lecturer. His *Gesamtausgabe* will consist of 102 volumes. From 1975 up to now, 90 volumes have been published. Both the title of each volume and the overall order of all volumes are of Heidegger's own arrangement. How are we to grasp the general orientation and fundamental concerns of Heidegger's life-long philosophical reflection?[1] H. W. Petzet chose the phrase "Towards a single star" (*Auf einen Stern zuge-hen*) as the title of his memoir on Heidegger (1993). This phrase comes from a series of poems entitled "The Thinker as Poet" Heidegger composed in 1947. The second part of the second poem runs,

> We are too late for the gods and too
>   early for Beyng. Beyng's poem,
>   just begun, is man.

> To head toward a star . . .

> To think is to confine yourself to a
>   single thought that one day stands
>   still like a star in the world's sky. ([1947, 4/76]; tr. m.]

This poem contains a number of key words of the later Heidegger: Beyng, gods, man, a single thought; and the "morning light" could be associated with *Morgenland* (that is, Greece)[2]. The "single star" is none other than the question of Being (Beyng). In the next poem, Heidegger sings,

> When thought's courage stems from
>   the bidding of Beyng, then
>   destiny's language thrives. [1947, 5/77]

It is clear that Being's disclosing is inextricably correlated with language. Therefore, reflection on the question of Being is at the same time reflection on the nature of language. In "A Dialogue on Language," Heidegger admits, "reflection on language and on Being has determined my path of thinking from early on, and therefore their exposition [*Erörterung*] has stayed as far as possible in the background" (*DL* 7/93; tr. m.). In his meeting (on 5 December 1963) with Bhikku Mahā Mani, a Buddhist monk and professor from Thailand, Heidegger states

> The experience of my deliberations is—and at the same time this means for Western philosophy: to reflect upon the history of Western thinking—that there was one question that had never been put so far, and that is the question of Being. [1963a, 590]

The central concerns of Heidegger's thinking cannot be more accurately captured by other remarks than these.[3] In this chapter I present a chronological account of Heidegger's intellectual development with reference to a few quasi-autobiographical materials.[4] Being aware that Heidegger sometimes modifies factual details for the sake of the overall purpose of his writing (this is especially so in "A Dialogue"), I do not completely rely on his own narratives. After reviewing these materials, I examine the two-fold meaning of the phrase "language is the house of Being," from which derives the presumption that "a dialogue from house to house is nearly impossible" (*DL* 5/90). One fold of meaning is that language constitutes the abode where Being discloses itself. In the meantime, language transforms itself into the essential saying. Another fold of meaning is that language is the essence of man. Only through language can man hear the message of Being and dwell in language as the guardian of Being; only by man can Being's saying be heard and make a claim. In the last section, I argue that both universalistic and relativistic readings are inadequate to Heidegger's thought.

LIFELONG CONCERN WITH LANGUAGE AND BEING

Embarking on the Way

Heidegger's intellectual journey can be traced back to his student years in the Gymnasium. At that time, he made friends with Dr. Conrad Gröber, a fellow Swabian, then vicar of Trinity Church in Konstanz, later archbishop of Freiburg. In the summer of 1907, he received as a gift from this paternal friend a copy of Brentano's dissertation entitled *On the Manifold Meaning of Being According to Aristotle* (1862). Heidegger's inscription in that book is, "My first guide through Greek philosophy in my Gymnasium days" (*DL* 7/92). In recollecting on this initial stimulation of mind, Heidegger cites Hölderlin's verse, " . . . For as you began [*anfängst*], so you will remain" (7/92). He certainly considers this occasion to be his philosophical *Anfang* (beginning), and characterizes the question of language and Being as "a gift of that light ray which fell upon [me]" (7/93; tr. m.). In "A recollection," Heidegger states,

> The quest for the unity in the multiplicity of Being, then only obscurely, unsteadily, and helplessly stirring within me, remained, through many upsets, wanderings, and perplexities, *the* ceaseless impetus for the treatise *Being and Time* which appeared two decades later. ([1957b, 21]; em. or.)

In defining his interest in the question of Being that is stimulated by Brentano's dissertation as "*the* ceaseless impetus" of the composition of his *magnus opum,* which was published exactly twenty years later, Heidegger obviously attaches great importance to the question that initiated his philosophical aspiration.

In his well-known letter to William Richardson, Heidegger cites Aristotle's aphorism quoted by Brentano on the title page of his dissertation, "A being becomes manifest (that is, with regard to its Being) in many ways," as the source for the "*question*" (em. or.) that determined the path of his thought from then on, namely, "What is the pervasive, simple, unified determination of Being that permeates all of its multiple meanings" [1962c, x]?

In "My Way to Phenomenology," Heidegger refers to another philosophy book he obtained around the same period. That was "On Being. Outline of Ontology" (1896) written by Carl Braig, then professor of dogmatics at Freiburg University. Heidegger was impressed by the extensive excerpts from Aristotle, Aquinas and Suárez, as well as the etymology of fundamental ontological concepts in that book [1963b, 74–5/81–2].

Another source of influence on the young Heidegger was his intensive religious and theological studies. From 1903 to 1906, Heidegger spent three years in a Catholic boarding school, and then another three years in the Gymnasium and archiepiscopal convent in preparation for a clerical career. He also spent a short period of time at the novitiate with the Jesuits until discharged because of health problems. Starting from the winter of 1909–1910, he studied theology and philosophy at the faculty of theology of the University of Freiburg. After four semesters he decided to discontinue clerical training and focus on philosophy. However, he did not completely stop studying Catholic philosophy and theology.

Around 1917–18, Heidegger underwent a transition from adhering to the Catholic faith and the neo-Scholastic philosophy to constructing a novel phenomenology of religion and phenomenological ontology.[5] In a letter to Karl Löwith on 19 August 1921, Heidegger writes,

> I work concretely and factically out of my "I am," out of my intellectual and wholly factic origin, milieu, life-contexts, and whatever is available to me from these as a vital experience in which I live. . . . To this facticity of mine belongs what I would in brief call the fact that I am a "Christian theo*logian.*" ([1921, 29]; em. or.)

In Heidegger's days, philosophy was said to have contributed to the degeneration of the original Christian experience. Heidegger sees in phenomenology a more adequate way of bringing out the *logos* in religious experience.[6] In "A Dialogue," he acknowledges that without his theological background he could never have "come upon the path of thinking" (*DL* 10/96). He states that at that time he was fascinated by the question of the relation between the word of the Holy Scripture and theological-speculative thinking. He thinks that the latter involves the same relation as that between language and Being (10/96).

It is no surprise that the first embodiment of Heidegger's exploration of the question of Being concerns Duns Scotus, an important medieval metaphysician. This is his habilitation dissertation *Duns Scotus' Doctrine of Categories and Theory of Meaning* (1915). As Heidegger explains in "A Dialogue," the doctrine of categories is the traditional name for the discussion of the Being of beings, whereas the theory of meaning, whose metaphysical name is *grammatica speculativa,* deals with "the metaphysical reflection on language in its relation to Being" (6/91–2).

Another source of decisive influence on Heidegger's intellectual *Bildung* is Husserl, whose *Logical Investigations* became Heidegger's frequent reading when he was a student of theology at the University of Freiburg in 1909. After Husserl came to Freiburg in 1916 as Rickert's successor, and especially after Heidegger became his assistant in 1919, Heidegger had the opportunity to delve into Husserl's method of phenomenological "seeing."

The major inspirations Heidegger drew from Husserl's work with respect to the question of Being are the following. First, Being itself is not a being. There is an essential difference between beings and Being, an ontico-ontological difference. This idea is what is at play in his discourse on Nothing. Second, Being is manifest in categorial intuition. In the factical life, the human being has an understanding of Being.[7]

In the meanwhile, Heidegger assumed a critical stance toward Husserl. For Husserl, phenomenon meant what appears to consciousness. He considered that his methodology of investigating what is given to consciousness is an antidote to the then widespread psychologism, which is related to the practice of analyzing all human undertakings, especially philosophy, logic and mathematics, in terms of human psychology. In Heidegger's view, in turning to a detailed account of the acts of consciousness that constitute knowledge in the second volume of the *Logical Investigations,* Husserl fell back on the position of psychologism that he had refuted in the first volume. Heidegger commented, "so it is a psychology after all" [1963b, 79/86]. He held to the position that what must be experienced and investigated as "things themselves" are not "consciousness and its objectivity," but "Being of beings in its unconcealedness or concealment" [79/86]. He considered this approach to be "a more faithful adherence to the principle of phenomenology" [1962c, xiv]. This difference of views led to Heidegger's parting company with Husserl. In a letter to Jaspers on 26 December 1926, Heidegger notoriously confessed that if *Being and Time* was "written against anyone, then it is Husserl, who immediately saw that too, but took a positive attitude from the start" (*HJC* 73/71).

Heidegger transformed (or "restored") the meaning of the word "phenomenon." He downplayed the role of consciousness and emphasized the self-manifestation of phenomenon itself. In the introduction to *Being and Time,* Heidegger provides an etymological analysis of the Greek word φαινόμενον, and concludes that phenomenon means "what shows itself in itself, what is manifest" (*BT* 51/28–9). Phenomenology means "to let that which shows itself be seen from itself in the very way in which it shows itself from itself" (58/34). This formula, Heidegger claims, expresses "nothing else than the maxim: 'To the things themselves!'" (58/34).

Another position that drew Heidegger away from Husserl was his view concerning the relation between phenomenological investigations and traditional Western philosophy. According to Heidegger, Husserl's programmatical explications and methodological procedure "strengthened the misunderstanding that through phenomenology a beginning of philosophy was claimed which denied all previous thinking." In contrast, his own conviction is,

> What occurs for the phenomenology of the acts of consciousness as the self-manifestation of phenomena is thought more originally by Aristotle and in all Greek thinking and existence as ἀλήθεια, as the unconcealedness of what is present, its being revealed, its showing itself. [1963b, 78–9/85–6]

For Heidegger, rejecting traditional metaphysics is not consistent with the principle of phenomenology. The purpose of phenomenology lies in a recovery of what shows itself in the beginning of Greek thinking and yet remains unthought in the metaphysical tradition. Much of Heidegger's work was devoted to re-appropriation of the work of past metaphysicians. In "A Dialogue," he claims that his philosophical praxis resides in an attempt to fit phenomenology "back into the place that is properly its own within Western philosophy" (*DL* 9/95).

In a text of 1937/38, Heidegger indicates "two directions" of his work until *Being and Time*: one is the historical direction, that is, "a resolute reverting to the Greek philosophy via the figure of its first foundational termination, Aristotle" [1937/38b, 365]; the other is "the direction of a serious engagement with the methodology of Husserl's 'phenomenology,'" which led him to "a mindfulness of history" [366].

THE TURN OF THE WAY

In his later writings, Heidegger dispenses with the term phenomenology. He dropped this word, "not—as is often thought—in order to deny the significance of phenomenology, but in order to leave [*zulassen*] my own path of thinking to namelessness" (*DL* 29/121; tr. m.).[8] He declares that the question of Being has been transformed from the "guiding-question" to the "grounding-question" (*CP* 52–54/74–77). For the purpose of indicating this change, he uses the archaic word *Seyn* (Beyng).[9] Beyng is Being in the grounding and originary sense. In view of Heidegger's *Denkweg* as a whole, it could be said that these two words identify two modalities of Being, or Beyng, or ~~Being~~, no matter which word is employed. As he writes,

> [T]he unfolding of the grounding-question at the same time proffers
> the ground for taking the whole history of the guiding-question back
> into a more originary ownership—instead of perhaps discarding it as
> something merely in the past. (*CP* 54/77)

The shift in Heidegger's approach to Being is often referred to as the turn (*Kehre*). Thomas Sheehan rightly stresses that the turn refers to the inner movement of Being, and cannot be identified as the movement that Heidegger's thought underwent in the 1930s. One needs to distinguish between Heidegger's thematic description of the self-movement (*die Kehre*) of Being's unconcealment and "the change in Heidegger's thinking" (*die Wendung im Denken*) (2001b, 3). The change in thinking means the shift in the way in which Heidegger formulated and expressed this internal movement of Being. It is a change in the thinking/saying of the *Kehre*. Sheehan's explanation points to an important question concerning the relation between Being and thinking. Heidegger himself explains,

> First and foremost the *Kehre* is not a process that took place in my thinking and questioning. It belongs, rather, to the very issue that is named by the titles "Being and Time" /"Time and Being." . . . The *Kehre* is at work within the issue itself. It is not something that I did, nor does it pertain to my thinking only. [1962c, xix]

It is clear that the *Kehre* does not reside in Heidegger's thinking; rather, Heidegger considers his thinking to be an attempt to emulate the essential movement of *die Sache selbst,* i.e. Being. In many of his writings, there is manifest a movement (*Kehre*), which, while gathering together the early and the latter halves of the text, moves away from essentialistic assumptions and directs toward *Gelassenheit,* toward ineffableness and vastness in which Being discloses itself. How this structure is at work in "A Dialogue" will be seen in Chapter nine. Furthermore, Heidegger may well have conceived the modification of his approach to the central question of Being in light of the *Kehre* of Being itself. Both early and later approaches, as well as modification and adjustment of formulations, arise out of necessity in accordance with the mode of movement of the *Kehre* itself.

For this reason, the distinction that Sheehan makes may not be sufficiently adequate for explicating the relation between the *Kehre* and Heidegger's approach to it. The way in which Sheehan sets out the distinction suggests a tenuous, external relation between the turn and the change of Heidegger's approach. Their internal connection is neglected. It better accords with Heidegger's ideas to attribute an internal bond to these two. Thinking in its essence is a correspondence to the call of what calls for thinking, i.e. *die Sache des Denkens* (Being), which resides in the turn. It is more appropriate to explain the relation of the turn and the change of Heidegger's approach to it in terms of the primordiality of the turn of Being itself and the derivativeness of the turn of thinking in relation to the primordial turn of Being itself, rather than in terms of a distinction.

Another point Sheehan argues for is that Heidegger's topic was not Being, either in its traditional ontological sense or in a transformed phenomenological sense. Instead, his question was: what brings about Being as the givenness or availability of entities? Heidegger's answer to this question was: Ereignis, the opening of a clearing (2001b, 5–9). As I see it, the dispute concerning the centrality of Being is mainly a matter of difference in formulations. In many places in his writings, Heidegger's thematization of Being is strikingly analogous to that of Ereignis. One could almost assert that, for him, Being is the "same" as Ereignis. In the *Contributions to Philosophy*, he writes,

> Beyng as Er-eignis. En-ownment [*Er-eignung*] determines man as owned by Beyng.
> Thus is Beyng then after all the other, over against Er-eignis? No, for ownhood [*Eigentum*] is belongingness into Er-eignis, and this itself is Beyng. (*CP* 185/263)

It is clear that, for Heidegger, Being (Beyng) and Ereignis are closely related notions. In any case, Sheehan cannot but use the word Being in his own formulation of Heidegger's basic question as cited above.[10]

It is well known that the later Heidegger devotes profound reflection to language and poetry. In 1934, Heidegger for the first time discussed in class his interpretations of Hölderlin's hymns.[11] In fact, before the First World War, Hölderlin had become one of his favorite readings.[12] In elucidating his poetry, Heidegger sees in language an abysmal source out of which an articulation of Being may become possible. Around the same time, he delivered a lecture series under the title "Logic," in which he explored the nature of language. This is suggested by the title under which the lecture notes were published, i.e. *Logic as the Question of the Nature of Language*.[13] In his "Letter to the Rector of Freiburg University" on 4 November 1945, Heidegger explains that by this course, he "sought to show that language was not the biological-racial essence of man, but conversely, that the essence of man was based in language as a basic reality of *spirit*" ([1945, 64/401]; em. or.). In the early 1950s, Heidegger states that the title "Logic" "conceals 'the transformation of logic into the question of the *essential nature* of language'—a question that is something else again than philosophy of language" (*WCT* 154/158). These statements again testify to the fact that Heidegger does not assume a simplistic "turning-away" attitude toward traditional metaphysics.

In his lecture course *Introduction to Metaphysics* in 1935, Heidegger systematically reconsidered the beginning of Western metaphysics. Concurrent with the composition of the *Contributions to Philosophy (From Enowning)* in 1936–38, his second *magnus opum*, Heidegger gave lecture courses on Nietzsche [1936/37], the lecture "The Origin of the Work of Art" [1935–36], and the lecture course *Basic Questions of Philosophy* [1937/38a]. These works were characterized with a rethinking of the beginning and end of Western metaphysics. In the *Contributions,* he initiated the thought of the other beginning (to be discusses in the next chapter), and sought its concrete possibilities through reflecting on the essence of language and Being.

Connected with Heidegger's reflection on the nature of language is the issue of hermeneutics. According to Gadamer, it was Heidegger who "introduced the concept of hermeneutics in philosophy, and not only in the methodology of the humanities" (1984, 58). Since the later Heidegger has almost completely dropped the term "hermeneutics," "A Dialogue" is a notable exception where he explicates his thoughts on hermeneutics. The question of an "authentic explanation" of the nature of hermeneutics constitutes one of the pair of clues in that essay (*DL* 11/98). Heidegger mentioned the inspiration he drew from his theological studies, and acknowledged his debts to Schleiermacher and Dilthey in this respect (10–11/97). He explains that what distinguishes him from these predecessors is that his primary concern is with the nature of interpretation (11/98), that he uses the term hermeneutics in a "broader" (*weiter*) sense, with broader meaning "from the vastness [*aus jener Weite*], which springs from the originary nature [*anfänglichen Wesen*]" (11/97; tr. m.).

Heidegger states that what concerns him in applying hermeneutics to philosophy is "to bring out the Being of beings . . . such that Being itself will shine out, . . . that is to say: the presence of present beings, the two-fold of the two in virtue of their simple oneness" (30/122). Language "prevails in and bears up the hermeneutic relation of human nature to the two-fold" (30/122). From these statements, it can be seen that Heidegger tended to regard his philosophical pursuit as one integral path of exploration of and rumination on the question of language and of Being.

EXPLORING THE NATURE OF LANGUAGE

Wesen is interrelated with other key notions of Heidegger's thinking such as Being (*Sein*), truth (*Wahrheit*), poetry (*Dichten*), language (*Sprache*) and technology (*Technik*). Heidegger claims, "in the concept of *Wesen* philosophy thinks *Sein*" (*ET* 153/200). It has been difficult to find a suitable English word that can convey all the complex and subtle nuances of *Wesen*.

Among the manifold senses of *Wesen*, what is the most central and prominent is originating, grounding, founding, presencing, or existing. In so far as this sense is close to the meaning of the Greek word φύσις,[14] since the standard translation of φύσις is "nature," in most cases I render *Wesen* as "nature." On the other hand, *Wesen* is essentially related to Being. Etymologically speaking, the perfect form of *Sein*, *gewesen*, relates very closely to *Wesen*. Thematically speaking, Being and language are the two sides of the same coin in Heidegger's thought. Language has its own mode of Being. Already in

Being and Time (section 34), he touches on the question as to "what mode of being language as language in any case has."[15] Therefore, sometimes I render *Wesen* as "essential being." For example, "In this case, the nature of language becomes the promise of its essential being, that is, becomes the language of being" (*OWL* 72/176; tr. m.).

Heidegger maintains that "reflection on the nature of language must also attain a different rank" (*LH* 243/318). In the lecture entitled "Language" delivered in 1950, he sets himself against three prevalent views of language. The first view regards language as external expressions of internal thought. The second view treats language as an activity of man. According to this view, one cannot say, "Language says," but has to say, "man speaks" [1950a, 190/14]. One cannot say that man is bespoken by language either. The third view considers language to be a presentation and representation of something. According to Heidegger, all these views fail to bring us to language as language.[16]

For Heidegger, to inquire into the *Wesen* of language means to explore the question "[h]ow does the nature of language arise in the essential swaying [*Wesung*] of Beyng" (*CP* 352/500; tr. m.). The essential unfolding of the nature of language is inextricably connected with Being. It is at the same time essentially involved with the unfolding of the nature of man. As Heidegger explicates, his phrase "Language says" means, "it is language that first brings man about, bring him into existence"; "To reflect on language means—to reach the saying of language in such a way that this saying takes place as that which grants an abode for the being of mortals" [1950a, 190/14].

These two sides of meaning are expressed in Heidegger's famous slogan "language is the house of Being." This phrase appears for the first time in the beginning of the "Letter on Humanism," and recurs many times in the 1940s and 1950s.[17] As Heidegger explains, it means two things. First, only by language can Being be shown forth, can the world be made to appear, and can the things be presented as the things they are. "Language is the clearing-concealing advent of Being itself" (*LH* 249/236). Second, only in language as language can man find the proper abode of his existence.[18] One could say, "language is the home [*Behausung*] of the nature of man" (*LH* 274/361).[19] These two dimensions can be re-formulated in one sentence as: "language is at once the house of Being and the home of man" (274/361).

Heidegger illustrates the co-perdurance of language and Being in terms of such a "guide word" (*Leitwort*): "The being [*Wesen*] of language: the language of being [*des Wesens*]" (*OWL* 94/200). In the first phrase, language is the subject whose being is to be determined. The whatness, τὸ τί ἐστιν, is at stake. By the second phrase one enters into what language is. In this phrase, the word "being" acts as a verb. It does not indicate a static whatness. "To be" means to perdure and to persist. "It is in being" means "it persists in its presence." "Being" is what "moves and makes a way for all things." "What moves all things moves in that it speaks."[20]

At the end of "The Way to Language," Heidegger recalls his famous phrase,

> Language has been called the "house of Being." It is the guardian of presencing, in that its coming to light remains entrusted to the appropriative showing of Saying. Language is the house of Being because, as the Saying, it is the mode of Appropriation. (*OWL* 135/267; tr. m.).

Here Heidegger correlates "language is the house of Being" with Saying, another famous word for the nature of language. Toward the end of "A Dialogue," the Inquirer finally improvises a more fitting word for language: "Saying" (*die Sage*).[21] Heidegger's dramatic introduction of this word is somewhat misleading, since he seems to find the "fitting word" (*DL* 8/89) for the nature of language just during his dialogue with the Japanese. In fact, the word "Saying" occurs to Heidegger almost twenty years before in "The Origin of the Work of Art,"

> Language, by naming beings for the first time, first brings beings to word and to appearance. This naming nominates beings *to* their Being *from out of* their Being. Such [S]aying [*die Sage*] is a projecting of the clearing, in which announcement is made as to what beings will come into the open as. ([1935–36, 46/61]; em. or.)

Heidegger associates the German word *Sage* to the old Norse word "Saga," and explains its meaning as "to show, to let appear, to let be seen as heard" (*OWL* 122/252). "Saying pervades and structures the openness of that clearing" (126/257). Language, as Saying, is closely related to thinking as the remembrance of Being, to the history of Being. The destiny of Being "comes to language in the words of essential thinkers" (*LH* 255/335). Thinking is a recollection of Being. Just as thinking is historic, for Heidegger, language is also historic (272–4/358–61). In its proper sense, the language that is to be the house of Being is not an arbitrary everyday language, but *the language* of Being, in which Being speaks itself. In the "Letter on Humanism," Heidegger makes this point clear. "Historically, only one Saying [*Sage*] belongs to the matter of thinking, the one that is in each case appropriate to its matter" (*LH* 272/358). That there is only "one Saying" that properly belongs to "the matter of thinking" implies that the language of Being has a singularity. There is something determinate that belongs to what is the own of language. It could be said, on behalf of Heidegger, that there is only one house of Being in the final analysis.

In discussing the nature of poetry, Heidegger states that "[the nature of poetry] is itself, in its nature, a founding [*Stiftung*]—that is, firm grounding [*feste Gründung*]" (*EHP* 63/45). He explains, "every founding remains a free gift. . . . This freedom, however, is not unrestrained arbitrariness and headstrong desire, but supreme necessity [*höchste Notwendigkeit*]" (63/45). Heidegger claims that the origination of the nature of poetry applies to the nature of language as well. There is "supreme necessity" involved in this event. In the *Contributions,* Heidegger writes,

> What is ownmost [*das Wesen*] to language can never be determined in any other way than by naming its origin [*Ursprung*]. . . . this relation of language to Beyng is generally not an arbitrary invention. . . . "The" language is "our" language; "our" language, not only as mother tongue, but also as the language of our history. . . . For all mindfulness of Beyng and of language is really only a thrust ahead [*Vorstoss*] in order to encounter our "standpoint" [*Standort*] in Beyng itself and thus our history. (*CP* 352–3/500–1)

The relation between language and Beyng is not without any rule. It is subject to supreme necessity. Exploration of the nature of language is at the same time an attempt to revive what is said in language in the beginning of history. Retrieval is owning (*Eignen*) and propriating (*Ereignen*). It is an act "to bring language (the nature of language [*das Sprachwesen*]) as language (the Saying) to language (to the sounded word [*zum verlautenden Wort*])" (*OWL* 130/261). The sounded word is what is heard in the inception of Western historicality. In "The Principle of Identity" (1957), Heidegger makes these points explicitly:

> Our Western languages are in different ways languages of metaphysical thinking. It must remain an open question whether the nature of Western languages is in itself marked with the exclusive brand of metaphysics, and thus marked permanently by onto-theo-logic, or whether these languages offer other possibilities of saying—and that means at the same time a telling unsaying [*sagenden Nichsagens*]. (*ID* 73/142; tr. m.)

Despite occasional criticisms of Western languages, Heidegger has the conviction that only through these languages could one find possibilities of a true Saying.

LANGUAGE AND MAN

By the claim "language is the home of the nature of man," Heidegger stresses the belongingness of man to language. He writes in the "Letter on Humanism,"

> Language is the house of Being. In its home man dwells. Those who think and those who create with words are the guardians of this home. Their guardianship accomplishes the manifestation of Being insofar as they bring this manifestation to language and preserve it in language through their saying. (*LH* 239/313; tr. m.)

This accent on man as the "guardians" of "the house of Being" has to be understood in light of what Heidegger considers to be the nature of man. Heidegger expresses discontent with the classical definition that man is *animal rationale*. For him, although traditional thinking acknowledges a difference between man and other creatures, as can be seen from this definition, it still determines man's essence in the dimension of *animalitas* by setting off man "as one living creature among others" and by "locat[ing] man among beings as one being among others" (*LH* 246/323). By this definition, "the nature of man is too little heeded and not thought in its origin, the essential provenance that is always the essential future for historical mankind" (246/323).

In the same vein, Heidegger opposes himself against humanism for the reason that it "does not set the humanism of man high enough," that it does not yet "realize the proper dignity of the human being" (*LH* 251/330). In refuting the prevalent conception of the human being from the perspective of anthropology, psychology, and biology, Heidegger attempts to grant the loftiest status to the human being. Any association of man to animal must be broken off. Man must be separated from beasts "by an abyss" (248/324).[22]

For Heidegger, "man essentially occurs only in his essence only where he is claimed by Being. Only from that claim 'has' he found that wherein his essence dwells" (*LH* 247/323). Man's nature has nothing to do either with his bodily features that can be analyzed by physiology, or with a Cartesian mind that is co-joined to an organic thing. Man's nature consists in standing outside (*ek-sistence*) into the "clearing of Being," or "the truth of Being." Only man is "destined to think the nature of his Being" (247/324). Language is not merely one capacity man possesses along with other capacities. Through language man can hear the message of Being; he dwells in language as the guardian of Being. Man and language are mutually indispensable.

Language seems to be granted the primal role in its relation to man. This is reflected in such remarks as "language speaks itself in us," and "language itself has woven us into the speaking" (*OWL* 112/242). However, man is indispensable. Man is given the dative role, so to speak, as the recipient of the message of Being, through whose experience alone can the event of occurrence be initiated. This role is co-primordial with the nature of language. "Language and man determine each other, mutually . . . by virtue of their belongingness to Beyng" (*CP* 351/499). In another place, Heidegger explains that "to discuss language, to place it, means to bring to its place of being not so much language as ourselves: our own gathering into the Ereignis" [1950a, 188/12].[23]

In accounting for the relation between man and language in terms of Ereignis, Heidegger suggests that man must "enter into the speaking of language in order to take up our stay with language" [1950a, 190/14]. In the founding act of Ereignis, man achieves his nature as man and becomes at home in the house of language. In this act, man is owned by Being and language as much as language is brought to language as language. This sense of Ereignis is similar to "it gives" (*Es gibt*)" (*TB* 5/6). Just as time and Being are both gifts of "it gives," language and man, for Heidegger, are also the gifts of "it gives."

Man must experience a transformation in order to dwell in language as the home of the nature of man. In "The Way to Language" [1959c], Heidegger writes:

> . . . a transformation of language is needed which we can neither compel nor invent. This transformation does not result from the procurement of newly formed words and phrases. It touches on our relation to language, which is determined by destiny: whether and in what way the nature of language as the arch-tidings of Ereignis, will retain us in Ereignis. (*OWL* 135/267)

In thinking experience, man responds to the Saying of language. Through the appropriating event (Ereignis), man is transported into the realm of the essential origin of language and Being. This event of appropriation is not an arbitrary happening, but is endowed with supreme necessity. As Heidegger emphasizes in "The Principle of Identity," Ereignis is a *singulare tantum*. It happens only in the singular (*ID* 36/101); it is essentially determined by destiny.

In a lecture on Heraclitus, Heidegger explains that the word *logos,* which is the guideword (*Leitwort*) of Heraclitus' thinking, names "that which gathers all present beings into presencing and lets them lie before us in it" [1951, 76/231]. It is the name for the Being of beings (77/232). In this sense, it is the nature of Saying as thought by the Greeks. "The Greeks *dwelt* in this nature of language. But they have never *thought* it—Heraclitus included" (77/232; em. or.). The Greeks experienced the nature of language, but they failed to think it through as the genuine *logos,* they failed to think it from out of the nature of Being. As a result, language comes to be represented as φωνή (*phone,* vocalization), γλῶσσα (*glossa,* tongue), and more predominantly, as expression. In this light, Heidegger claims that "Λόγος conceals within itself the essential origin of the imprint of the nature of language, and thus determines the way of saying as a logical one in the broader sense" (*ID* 69/137; tr. m.).

The task of thinking, for Heidegger, is for man (Western man) to experience and to think what remains unthought in the beginning of Western historicality. This endows the supreme necessity and rule to the appropriating event in and through which man dwells in the house of Being. Heidegger stresses, "The reflection on language [is] a decisive way toward the leap into the completely other, namely being-historical thinking" [1939a, 5/5].

RELATIVISM OR UNIVERSALISM?

Although Heidegger's thinking on the nature of language is intimately related to the history of Being, the importance he attaches to the role of language is so omnipresent that his philosophy has been characterized as "linguistic phenomenology," or "linguistic idealism."[24] Richard Rorty (1989) and Christiana Lafont (2000) find in Heidegger a "reification of language."[25] Lafont claims that language plays the role of world-disclosure in his philosophy, that language is "the court of appeal that (as the 'house of being') judges beforehand what can be encountered within the world" (7). These comments convey an aspect of Heidegger's reflection on language. Heidegger articulates a holistic idea of language, that is, language is an exclusive whole. He thus explicates the relation between word and thing:

> This relation is not, however, a connection between the thing that is on one side and the word that is on the other. The word itself is the relation

which in each instance retains the thing within itself in such a manner
that it "is" thing. (*OWL* 66/170)

These statements are strongly suggestive of linguistic holism.

In the essay "Words" [1958a], Heidegger modifies the last verse of Stefan
George's poem "Words," "Where word breaks off no thing may be," as "No
thing is where the word breaks off" (*OWL* 60/163). According to him, "breaks
off" means "is lacking." "No thing is where the word is lacking, that word
which names the given thing" (60–61/163). Heidegger elaborates further, "the
being of anything that is resides in the word. Therefore this statement holds
true: Language is the house of Being" (63/166). The word serves as the enlightenment that brings beings into Being, or, alternatively speaking, lets Being present in beings. In "A Dialogue," Heidegger remarks, "the word is a hint and not
a sign in the sense of mere signification" (*DL* 27/119). "Hints need the widest
sphere in which to swing, where mortals go to and fro only slowly" (27/119).
Only language as the word can bring Being as a whole to presence.

Heidegger's emphasis on the grounding nature of words accords with
Lafont's observation that for him language is the site of world-disclosure. However, if Heidegger's reflection on language is to be characterized as reification,
one needs to differentiate it from the usual understanding of reification which
Heidegger himself depreciates. In *Being and Time*, Heidegger opposes "reification [*Verdinglichung*] of consciousness" or the notion of "substantial soul" (*BT*
72/46). As Kisiel explains,

> [T]he light of reason interpreted as a *reified* power somehow implanted
> in us is precisely what Heidegger from the beginning strives to surpass,
> in order to establish the ontological ground for any act of illumination or
> intuitive seeing. (1970, 91; em. ad.)

Indubitably, Heidegger does not appreciate a "reification" that fixates and
substantializes consciousness and reason, or the power to know. He underscores
this point,

> Thingliness [*Dinglichkeit*] itself needs to be demonstrated in terms of its
> ontological source in order that we can ask what is now to be understood
> *positively* by the non-reified *being* [*nichtverdinglichten Sein*] of the subject,
> consciousness, the spirit, the person. (*BT* 72/46; em. or.)

Heidegger is also against the kind of reification that objectifies. In "A
Dialogue," he emphasizes that "[s]peaking *about* language turns language

almost inevitably into an object . . . and then its nature [*Wesen*] vanishes" (*DL* 50/149; em. or.).

The kind of reification that characterizes Heidegger's reflection on language is connected with the idea that the nature of language is nothing linguistic, but is essentially bound up with the inception of the history of Being. With Heidegger, language seems to have its own existence that is independent of human beings and the world. It is something that can be referred to, or, to use Heidegger's phrase, can be hinted at. It speaks. Heidegger states that there can only be "a speaking *from* language," "*from out of* language's nature, be led to its nature" (*DL* 51/149–50; em. or.).

Lafont argues that Heidegger's treatment of language as the site of world-disclosing leads to "extreme relativism" (xv), and "radical incommensurability" (xvi). The implication of this is, "There is no absolute truth across incommensurable understanding of being or world-disclosures. They are unrevisable from within and inaccessible (meaningless) from without" (xv).[26] In light of this neutralized reading, which considers language and Being as neutral, replaceable, potentially countable nouns, the West and the East are considered to be self-enclosed houses because of the radical difference of their languages.[27] Consequently, a dialogue from house to house is "nearly impossible" (*DL* 5/90).

Some aspects in Heidegger's writings are strongly suggestive of a relativistic stance. However, one should notice that the relativistic strand in his work is not the ordinary version. For Heidegger, the East does not share what is constitutive of the West. That is the history of Being as articulated by Western languages. Only Western languages are the languages of Being. I will elaborate on Heidegger's understanding of philosophy and thinking in relation to the history of Being in the next chapter.

During his meeting with the Thai monk (Mani) in 1963, Heidegger emphasizes that "vis-à-vis Eastern thinking, it is [Western] history that actually separates East and West" (Petzet, 176; em. ad.). After Mani responds that with Eastern thinking there is not such a concept of history but only passages through the world, Heidegger seems to have found evidence for his conviction. He claims that it is different attitudes toward history and the world that "makes impossible a simple comparison of the theses of philosophy in West and East" (Petzet, 176). Since the presuppositions are different, any such comparison will cause falsifications. This sounds as if it is a relativistic stance. However, Heidegger's point is that, because the history that the West possesses is the sole genuine history, any attempt at an immediate comparison with the East would be wrong-headed.

In the same conversation with Mani, Heidegger states, "what matters is whether one can co-enact [his] path of thinking" and that "the only significant thing is 'to be on the way'" (Petzet, 176). This remark is made in response to the question whether he considers it more important to set up a new system of thinking or whether he would stress the necessity of religion. However, since this exchange occurs immediately after the discussion of East-West difference as cited in the foregoing, Heidegger may have made this remark in relation to the East-West relation as well. On the presumption that Eastern and Western thought are completely different and incomparable, Heidegger seems to be suggesting that only by initiating his way of thinking can there be a possibility of engagement between East and West.

Therefore, although there are clear signs of relativism in Heidegger's thought, his position is more complicated than that. He would not take himself to be a relativist in the ordinary sense of the word. In his lecture to the Marburg Theological Society in 1924, he states, "anxiety in the face of relativism is anxiety in the face of Dasein" [1924, 20/123]. Following Husserl, albeit in a quite different way, Heidegger considers that one of his tasks of thinking is to combat relativism. For him, the validities of truth only reside in the single house of Western language and tradition. The history that plays an indispensable role in his thinking has an abysmal difference from the historian's history. It is the history of truth, the history of Being. It is not possible for him to embrace the idea that meaning should be "contingent and historically alterable," to use Lafont's words (xv). Neither would he ponder over the question of "radical incommensurability." For him, what is more important than dealing with the question of incommensurability is to follow his path of thinking, which emulates the essential movement of Being.

Some scholars focus on the feature of essential openness in Heidegger's writings on language. Authors such as Richard Polt (1999) and Joseph Kockelmans (1972) argue that Heidegger's ideas are radically opposed to the classical view of language that treats it as an empirical object. They draw on the primacy Heidegger ascribes to the originary (*anfänglich*) nature of language by which what has been said in the Sayings of Greek thought is to be retrieved and thought anew. This aspect is consonant with Heidegger's privileging of the transformative experience that carries thinkers into the region of their proper abode—the unconcealment of Being in its concealedness, and with his emphasis that what he is considering is not language in the sense of a biological and racial feature of human beings, but only language itself. However, these authors have refrained from assessing the implication of their interpretation of Heidegger's view for East-West dialogue.

A few authors who are concerned with transcultural issues present Heidegger as a universalist by focusing on this aspect of fundamental openness of language, Being and tradition. In doing this, they have either implicitly or explicitly regarded the question of Being and of language as a universal concern of human beings, instead of a Western privilege. J. L. Mehta can be said to be the pioneer who ascribes this version of universalism to Heidegger. According to him, Heidegger's project of "planetary construction" is "the construction of a *universal,* basic language of Truth [*sic*] from which the languages of different philosophical and religious traditions can be derived" (1976, 465; em. ad.). More importantly, Mehta obviously considers that the "region of all regions" Heidegger aims to leap into lies beyond the opposition of East and West. He writes,

It is the realm of that *universality* and simplicity of primordial truth, . . . where alone divergent traditions, disfranchised of their exclusive claims and yet without losing their own identity, can meet together as one, as belonging-together in the Self-same. If there is any hope of an ultimate unity of divergent philosophies and religions, it lies . . . solely through a going back of each to its own origins, in the leap into this swaying region, vibrant with the possibility of giving voice to its primordial word in a multiplicity of tongues. (Mehta 1976, 463–64; em. ad.)

Clearly, Mehta has perceived the possibility in Heidegger's thinking that point in the direction of relativism. By granting the "region of regions" a unifying power that can reconcile exclusive claims from different traditions, Mehta attempts to explain away the potential relativism. Although the idea of divergent traditions going back to their respective origins seems to entail relativism, as long as these traditions are able to leap into this unifying primal region, differences will become insignificant and will not contradict claims of universalism. With the opening up of this region, divergent traditions can be said to achieve unity in each of their differences. Such an interpretation or extension of Heidegger's thought rightly conveys some of the central features of his philosophy, although it may be more suitable for Mehta to use the term "phenomenological" rather than "universal." The focus falls upon the opening up of a phenomenological horizon that has been anticipated.

It is necessary to distinguish between two kinds of universalism that are both involved in this Heidegger-inspired discourse. According to one kind of universalism, there is something determinate and substantial that is shared, for example, a concern with the question of Being. The other kind of universalism accentuates the movement by means of which all traditions leap into the primal region. It seems that Heidegger would have stronger objections against the first kind than against the second. He would resolutely oppose himself against the idea that Being has shown itself to peoples other than the Greeks. For him, it is a historic fact that Being shows itself *only* to the Greeks; the history of Being is intimately bound up with the West.

The problem with the second kind of universalism is that: if what is shared is the movement as such, then there does not seem to be a basis on which the region into which each tradition leaps is guaranteed to be the same region. The implication of this is: with this kind of universalism, the shadow of relativism remains, since it can well be the case that each tradition leaps into a different region of their own.

Heidegger would consider both universalistic and relativistic readings of his thought to be inadequate and superficial. For him, the urge toward universalism, toward sameness and communication goes against the historic character of language and truth. As he states in the lecture "Language,"

> Reflection tries to obtain an idea of what language is universally. The universal that holds for each thing is called its essence or nature. To represent universally what holds universally is, according to prevalent views, the basic feature of thought" [1950a, 187f/11f].

Against this universalistic stance, Heidegger underlines that the title of his lecture is not "On the nature of language," but only "Language," which is "far more presumptuous" (188/12). Certainly, the universalism as Mehta describes is more complicated than this version (I will explore related issues in Chapter nine). In the meantime, the relativistic presumptions also fail to capture the singularity of Heidegger's thought. For him, language does not speak many languages, but speaks only one language, the language of Being. Heidegger's reflection on language is indeed radically "presumptuous."

Chapter Three
Philosophy, the *Ge-stell,* and East-West Dialogue

In the *Spiegel* interview, Heidegger defends himself against the accusation that his project of overcoming metaphysics is damaging Western philosophical tradition. He explains,

> My whole work in lectures and exercises in the past 30 years has been in the main only an interpretation of Western philosophy. The regress into the historical foundations of thought, the thinking through of the questions which are still unasked since the time of Greek philosophy—that is not a cutting loose from the tradition. [1966a, 109/674]

The orientation of Heidegger's path of thinking is integrally bound up with a retrieval of resources in the Western philosophical tradition. His thoughts on the origin and transformation of philosophy are concentratedly thematized in terms of the first and the other beginning. From this perspective, he ascribes central importance to the early Greek philosophers, whom he regards as the inceptive thinkers of the first beginning.

In the meantime, Heidegger claims an intimate relation between technology on the one hand, and Being, metaphysics, and philosophy on the other. According to him, the present world, which has been in the grip of the *Ge-stell,* is a necessary unfolding of the history of Being (*Seinsgeschichte*). Almost all of Heidegger's fleeting references to East-West dialogue occur in the context of his concern with the *Ge-stell* and with the necessity of a dialogue with early Greek thinkers. After elucidating his reflection on the first and other beginning, philosophy and thinking, and the *Ge-stell,* I will discuss those passages from Heidegger's writings that contain references to East-West dialogue.

THE FIRST AND THE OTHER BEGINNING

The Positing of the First Beginning

In a narrow sense, the first beginning indicates the appearance of the originary thinking of the Pre-Socratic thinkers. In a wide sense, it encompasses
the entire history of metaphysics up to the post-Nietzschean time. In *Parmenides,* Heidegger claims that the first beginning can only occur to "a historical people of thinkers and poets in the West" [1942/43, 77/114]. He
distinguishes the word *Anfang* from *Beginn.* According to him, *Beginn* (outset) refers to the coming forth of the early thinking at a definite time. Thinking does not mean the course of psychologically represented acts of thought,
but the historical process in which a thinker appears, articulates his word,
and gives truth a place within a historical humanity.

Outset has to do with the debut and the emergence of thinking. In
contrast, *Anfang* (beginning, or inception) is "what, in this early thinking,
is to be thought and what is thought" [1942/43, 7/9–10]. This means,
"Being is the beginning" [7/11]. Not every thinker, who has to think
Being, thinks the beginning. A primordial thinker is one who expressly
thinks the beginning. The beginning is not something like an object the
thinkers take up, nor is it a construction of thought. Etymologically speaking, the German word *Anfang* derives from *an-* (in, at, to) and *-fangen* (to
seize, take, catch). This supports Heidegger's claim that primordial thinkers do not rely on their own resources in carrying out the beginning of
thinking. Instead, they are seized and taken up by *the* beginning. In his
own words, "The thinkers are begun by the beginning, incepted [*An-gefan-
genen*] by the in-ception [*An-fang*]; they are taken up by it and are gathered
into it" [1942/43, 7–8/11].

Being is the central concern of early Greek thinking. In his interpretation of the pre-Socratic thinkers and of the chorus of Sophocles' *Anti-
gone,* Heidegger explains that in the first beginning Being is conceived
as φύσις, which is rendered as *natura* when it was translated into Latin
(meaning "to be born," "birth"). With this Latin translation, Heidegger
asserts, "the originary content of the Greek word φύσις is already thrust
aside, the authentic philosophical naming force of the Greek word is
destroyed" (*IM* 14/10). According to him, φύσις in its true sense names
"the unfolding that opens itself up, the coming-into-appearance in such
unfolding, and holding itself and persisting in appearance—in short, the
emerging-abiding sway" (*IM* 15/12). When φύσις is translated as *natura,*
the inceptive philosophy of the Greeks is misrepresented as a philosophy of

nature, a philosophy that is concerned with representing all things as things of a material nature. This, according to Heidegger, gives rise to a distorted image of Greek thought (16/12).

Φύσις can be experienced in the abundance of natural phenomena where emergence is involved, such as the rising of the sun, the surging of the sea, and the growth of plants. Heidegger stresses that the process of φύσις *itself* should not be understood under the same term as other processes, that is, as one process among others. This is because "φύσις is Being itself, by virtue of which beings first become observable and remain so" (*IM* 15/12; tr. m.).

The Greek philosophers experience the truth of Being through the notion of φύσις and ἀλήθεια, through the experience of the overpowering of φύσις through τέχνε, of the breakdown of ἀλήθεια, and of the differentiation of being and thinking (that is, between φύσις and λόγος). This experience marks the decisive moment of the first beginning. Greek thought is born of this originary experience of the truth of Being, an experience of the presencing that belongs to Being, and of its occurrence as withdrawal. The Greek word for truth, ἀλήθεια, which Heidegger translates as "un-concealment," points to the dual aspect of the truth of Being. "Un-concealment" entails the pre-existing experience of concealment. Although the Greeks experienced concealment, they have failed to conceive it as essentially belonging to the truth of Being. This does not mean that Greek thought is imperfect or disabled. Rather, their failure derives from the necessity of the history of being; it belongs to the ways in which the truth of Being enacts itself in the first beginning. As Heidegger affirms unequivocally, "*Only what is unique is retrievable and repeatable.* Only *it* carries within itself the ground of the necessity of going back to it and taking over its inceptuality" (*CP* 39/55; em. or.).

The Transition to the Other Beginning

It is important to note that both the first and the other beginning (*der andere Anfang*) are singular. Heidegger stresses the existence of the internal connection between the first and other beginning. The first beginning refers to what is thought and what is to be thought by the Greek thinkers. The other beginning acquires meaning from its essential connection with the first beginning. In the first section of the *Contributions,* Heidegger explicates,

> The "other" beginning of thinking is named thus, not because it is simply shaped differently from any other arbitrarily chosen hitherto existing philosophies, but because it must be the only other beginning according to the relation *to* the only one and first beginning [*er der einzig andere aus dem Bezug* zu *dem einzig einen und ersten Anfang sein muss*]. The

style of thoughtful mindfulness in the crossing from one beginning to the other is also already determined by the allotment [*Zugewiesenheit*] of the one beginning to the other beginning. (*CP* 4/5; em. or.)

Heidegger makes it clear in this passage that the other in the formulation "the other beginning" has no association with the suggestion that it is other than any existing philosophy. Instead, it obtains its validity from its relation to the first beginning. Moreover, the manner of thinking in the transition from the first to the other beginning is decided by the "allotment" of the former to the latter.

One should comprehend such words as "beginning," "first," and "other" originarily. Do the first and the other beginning represent two beginnings respectively, or are they inextricably intertwined with one another such that speaking of them as separate terms would already miss Heidegger's point? Notably, Heidegger has never spoken of a/the *second* beginning. He explains that the other beginning is named thus "because it must be the only other out of the relation *to* the only one and first beginning" (4/5; em. or.; tr. m.).[1] This implies that the first and the other beginning designate one single event. In the most originary sense, one could say that there is only one beginning. The beginning that is one grounds the space where "the first beginning" and "the other beginning" enact themselves in the movement of the playing-forth. The sense of the "one" conforms to the sense in which there is only one first beginning and only one other beginning.

That there is only one first and other beginning should not be taken to be a transcendent or transcendental beginning that subsequently divides into the first and the other. It is an occurrence that occurs when one discards representational thinking and enters into Being-historic-thinking. This is the inceptive thinking. As one thinks inceptively, the differentiation between the first and the other occurs, and the in-between of the grounding attunement to the happening of the truth of Being as Ereignis opens up. Originarily speaking, the other beginning arises in the decisive encounter with the history of metaphysics, while the first beginning comes to be only at the intimation of the inception of the other beginning. The other as articulated in terms of the other beginning is not something alien to Western metaphysical tradition. Rather, it occurs in the inceptive understanding of it.

Heidegger stresses that the transition into the other beginning is not a "counter-movement" (*Gegenbewegung*) (130/186). Counter-movements and counter-forces remain to be determined by what they are against, and consequently are confined by what they conquer. This cannot be the case with an essential transformation. True transformation demands that future decisions be disentangled in the hitherto existing domains. The other beginning "as the other [*als anderes*] stands outside the counter [*gegen*] and outside immediate comparability" (131/187). The encounter (*Auseinandersetzung*) between the first and the other beginning (8/10), Heidegger explains, is neither a crude rejection, nor a sublation of the first in the other. The other beginning "helps the first beginning to [enter unto] the truth of its history—and thus unto its inalienable and ownmost otherness" (131/187). From this perspective, it becomes clearer that the other of the other beginning already has its seeds in the first beginning. The other is not an alien external other, but an internal otherness, though it could be said to be alien in the sense of being inexhaustible.[2]

My last remark on Heidegger's thematization of the other beginning is the following. There is a subtle tension within the temporal structure of the occurrence of the other beginning. This tension concerns the sense in which the other beginning is "not yet" and the sense in which it "has already been." On the one hand, Heidegger speaks of the "transformation-initiating preparation for the other beginning" (119/169). This implies that the other beginning has "not yet" been enacted. The truth of Being has not yet occurred as Ereignis that makes concealing unconcealment possible. The end of metaphysics has not yet awakened man to the withdrawal of Being. Man clings to representational thinking and has not yet surpassed into Being-historic-thinking. On the other hand, although the other beginning in the futuristic "not yet" sense is only intimated, in the in-between of the transition from the first to the other beginning, it "has already been" decided as Being-historic-thinking; it "has already" surpassed the first beginning. This is because, historically speaking, Being-historic-thinking has been set out into the realm of the truth of Being.

PHILOSOPHY AND THINKING

Heidegger's thinking on the first and the other beginning is intimately related to a unitary history of Being, which belongs solely to Western thinking. This is the necessary background against which one should understand his discourse on the relation between philosophy and thinking. Among the writings that focus on or devote attention to Heidegger's Asian connection, his reflection on the other beginning, or the new beginning, have occupied a prominent place.[3] It is considered to be an effort to break away from traditional metaphysics and open up the possibility of allowing other traditions to play a role in the construction of a new beginning. This new beginning is not philosophy any more, but a non-metaphysical thinking that is inclusive of the sources and resources from other traditions. According to this view, Heidegger's thinking opens up a possibility for the Western tradition to understand its own limit and to enter into an essential dialogue with other non-Western traditions. However, this line of thought has ignored Heidegger's emphasis on the unitary relation between the first and the other beginning, and between philosophy and thinking.

One must be aware that what Heidegger calls "thinking" is not completely distinct from "philosophy," but instead is intrinsically united with it. As philosophy is, thinking is a correspondence to the claim of Being. True thinking is an *Andenken* (remembrance) of what is said by the Greek thinkers. It allows man to be transported into the realm of Being's unconcealment. Heidegger asserts, "with the end of philosophy, thinking is not also at its end but in transition to the other beginning" (*OM* 77/81).[4] The word "philosophy" in the phrase "the end of philosophy" refers to traditional metaphysics that treats Being as Being of beings without thinking about Being itself. With traditional metaphysics coming to an end, true philosophy (which is recollective, world-historic thinking) is to be initiated into the other beginning. Thinking is philosophy in the authentic sense.

In "Europe and German Philosophy," Heidegger writes, "each new beginning of philosophy *is* and *can* only be a repetition of the first—a regurgitation of the question: what Being might be—a saying the truth of Being" ([1936b, 34]; em. or.). In this statement, Heidegger is obviously using "philosophy" in the broad sense. A new beginning, a new era of philosophy *can* only grow out of the soil of what precedes it; and it continues to have the question of Being as the central question. In "A Dialogue on Language" [1953/54], Heidegger affirms that when he speaks of overcoming metaphysics, what he purports to do is to bring out the "essence of metaphysics, and only thus brings metaphysics back within its own limits" (*DL* 20/109). He emphasizes that his project is "neither a destruction nor even a denial of metaphysics," and that "[t]o intend anything else would be childish presumption and a demeaning of history" (20/109). It is clear that Heidegger's "seemingly subversive will tries above all to recover the things of the past in a more originary form" (36/130). The rhetoric of overcoming metaphysics is formulated in order to call attention to the urgency of a true transformation of metaphysics, of a thinking that thinks of the most sublime question of philosophy (that is, the question of Being) and, in doing this, brings out the essence of philosophy.

Philosophy, thinking and metaphysics share the same realm of reflection. This is because, as Heidegger states, "insofar as thinking is originally performed as λόγος, a change of the thinking process can consist only in a transformation of the λόγος" (*WCT* 156/101). In view of this continuous trajectory of the development of thinking, philosophy is exclusively Western. Heidegger makes this point emphatically in the lecture series on Heraclitus,

> The expression "Western philosophy" is avoided; because this notion is rigorously thinking an overladen term. There is no other philosophy than the Western one. "Philosophy" is in its essence so originally Western, that it carries within itself the history of the Western world. [1943a, 3]

In this passage, Heidegger explains that he refrains from using the expression "Western philosophy" because it may misleadingly suggest that the term philosophy is a genus with different species, and that the so-called "Western philosophy" is only one such species. It is for this reason that he dispenses with the modifier "Western." For Heidegger, philosophy is not something without proper historical and cultural determinations. Nor does it come to any people impartially. It appears only in the West and grounds the unfolding of the whole of the Western world. Furthermore, it is essentially entangled with the question of Being: "Philosophy means to be addressed by Being itself" [1942/43, 120/179].

In *What is Called Thinking?* Heidegger claims that Parmenides' saying that "it is useful to let-lie-before-us and so taking-to-heart also: beings in being" has already taken heed of the Being of beings. To the point where the Being of beings can be taken to heart, the duality of beings and Being has emerged. However, there have been no further inquiries and thinking about this duality itself, neither in relation to its nature nor in relation to its origin. In this context, Heidegger comments,

> Thus it is that the one thing which remains to be asked—what are particular beings in their Being?—comes to the fore within the sphere of this duality. The style of all Western-European philosophy—and there is no other, neither a Chinese nor an Indian philosophy—is determined by this duality "beings—in Being." Philosophy's procedure in the sphere of this duality is decisively shaped by the interpretation Plato gave to the duality. That the duality appears as participation does not at all go without saying. (*WCT* 224/228)

The statement that there is no Chinese or Indian philosophy can be facilely taken to be an indirect compliment Heidegger makes to Asian thought. That is, Western-European philosophy has been totally contaminated by dualistic metaphysical thinking that has forgotten Being itself, whereas ancient Asian traditions have been fortunately exempt from this kind of deterministic metaphysical thought. This explanation *seems* to be quite convincing, however, things are seldom what they seem in this philosopher's writings.

It is certainly true that on this occasion, as on many other occasions, Heidegger is criticizing the Western philosophical tradition after the pre-Socratic period. In this case, his criticism is related to the lack of thought concerning the duality of beings and Being. The Platonic characterization of the duality as participation, in Heidegger's eyes, is not an adequate interpretation. According to him,

> In order that a Western-European metaphysics can arise, in order that a meta-physical thinking can become the mission and historic fate of mortal man, is necessary before all else that a call summon us into the λέγείν τε νοεῖν τ᾽ ἐὸν ἔμμεναι [letting-lie-before-us and so taking-to-heart also: beings in being]. (*WCT* 224/228)

Heidegger explains, "thinking" means "letting-lie-before-us and so taking-to-heart also: beings in being." Despite the inadequate reflection on this duality itself, the duality of beings and Being has made possible and pervaded the foundation of the whole of Western-European philosophy. Thinking is determined to conduct its course within what is set down as the duality in the beginning of Greek thinking. It is necessarily related with renewed interpretations of Western thinkers since Parmenides. Such terms as "Being," "to be" are the rubrics of metaphysical language. Discarding them would cause the temple of perennial philosophy to crumble. Without this language, one cannot understand the simplest proposition that is in use for centuries such as: This summer is hot (*WCT* 225/229).

It is mistaken to take a few words by Heidegger out of their context, draw the conclusion that what Heidegger calls thinking is totally different from and discontinuous with what he calls philosophy, and on this basis argue that his notion of thinking has opened up space for including non-Western traditions. For Heidegger, thinking shares with philosophy the same topic of reflection: the question of Being. It is impossible to discard Western metaphysical tradition because one is tied to one's heritage. The relation between thinking and philosophy is comparable with that between the first and the other beginning.

Certainly, Heidegger does use the word "thinking" (*Denken*) with respect to Asian thought. A good example is:

"Thinking"—that is, our Western thinking, is determined by and attuned to *logos*. Definitely this does not mean that the ancient world of the Indies, China and Japan remained without thinking. [1957a, /145]

It can be seen that the first occurrence of "thinking" refers to thinking *propre*. Heidegger is making a similar point as he does in affirming that the word "Western" is left out because it may mislead one to consider that there are other forms of philosophy or thinking. The second occurrence of "thinking" refers to thinking in the non-technical, ordinary sense, which is not inherently related to (Western) philosophy. It is perhaps because he is using "thinking" in a different sense in regard to Asian thought that Heidegger on at least two occasions places this word in quotation marks.[5] For sure, as Heidegger admits, it seems implausible to deny the existence of thinking in the ancient Asian world. However, one must distinguish Asian "thinking" from the thinking that is in its essence continuous with philosophy.

After delivering his lectures *What is Called Thinking?* in 1951/52, Heidegger makes the word "philosophy" the central word in the lecture "What Is Philosophy?" given in 1956. He explicates at length his view on philosophy and its origin and nature.

"What is philosophy?" We have uttered the word "philosophy" often enough. If, however, we use the word "philosophy" no longer like a worn-out title, if, instead, we hear the word "philosophy" coming from its source, then it sounds thus: φιλοσοφία. Now the word "philosophy" is speaking Greek. (*WIP* 29/28)

Heidegger suggests that, if we hear it from its source, the word philosophy is φιλοσοφία. This word is Greek; therefore, in its origin and essence, philosophy speaks the Greek language. Heidegger emphasizes,

The word φιλοσοφία tells us that philosophy is something which, first of all, determines the existence of the Greek world. Not only that— φιλοσοφία also determines the innermost basic feature of our West ern-European history, The often-heard expression "Western-European philosophy" is, in truth, a tautology. Why? Because philosophy is Greek in its nature; Greek, in this instance, means that in origin the nature of philosophy is of such a kind that it first appropriated the Greek world, and only it in order to unfold. (*WIP* 29/28)

For Heidegger, the question of the origin and the question of the nature of philosophy ask about the same thing. He attributes a unique historic character to the fact that philosophy came into being in ancient Greece. That is not a contingent event. To think of philosophy in regard to its nature, one has to think of it in regard to its origin, which is not a historical occurrence in the ordinary sense, but an event of world-historic importance.

Heidegger establishes an important connection between the beginning of the West, the question of Being, and modern technology. This point will become clear in the subsequent explications on Heidegger's view of the essence of technology.

THE ESSENCE OF TECHNOLOGY

Modern Technology

The later Heidegger develops a novel discourse on the essence of technology and its relation to the history of Being. His writings on this subject span from the mid-1930s to his last years. As a German citizen who lived through two devastating world wars that happened within less than half a century, Heidegger's philosophical reflection has been inextricably connected with his consideration of the world situation and his concern about humanity's fate in the modern world.[6] In the essay "The Age of the World Picture" [1938], he enumerates five characteristics of the modern world, namely, the mathematical science of nature, machine technology, the loss of the gods, the attempt at universal cultural formation for everyone, and the conversion of the realm of art to that of aesthetic experience.[7] What underlies all these characteristics is the relation between humanity as the dominating subjectivity and the realm of objects.

Not only nature but also education, political processes, arts, the whole sphere of human practices are submitted to human control. Heidegger uses the word "technology" in a very broad sense to refer to this phenomenon. Technology "includes all the areas of beings which equip the whole of beings: objectified nature, the business of culture, manufactured politics, and the gloss of ideals overlying everything" (*OM* 74/78). He even claims that "[c]ulture is the same in essence as modern technology," both being "forms of barbarism" when thought in the Greek way [1941/42, 70/103].

In addition, the human being has also become part of the system of calculables that is governed by orderability and deliverability,

> Man is the "most important raw material" because he remains the subject of all consumption. He does this in such a way that he lets his will

be unconditionally equated with this process, and thus at the same time become the "object" of the abandonment of Being. (*OM* 85/91)

In submitting his will to the process of objectification, man surrenders himself as raw material to the overarching power of technology.

It is interesting to note that Heidegger perceives an inner connection between submission to modern technology and the distortion of "the word." This consideration consists in the following series of claims. According to Heidegger, in its originating essence, writing is handwriting. The hand indicates and in indicating discloses what was concealed, and thereby marks off and forms the indicating marks into formations. It is by handwriting that the word is indicated and brought to appearance. There is an essential correlation of the hand and the word. "[T]he original unity of both in their separation" [1942/43, 80/119] is, according to Heidegger, the original meaning of the Greek word πρᾶγμα. Both the hand and the word are the essential distinguishing marks of man. As Heidegger states,

> Man does not "have" hands, but the hand holds the essence of man, because the word as the essential realm of the hand is the ground of the essence of man. The word as what is inscribed and what appears to the regard is the written word, that is, script. And the word as script is handwriting. [1942/43, 80/119]

With the invention of modern printing presses at the inception of modernity, writing strokes disappear. Word-signs become type, type is set and set is "pressed." This mechanism of setting, pressing and printing is the preliminary form of the typewriter. With the typewriter going into use, typesetting machinery and technology is born. Words are no longer brought about by the writing hand, the properly acting hand, but by the mechanical forces the typewriter releases. Heidegger calls this "mechanical writing." He writes,

> Mechanical writing deprives the hand of its rank in the realm of the written word and degrades the word to a means of communication. In addition, mechanical writing provides this "advantage," that it conceals the handwriting and thereby the character. [1942/43, 81/119]

With mechanical writing, words are disconnected from the hand, from the origin of its essence, and transferred to the machine. This is one of the major causes for the increasing destruction of the word.

Furthermore, Heidegger depicts an internal connection between technology on the one hand, and philosophy and metaphysics on the other.

> [T]hat in Greek antiquity the Being of beings becomes worthy of thought *is* the beginning of the West [*das Abendland*] and *is* the hidden source of its destiny. Had this beginning not safeguarded what has been, i.e. the gathering of what still endures, the Being of beings would not now govern from out of the essence of modern technology. ([1951, 76/232]; em. or.)

For Heidegger, the rise of modern technology is the inevitable result of the unfolding of the history of Being. The meaning of the name "technology" as understood in an essential way coincides with that of the term "completed metaphysics" (*OM* 75/79). Heidegger asserts that metaphysics "achieves its supreme and utter triumph in our century as modern machine technology" (*HHI* 53/66).

According to Heidegger, Being has shown itself to the Greeks for the first time. However, it has not been thought through and has been forgotten. What results from this forgottenness is metaphysics in which Being shows itself in an oblique and distorted way. Because of the inner relation between technology and philosophy, the fate of technology is at the same time the fate of metaphysics. The task of overcoming metaphysics, an urgent necessity, involves not only an exploration of the essence of language, but also a confrontation with the essence of modern technology.[8]

The Ge-stell

Heidegger gives a new meaning to τέχνε, the Greek word for "technology" (*Technik*).[9] He writes,

> τέχνε, as knowledge experienced in the Greek manner, is a bringing forth of beings in that it brings *forth* what is present, as such, *out of* concealment specifically *into* the unconcealment of its appearance; τέχνε never means the action of making. (*OM* 35/46; em. or.; tr. m.)

Heidegger ignores the original meaning of τέχνε as making, and provides it with an innovative interpretation in terms of the unconcealment of beings. This new explanation of τέχνε is brought to bear upon his reflection on modern technology.

In the essay "Traditional Language and Technological Language," Heidegger lists five features of the current conception of modern technology:

first, it is "the constant, gradually increased development of the old manual technology"; second, it is "an instrument for the realization of industrial ends"; third, it is the "practical application of modern natural science"; fourth, it is "a special province within the modern cultural fabric"; fifth, it "requires that it be brought under human control" [1962b, 133/11]. According to Heidegger, this conception of technology is an "anthropological-instrumental" one. It is correct, but not true [1962b, 134/14]. Heidegger reiterates that technology "is not identical [*nicht das Gleiche*] with the essence [*Wesen*] of technology" (*QT* 311/7; tr. m.).[10] One must consider technology in view of the essence that holds sway in it, and in view of its internal relation with the unconcealment of Being.

Heidegger uses the term *Ge-stell,* usually translated as "enframing," to represent the phenomenon of expansionist enclosure of all beings, which turns beings into utter availability and sheer manipulability. The enduring of technology is one in which enframing (*Ge-stell*) propriates (*ereignet*) as a destining of revealing. In conformity with the propriating unconcealment, modern technology reveals the actual as standing-reserve. By the term "standing-reserve" (*Bestand*) [1969a, 61/368] or "calculable resource" (*EHP* 202/178), Heidegger refers to the way in which everything presences in such a way as to be wrought upon by the challenging-forth of revealing. The *Ge-stell,* "the gathering unity of all ways of positing" ([1969c, 60/366]; cf. *QT* 324/20) is more real than all atomic energy and the whole world of machinery, more real than the driving power of organization, communication, and automation.

The revealing of modern technology is a challenging-forth (*Heraus-fordern*). It demands of nature extractable and storable energy. The pre-modern technical device uses natural energy as it is without trying to store it away. With modern technology, everything is regarded as a kind of resource to be set in order (*Bestellen*). Everything is ordered to stand by (*auf der Stelle zur Stelle zu stehen*), to become available for the maximum yield. As Heidegger describes,

> The energy that is locked in nature is unlocked, what is disclosed is transformed, what is transformed is reinforced, what is reinforced is stored, what is stored is distributed. These ways, according to which nature is secured, are controlled. This controlling, in its turn, must secure itself further. [1962b, 137/18][11]

According to Heidegger, man himself is under the challenging-forth as well, and even more originarily belongs to the process of ordering than nature. In *Identity and Difference,* he writes,

> Is it that Being itself is faced with the challenge of letting beings appear
> within the horizon of what is calculable? Indeed. And not only this. To
> the same degree that Being is challenged, man, too, is challenged, that
> is, forced to secure all beings that are his concern as the substance for
> his planning and calculating; and to carry this manipulation on past all
> bounds. (*ID* 35/99)

Man is inevitably subject to the sweeping power of *das Ge-stell*. Unlike
nature, man is not merely transformed into standing-reserve. Man himself
participates in the ordering that is a way of revealing. The modes of revealing that belong to the essence of technology are allotted to man as well. The
unconcealment of the unconcealed places a claim on man to respond to its
call, to investigate nature as an object of research. The challenging-forth
gathers (*versammelt*) man into the ordering of nature as standing-reserve.
As Heidegger states, "Today's humans are themselves challenged forth by
the demand to challenge nature forth into preparation [*Bereitstellung*]"
[1962b, 138/20].

While being subject to the *Ge-stell,* man has an important role to
play in restoring a free relationship to Being. This free relationship to
Being cannot be obtained by way of man's getting control over technology,
since man is himself in the hands of the power of the *Ge-stell*. Rather man
is needed and called to think on the essential unfolding of technology. In
order that man in his essence may become attentive to the essence of technology, and in order that there may be established an essential relationship between technology and man in regard to their respective essence,
modern man must find his way back into the full breadth of the space
that is proper to his essence. That essential space of man's essential being
receives its dimension solely from out of the conjoining relation between
Being and man, out of the way in which the safekeeping of Being itself is
given as belonging to the essence of man (*QT* 339/35). In order to achieve
a free relation to Being, to the modern world which arises out of the two-
fold concealment-unconcealment movement of Being itself, man should
let himself be appropriated by Being.

Danger and Destining

When man reflects upon the essence of technology, man experiences himself
as the one whose activities are challenged forth by the *Ge-stell*. As a result,
man comes to realize that the *Ge-stell* is a destining of revealing, and that
his own essence, out of necessity (that is, by destiny [*Geschick*]), belongs to

revealing and must be open to the freeing claim of unconcealment. Destining means sending. Since Heidegger characterizes Being also as sending, an internal relation is hence established between the promiscuous phenomena of technological appliances and development on the one hand, and the history of Being on the other.

The disclosing of Being has a two-fold character. It reveals; yet in the meantime it conceals. The unconcealment of Being is possible only when the call of Being is heard by man. The *Ge-stell* as destining is not an ordinary historical happening. Destining is essentially the destining of Being [1949b, 37/68]. There harbors a danger within the unconcealment because man may easily misconstrue and misinterpret the unconcealed. In this context, Heidegger is not using the word "danger" in its ordinary meaning; he is employing it as a technical term to express a particular consideration. He emphasizes, "The destining of revealing is in itself not just any danger, but *the* danger" (*QT* 331/27; em. or.). Moreover, as he explains,

> The danger consists in the threat that assaults man's nature in his relation to Being itself, and not in accidental perils. This danger is *the* danger. It conceals itself in the abyss that underlies all beings. ([1946c, 222/295]; em. or.; tr. m.)

The word "danger" is obviously a unique metaphysical term in Heidegger's texts. It does not refer to something that may cause injury, suffering or loss of life. Neither a catastrophe in the natural world nor the dominating individuality of man constitutes the decisive danger. Both of these are already the consequence of the destiny (*Geschick*) that exposes man to the power of the *Ge-stell* (*des Stellens*) and occupies him in the business of organizing the orderable stockpiles.

To Heidegger, "destining" and "danger" are the two words that well capture the nature of the *Ge-stell* as the essence of modern technology. The danger with which he is concerned is that man may be denied the access to a more originary revealing and the experience of the call of the primal truth. Sometimes Heidegger uses "danger" as a synonym of Being: "But *the* danger, namely, Being itself endangering itself in the truth of its coming to presence, remains veiled and disguised. This disguising is what is most dangerous in the danger" ([1949b, 37/68]; em. or.). In any case, the danger is a critical and necessary occasion where Being can be revealed. It is "the essential unfolding of technology" itself that harbors "the possible rise of the saving power" (*QT* 337/33). On several occasions, Heidegger cites Hölderlin's verse,[12]

> But where the danger lies, there also grows
> that which saves.

He explains, "to save" (*retten*) means "to fetch something home into
its essence, in order to bring the essence for the first time into proper
appearing" (*QT* 333/29). The saving power takes root and thrives where
the danger is.

In view of these complexities and subtleties of Heidegger's reflections, one cannot reduce his attitude toward modern technology to simplistic protest and criticism. He establishes an intrinsic relation between
the emergence of modern technology and the destiny of Being. Technology
is a mode in which the totality of beings is revealed; at the same time, it is
also the place where the event of appropriation could be brought about. At
the Le Thor seminar given in 1969, Heidegger explicitly connects the *Ge-
stell* with Ereignis:

> Enframing [*Ge-stell*] is, as it were, the photographic negative of *Ereig-
> nis*. . . . enframing (the gathering unity of all ways of positing [*Weisen
> des Stellens*]) is the completion and consummation of metaphysics and
> at the same time the disclosive preparation of enowning. *This is why it
> is by no means a question of viewing the advent of technology as negative
> occurrence* . . . ([1969c, 60/366]; em. ad.)[13]

It is clear that Heidegger does not subscribe to the view that technology
is simply something negative. Technology represents the completion and
consummation of metaphysics. As such, it is the necessary preparation for
the appropriating event (Ereignis) through which man and Being obtain
their ownness. This is a step out of technology in the ordinary sense of the
word, and at the same time a step into the essence of technology. As Heidegger remarks,

> Viewed from the present and drawn from our insight into the present,
> the step back out of metaphysics into the essential nature of metaphys-
> ics is the step out of technology and technological description and inter-
> pretation of the age, into the *essence* of modern technology which is still
> to be thought.[14] (*ID* 52/118; em. or.)

The power of the *Ge-stell* hides in itself the promise of salvation.
By attending to the prevailing power of the *Ge-stell*, that is, to the most
characteristic feature of the technological world, man can hear the claim

of Being in the *Ge-stell*. This makes it possible for man and Being to attain their essence.

HEIDEGGER, JASPERS, AND THE "AXIAL PERIOD"

Heidegger is well aware of Jaspers' idea of the "Axial Period." This idea refers to circa 5th century BC, when ancient Chinese, Indian, and Greek civilizations grew into full bloom. Jaspers' idea is conceived in opposition to the Christian faith that the appearance of Christ is the axis of world history. This faith finds reflection in Hegel's statement that all of history comes from and goes toward Christ. Jaspers insists, "An axis of world history, if such exists, would have to be arrived at *empirically*, as a factual situation that as such can be valid for all men, Christians included" (1986, 382; em. or.).[15] Contrary to Jaspers' position, Heidegger sets himself radically against anything like an empirical approach to history. For him, this approach presupposes a paradigm of universal history, according to which facts about other traditions are considered as neutral materials that can be laid side by side and compared with one another. Heidegger deems that this paradigm fails to consider history as the destiny of the world. As he states in *What is Called Thinking?*

> Our age rages in a mad, steadily growing craving to conceive history in terms of universal history [*Universalhistorie*], as a happening [*Geschehen*]. Its frenzy is exacerbated and fed by the quick and easy availability of sources and means of presentation. . . . Universal history, operating with the most comprehensive means, assumes that a comparative portrayal of the most varied cultures, from ancient China to the Aztecs, can establish a relation to world history [*Weltgeschichte*]. This world history, however, is not the destiny of a world but rather the object established by conceiving world in terms of universal history. . . . World history, however, is the destiny whereby a world lays claim to us. We shall never hear that claim of the world's destiny while we are engaged on world-historical—which in this context always means universal-historical—tours [*Rundfahrten*]. (*WCT* 166/104)

It is clear that, for Heidegger, the message sent from Being lies at the core of authentic history. The narrative and comparative descriptions of historical facts about China and other traditions lack the essence of authentic world history. One must disentangle oneself from those empirical investigations that are characterized by the richness of sources and the variety of means of conveyance, and strive to put oneself in a position to be able to give heed to the claim of Being from which is derived the authentic world-historic.

In a letter of 21 September 1949, after reading Jaspers' *The Origin and Goal of History* and *The European Spirit,* in which Jaspers elaborates the idea of "Axial Period," Heidegger writes,

> That you think the simultaneity and synchronicity of Chinese, Indian, and Western centuries as axial time seems essential to me, for here a world axis conceals itself, which could become a pivot upon which modern world-technology turns.
>
> I also agree with you, as you will soon see more clearly, that modern technology is something essentially other than all previous technology.
>
> But this *other* has its *essential* origin in the Greek inception of the West, and only here. I know too little to decide whether this technology could ever have originated from the other two spaces of axial time, but where is the measure for interpreting these three simultaneous spaces of time?
>
> I cannot hold back the reservation that your interpretation of these spaces, even especially the Greek, perhaps moves within a too-traditional sphere of representation, wherein it indicates more similarity between them than, perhaps, they have. (*HJC* 176/185; em. or.)

After half-heartedly praising the idea of the "Axial Period" as "essential," Heidegger points out that it is confined to traditional historical ways of representation in that it attempts to demonstrate similarities of civilizations through empirical and comparative surveys. This approach cannot reveal what is genuinely historic about world and history.

According to Jaspers, there exist striking similarities between the three major traditions (that is, Chinese, Indian, and Western traditions); only with the emergence of modern technology did a radical gap appear. Contra Jaspers, Heidegger ascribes a unique significance to the Western tradition. He describes the origin and development of modern philosophy and technology as a continuous and inter-related process, and insists that modern technology originates only in the Greek inception of the West. It is quite probable that, for Heidegger, the similarities between Chinese, Indian and Greek traditions as perceived and presented by Jaspers are not far from the "assimilations and intermixtures" (*DL* 3/87) that result from the superficial encounter between East and West, both being subject to the *Ge-stell.*

Heidegger and Jaspers' discussion about monologue in their correspondence in August 1949 sheds light on Heidegger's concerns that a new beginning, or the other beginning, can only be enacted from within the purity and immanence of the "european-occidental-grecian" *axis* (to borrow Jaspers' phrase). After commenting on his reading of Heidegger's recent writings, Jaspers remarks, "the question as to how we are to emerge out of the monologue—and the repetition of the monologue by others—is indeed a vital question for our current philosophizing" (*HJC* 169/178). In reply, Heidegger writes,

> What you say about monologue is right. But much would already be gained if monologues may remain what they are. It almost seems to me that they *aren't* this yet at all; they are not yet strong enough for this.
>
> With the arrival of your letter, a saying of Nietzsche occurred to me that you are naturally familiar with: "A hundred deep solitudes together form the city of Venice—this is its magic. A picture for the human beings of the future."
>
> What is thought here lies beyond the alternative of communication and non-communication. (*HJC* 171/181; em. or.)

Jaspers is concerned with the question how to transcend the monologue of Western philosophy and enter into dialogue with other intellectual traditions. In response, Heidegger emphasizes that currently the Western monologue has not yet attained maturity. Authentic thinking can only arise from within profound solitude. This is the essential something that the rhetoric of dialogue and communication fails to capture. From the perspective of his discourse on the first and the other beginning, Heidegger's notion of monologue can be explained as the encounter between these two beginnings. This is a monologue with positive and creative significance. Heidegger strongly believes that truth can only originate from within its homeland. The future of the West, as world-historic, resides in a quasi-totalistic renewal of its own heritage. This will be a movement of purity and simplicity, precluding promiscuous elements from non-Western traditions.

Heidegger's idea of history and monologue are also at play in his most famous remark in the *Spiegel* interview. Considering that a remark by Heidegger in his Nietzsche lecture, "The Will to Power as Art" [1936/37], discloses his idea that the Germans bear a unique destiny, the journalist asks for an explication of it. In this context, Heidegger makes the following remark as a response to the journalist's query,

> I could explain what was said in the quotation in the following way: it is my conviction that a reversal [*Umkehr*] can be prepared only in the same place in the world where the modern technological world originated, and

that it cannot happen through any takeover [*Übernahme*] by Zen Buddhism or any other Eastern experiences of the world. There is need for
a rethinking which is to be carried out with the help of the European
tradition and of a new appropriation [*Neuaneignung*] of that tradition.
Thinking itself can be transformed only by a thinking which has the same
origin and calling. [1966a, 113/679]

Because the history of Being, which constitutes the essence of the
West, is the true history that has unfolded into the planetary *Ge-stell*,
only from its own origin can the present technological world transform
itself. This transformation cannot be substituted by a takeover of Eastern
traditions. Heidegger's reference to "Zen Buddhism or any other Eastern
experiences" illustrates the wide spread of Eastern thought in the West.
Heidegger deems both a simplistic comparison with Eastern thinking or a
takeover by it to be superficial. However, this does not prevent him from
pondering whether a "realm of possible dialogue" with the East could be
opened up.

THE *GE-STELL* AND EAST-WEST DIALOGUE

In his correspondence with his Japanese friends, Heidegger frequently expresses
his anxiety concerning the *Ge-stell*. In a letter to Kojima Takehiko in 1963,
he remarks that the Europeanization of the world consists in the planetarian
domination of the *Ge-stell*. The *Ge-stell* is spreading out from the contemporary *Abendland* (Evening-Land) throughout the world. As a consequence of
the domination of the power of the *Ge-stell*, "national cultures," which grow
out of the natural environment of human beings, are disappearing; at the
same time, a world civilization is in the shaping [1963c, 222–23].[16]

That the *Ge-stell* has spread all over the globe is manifest not only in
the global domination of technology, but also in the dissemination of Western metaphysics. As Heidegger states,

> Through technology the entire globe is today experienced in Western
> fashion and represented on the epistemological models of European
> metaphysics and science. ([1951, 76/232]; tr. m.)

In the last stage of his career, Heidegger's anxiety about the development
of the contemporary "interstellar-cosmic space" (*EHP* 201/177) does not
dwindle, but seems to be exacerbated. In a letter in 1974 to *Risō* (a Japanese
journal), which was published in its first issue of 1975, Heidegger reiterates,

The age of technological-industrial civilization holds a steadily increasing danger, whose foundations are thought about all too little. . . . Presumably modern world civilization is executing the transition to the final phase of the epochal destiny of Being in the sense of a determination of Being as the unconditional orderability of what is, including human being.[17] [1974a, 744]

It is notable that Heidegger is using the word "world civilization" in a negative sense. Due to the spread of the *Ge-stell,* each "national culture" is deprived of its individual characteristics. Things are treated as orderable and disposable neutral entities. This results in a world civilization that is encompassing the whole earth, including East Asia. In a letter addressed to the participants of the tenth Heidegger colloquium held in Chicago, dated 11 April 1976 (six weeks before his death), Heidegger makes the following remark:

In the age of a world civilization stamped by technology, forgottenness of Being is oppressive in a special way for the asking of the question of Being. [1976a, 3]

In this place, "world civilization" is related to technology and "forgottenness of Being." Its negative sense is similar to that of the word "planetary," as we will see in a moment.

Heidegger's reflection on the *Ge-stell* lurks in the background of his fleeting references to East-West dialogue. In detailed studies of Heidegger's view of modern technology, the connection Heidegger makes between the *Ge-stell* and East-West dialogue has not been taken into account.[18] In the following I examine some of the relevant passages in which the themes of modern technology and East-West dialogue are configured together in Heidegger's writings.

The Realm of Possible Dialogue

The remark on the "realm of possible dialogue" between East and West appears in "On the Question of Being" written in 1955. This essay first appeared under the title "Concerning 'The Line'" (*Über 'Die Linie'*) as a contribution to *Freundschaftliche Begegnungen,* a *Festschrift* for Ernst Jünger (1895–1998) on his sixtieth year.[19] In this contribution, Heidegger explicates how meditation on the essence of nihilism is closely connected with reflection on Being as Being. According to him, Western philosophical tradition has approached the question of Being as the question concerning beings as beings. This approach has remained unquestioned. Therefore, metaphysics has to trace back into its ground.

Heidegger's essay takes the form of a letter to Jünger, in response to the latter's article "Across the line" (*Über 'Die Linie'*), which was written in 1949 as a dedication to Heidegger's sixtieth birthday. For Jünger, the line is the zero point surrounded by the realm of the consummation of nihilism. Two possibilities lay open for the movement of nihilism: one is that this movement comes to end in a nihilistic nothing; the other is that this movement constitutes the transition to the realm of a new turning of Being.

Heidegger thus evaluates Jünger's idea: "your assessment of the situation follows the signs whereby we may recognize whether and to what extent we are crossing the line and thereby exiting from the zone of consummate nihilism" [1955a, 292/386]. His idea differs from Jünger's in that the word *über* in the title *Über 'Die Linie'* means *trans-*, across for Jünger, whereas for Heidegger *über* means *de-*, about, concerning. While Jünger is concerned with how to cross the line and arrive at a new realm of Being, Heidegger addresses problematics concerning the line itself, concerning the zone of self-consummating nihilism. Precisely in the zone of nihilism resides the possibility of the turn of Being. Heidegger repudiates the idea that there is another realm of a new turning of Being into which the movement of nihilism has to enter. Instead, one should inquire into the essence of nihilism in the very locale of nihilism. It is in this locale itself that thinking must be brought back to the ground of Being. Thinking and poetizing must return to where they originated and prepare for a dwelling in the locality of the essence of Being (the essence of the oblivion of Being is at the same time the essence of Being). They must build the path leading to a renewal of metaphysics that is at the same time the overcoming of nihilism. In this context, Heidegger invokes the theme of East-West dialogue,

> Your [Jünger's] assessment of the situation *trans lineam* and my discussion *de linea* are referred to one another. Together they are directed not to cease the endeavor to practice planetary thinking [*planetarische Denken*] for part of its path, however short in measurement. And here no prophetic talents and demeanor [*Gaben und Gebärden*] are needed in order to realize that planetary building [*planetarische Bauen*] will bring about encounters [*Begegnungen*], for which neither of those involved today are able to cope with. This is equally true for both the language of Europe and that of East Asia, and is true above all for the realm of possible dialogue between them [*ihrer möglichen Zwiesprache*]. Neither is able on its own to open or to found this realm. [1955a, 321/424; tr. m.]

To understand this passage, it is crucial to make clear what Heidegger means by "planetary" or "planetarization." Scholars such as Mehta (1970, 312–13; 1976, 463–68), Parkes (1996, 108) and Vetsch (1992, 85) treat these terms as synonyms of "intercultural" or "transcultural" in the positive sense of the word. A careful reading of Heidegger's texts reveals that the word "planetary" is fundamentally related to the totalization of the whole of actuality and to the domination of the European way of thinking. It can well be said that "planetary" is an alternative expression Heidegger employs to illustrate his idea of the *Ge-stell.*

In "On the Question of Being," "planetary" is more directly involved with the spread of nihilism, which results from the withdrawal of Being. Heidegger deplores, "Nihilism, at first merely European, thereby appears in its planetary tendency" [1955a, 294/389]. Following this, he states that Jünger's work has not been read with "a sufficiently broad, i.e., planetary, horizon" (295/389). This statement is connected with Heidegger's view that Jünger's essay "The Worker" (1933) has provided a description of European nihilism after the First World War.

In "Principles of Thinking," Heidegger states that "European thinking is also threatened to become planetary in that contemporary Indians, Chinese and Japanese can usually bring to us what is experienced by them only through our European way of thinking" [1957a, /145]. In this place, planetary is connected with the fact that Asian thought is not available in its authenticity. What is authentic has been distorted by dualistic European metaphysical systems.

In "Hölderlin's Earth and Heaven" (1959), Heidegger remarks, "The fact consists in this: In its essential beginning, which can never be lost, the present planetary-interstellar world condition is thoroughly european-occidental-grecian" (*EHP* 201/177). Here "planetary" is related to the Greek and its unfolding as the occidental and European. The planetary world has been internally brought about by world-historical development. The nature of planetarization is european-occidental-grecian. For this reason, a reversal can only come from where planetarization originated.

Now we return to the passage in focus. Heidegger sees a connection between his view and Jünger's. They entail each other and are directed toward each other. Their aim is not to put an end to the planetarization that is taking hold of the planet. Planetarization will bring about *Begegnungen* (encounters). What does "encounters" mean? It is not unreasonable to relate it to a passage from "A Dialogue," which passage I will discuss in detail in the next section. For the moment, suffice it to say that, in this context, "encounters" refers to superficial contact between East and West. It is subject to the domination of the *Ge-stell.* Contemporary European thinking is unable to cope with the present situation, neither is East Asia, the other side of the globe. This is because East Asia has also been subjugated to the dissemination of the *Ge-stell.* Therefore, neither side is in a position to open or to found "the realm of possible dialogue [*Zwiesprache*] between them."[20]

Immediately after this remark, Heidegger advocates recollective thinking (*Andenken*) that recalls the "ancient provenance" where reflection on the essence of nihilism originates. Then he closes his essay with a passage from Goethe, which speaks of the damaging influence of conventional expressions. This again reveals Heidegger's pessimism regarding the dominating power of the *Ge-stell* from which no one can escape.

The Inevitable Dialogue

Another famous reference to East-West dialogue can be found in Heidegger's lecture "Science and Reflection" initially delivered in 1953. It occurs in the context of the question of modern science and globalization,

> Whoever today dares, questioningly, reflectingly, and, in this way already as actively involved, to respond to the profundity of *the world shock that we experience every hour,* must not only pay heed to the fact that our present-day world is completely dominated by the desire to know of modern science; he must consider also, and above else, that every reflection upon that which now is can take its rise and thrive only if, through *a dialogue [Gespräch] with the Greek thinkers and their language,* it strikes root into the ground of our historical existence. That dialogue still awaits its beginning. It is scarcely prepared for at all, and yet it itself remains for us the precondition of *the inevitable dialogue with the East Asian world.* ([1953b, 157f/41]; em. ad.)

After this remark touching on East-West dialogue, Heidegger elaborates on the nature of the necessary dialogue with Greek thinkers and poets, and then proceeds with the main topic of his lecture, that is, the nature of modern science. Most of the subsequent discussions are devoted to the etymological roots in Greek of such notions as "theory" (*Theorie*), "reality" (*das Wirkliche*), "object" (*Gegenstand*) and their translations into Latin. There is no more reference to East Asia.

At the beginning of the cited passage, Heidegger speaks of the "world shock" that is being experienced every hour and the complete domination of modern science. Then he stresses that only through a dialogue with the Greek thinkers and their language can one touch the ground of Western people's historic existence, and can the reflection on beings in the contemporary *Ge-stell* rise up and sustain. After this, Heidegger speaks of the necessity of a dialogue with Greek thinkers as the precondition for a dialogue with the East Asian world. It is clear that the topic of the *Ge-stell* and the dialogue with Greek thinkers often appear in tandem and constitute the most common context of Heidegger's oblique references to East Asia. Citing phrases such as "the inevitable dialogue with the East Asian world" in isolation from their context easily leads to inadequate representation of his ultimate concern.

In order to obtain a well-grounded and convincing interpretation of this remark, a number of things call for attention. First, the phrase "the inevitable dialogue with the East Asian world" (*das unausweichliche Gespräch mit der ostasiatischen Welt*) occurs only once in the whole essay. Heidegger neither comes back to it later nor provides any explanation about the import of this rather abrupt reference. Parkes has noted this detail and remarks that Heidegger adds the remark "almost in passing" (1992, 396). Second, Heidegger's focus falls upon "a dialogue with the Greek thinkers," which is the precondition for the dialogue with the East Asian world. Third, the dialogue with the Greeks "still awaits its beginning" and has been scarcely prepared for at all. Fourth, this remark on these two stages of dialogue are preceded by a reference to the *Ge-stell*. Commentators have either overlooked or inadequately accounted for these points.

Heidegger's aim is to call attention to the neglected fact that, in the present world dominated by scientific knowing, only a reflection on the historic being of the Western people can make possible and sustain a reflection on beings. Because the Western people have inherited the concern with Being from the Greek people, a dialogue with Greek thinkers and their language is of primary urgency, although this dialogue is barely prepared for at all. It is in this context that Heidegger mentions that this dialogue is the precondition for the "inevitable dialogue with the East Asian world." One should not place overdue weight upon this marginal note. On the other hand, it is clear that in Heidegger's eyes, East-West dialogue, no matter how inevitable it is said to be, is secondary to the dialogue with Greek thinkers and thus to the self-transformation of the Western tradition.[21]

In "A Dialogue," there is a discussion concerning East-West encounter in the context of the rhetorical question whether the alleged incapacity of the Japanese language should be regarded as a deficiency:

> J: . . . since the *encounter* with European thinking, there has come to light a certain incapacity in our language."

I: In what way?

J: It lacks the delimiting power to represent objects related in an unequivocal order above and below each other.

I: Do you seriously regard this incapacity as a deficiency of your language?

J: Considering that the *encounter* [*Begegnung*] of the East Asian with the European world has become inevitable [*unausweichlich*], your question certainly calls for searching reflection. (*DL* 2/87; em. ad.)

Cho takes the last passage in this conversation to be the evidence that Heidegger's promise concerning the "inevitable dialogue with the East-Asian world" made in "Science and Reflection" has come to fruition in "A Dialogue" (1993, 149). Cho's claim is groundless. In the foregoing citation, Heidegger is not asserting that a genuine East-West dialogue is actually happening, although in this place he also uses the word "inevitable." After a few passages on the pervasiveness of "modern technicalization and industrialization of every continent" (*DL* 3/87), there is the following exchange:

J: [. . .] the possibility still always remains that, seen from the standpoint of our East Asian existence [*Dasein*], the technical world which sweeps us along must confine itself to what is foregrounded, and . . . that . . .

I: . . . that for this reason a genuine [*wahrhafte*] encounter with European existence *is not yet taking place,* in spite of all assimilations and intermixtures. (*DL* 3/87; em. ad.; tr. m.; omission signs original, except for those in square brackets)

Here Heidegger is explicit in observing that a genuine encounter is *not yet* taking place. Immediately after the passage Cho quotes, the Inquirer states,

Here you are touching on a controversial question which I often discussed with Count Kuki—the question whether it is necessary and rightful for East Asians to chase after the European conceptual systems. (*DL* 3/87)

It seems very plausible that the "encounter" in "A Dialogue" refers to situations in which East Asian people are pursuing European conceptual constructs, which result in numerous "assimilations and intermixtures" (*DL* 3/87). It is not possible for Heidegger to treat these superficial happenings as East-West dialogue, which for him should be engaged in "from a deeper place" [1958d, 192]. In describing these happenings as inevitable,

Heidegger is hinting at the *Ge-stell,* as he always does. Non-European people have been unavoidably subordinated to the sweeping power of the *Ge-stell.* This is manifest in their trying to adopt European metaphysical system. The so-called inevitable "encounter of the East Asian with the European world" (*DL* 2/87) is a depiction of the ontic, inauthentic encounter. It cannot, in any case, be regarded as a synonym of a true dialogue between East and West.

Deep Encounter

On 18 May 1958, Heidegger co-held a colloquium on the theme "Art and Thinking" together with Hisamatsu Shinichi (to be discussed in Chapter seven). In the evening of the same day, Hisamatsu had a conversation with Heidegger at his house in Freiburg. A transcript of part of their conversation was published in *Japan und Heidegger* with the title "Mutual Mirroring" [1958d]. During their conversation, it was mentioned that Hartmut Buchner, one of Heidegger's former students, had gone to Japan to obtain a promotion to Doctor of Letters from the National University of Kyoto.[22] Hisamatsu expressed his hope that Buchner's stay in Japan would contribute to the cultivation of East-West dialogue. Following this remark, there was an interesting exchange on the topic of East-West dialogue.

> Hisamatsu: What I wish is, that one day the East would encompass [*einschliesst*] the West, and reversely the West the East, so that we could see the unfolding of East-West exchange of thought in this way.
>
> Heidegger: I thank you for those words. I feel that such an encounter [*Begegnung*] between East and West is more important than economic or political contacts.
>
> Hisamatsu: I am of the same opinion. Presumably such meetings would have an influence even on politics.
>
> Heidegger: That goes without saying. It would not work the other way round. We would not make any progress if we looked upon economics and politics as the starting point. We must begin from a deeper place [*von einem tieferen Ort*].
>
> Hisamatsu: Indeed, I fully agree with this. Your words are a great present for my return to Japan. [1958d, 191–92]

It seems that the two interlocutors place different emphases on East-West dialogue in this friendly exchange. With Hisamatsu, the emphasis falls on the mutuality of East-West exchange; he conveys an optimistic vision of East-West dialogue in which both sides are equals. With Heidegger, the emphasis falls on the depth of this encounter. Once again he expresses disapproval of superficial encounters between East and West, such as economic or political contact, and points to a deep-level encounter.[23]

It is not easy to decipher the nature of such deep encounter. On other occasions, Heidegger seems to be entertaining the possibility that Eastern traditions may be able to lend a hand to the transformation of thinking. In the *Spiegel* interview, he wonders "who of us can decide whether or not one day in Russia and China the ancient traditions [*uralte Überlieferungen*] of a 'thinking' will awaken which will help make possible for man a free relationship to the technical world?" [1966a, 111/677]. In his response to Tsujimura Kōichi's talk at the evening gathering in Messkirch in celebration of his eightieth birthday, Heidegger stresses,

> In [the middle of] this world civilization we stand. This fact concerns the confrontation of thinking [*Auseinandersetzung des Denkens*]. Meanwhile this world civilization has reached the whole earth. Hence our distress, Mr. Tsujimura, is the same as yours. [1969a, 166]

It is ambiguous whether Heidegger was thinking of East-West dialogue in speaking of "confrontation of thinking." What is clear is the view that, with the spread of the *Ge-stell*, Asian people come to live in the same world condition as Western people, that is, their old traditions are not available because of the domination of the *Ge-stell*.

Heidegger's concern is more explicitly expressed in what was intended to be a foreword to the Japanese translation of his lecture "Toward the Question of the Determination of the Matter of Thinking" [1965a]. In this short piece, he explains that the "the matter [*die Sache*] of thinking" refers to that to which thinking is being claimed. Through this claim, thinking is tuned to what it has to think. If human beings attempt to listen to the voice of the claim, they will reach what is called the Clearing (*die Lichtung*). Heidegger states that he addressed this phenomenon in *Being and Time* for the first time and has continued to think about it repeatedly. Following this, he writes,

> By thinking the clearing and characterizing it adequately, we reach a realm that can perhaps make it possible to bring a transformed European thinking into a fruitful dialogue with East Asian "thinking" [*eine fruchtbare Auseinandersetzung mit dem ostasiatischen „Denken"*]. Such a confrontation could help [*könnte mithelfen*] with the task of saving the

essential nature of human being from the threat of an extreme technological calculation and manipulation of human Dasein. [1968, 230]

Here we have again a passage in which the threat of the *Ge-stell,* the
need of a transformation of European thinking, and a reference to East-
West dialogue (or confrontation) occur together, the transformation of
Europe being a necessary precondition for East-West dialogue. The control
has brought about East-West encounters of a superficial nature. In order
to alleviate or overcome the increasingly omnipresent *Ge-stell,* Heidegger
sometimes entertains the idea of "a fruitful dialogue," "deep encounter," or
"inevitable dialogue" between East and West, as distinguished from their
superficial encounters under the control of the *Ge-stell.* In subsequent chapters we will come across a few more hints at this idea, which nevertheless has
never been elucidated by Heidegger. In Chapter nine we will see the problematics involved in Heidegger's notion of a genuine dialogue with the East.
For the moment, I have one comment concerning the phrase "could help"
(*könnte mithelfen*) in the last sentence of the preceding citation. This phrase
is set in subjunctive mode, and the word "help" suggests something external
as compared with such words as "engage" and "interact."

Chapter Four

The Journey Abroad and "The Few Other Great Beginnings"

In this chapter, I discuss two prominent issues in Heidegger's elucidation of Hölderlin's poetry. One is the tripartite theme of homeland, homecoming and the journey abroad. Heidegger relates the homeland with the "nearness to Being." The journey abroad is the necessity for becoming at home. The ontologically necessary process of not-being-at-home, passing-through-the-foreign, and becoming-at-home, has a particular ontic reference to the intrinsic link between the Greek and German *Dasein.* In this connection, I comment on Vetsch's construction of an account of intercultural dialogue that is ascribed to Heidegger. The other issue concerns the meaning of "the few other great beginnings," which some authors identify with East Asian traditions or non-Western thought in general. Through a careful reading of the text, I demonstrate that the most plausible reference of this phrase is the four-fold of heaven, earth, god and man, which is closely related to Greece. I also discuss similar misreading of other phrases such as the *Morgenland* and the *Orient.*

POETRY, POET, AND THINKING

Heidegger claims, all art, "as the letting happen of the advent of the truth of beings," is in essence poetry [1935–36, 44/59]. His usage of the word *Dichtung* (poetry) is close to the Greek notion *poiesis,* which means both "making, fabricating, producing" and "poetry, poem." In his view, it is in language that the primordial essence of *Dichtung* is preserved. Language first brings the entity as an entity into the clearing by naming it. This is an act of projective saying, which is *Dichtung.* Heidegger perceives an essential connection between poetry and the nature of language in observing that "language itself is poetry in the essential sense" [1935–36, 46/62], and that "the primary language is poetry as the founding of Being" (*EHP* 61/43). Poetry is as closely related with Being as language is. As Heidegger remarks, "Poetry that thinks is in truth the topology of Being" [1947, 12/84]; "Poetry is the saying of the unconcealment of beings" [1935–36, 46/61].

Heidegger considers that thinking (or philosophy) and poetry are intimately connected with each other. He uses the notion of the Same (*das Selbe*) to explicate the relation between poetic and philosophical thinking: "Only poetry is of the same order [*in derselben Ordnung*] as philosophical thinking, although thinking and poetry are not identical [*gleich*]" (*IM* 28/28). The bond between poetry and thinking is a gathering that shelters and grounds both of them. At the same time, Heidegger maintains their distance. In the "Postscript to 'What Is Metaphysics?,'" he stresses the separateness between philosophy and poetry,

> The Saying of the thinker comes from a long-protected speechlessness and from the careful clarifying of the realm thus cleared. . . . Of like provenance is the naming of the poet. Yet because that which is like [*das Gleiche*] is like only as differentiating, and because poetizing and thinking are most purely alike in their care of the word, they are at the same time farthest separated in their essence. . . . the manner in which—thought from out of the essence of Being—poetizing, thanking, and thinking are directed toward one another and are at the same time different, must be left open here. Presumably thanking and poetizing each in their own way spring from originary thinking, which they need, yet without themselves being able to be a thinking. ([1943e, 237/312]; tr. m.)

There exists an essential distance between poetry and thinking. This distance does not arise from their respective distinctiveness, but from their likeness. On this occasion, Heidegger uses *das Gleiche,* a word that belongs to traditional metaphysics, rather than *das Selbe,* a word that initiates being-historic thinking, to characterize the mode of togetherness between poetry and thinking. This is probably because here what is under emphasis is the "farthest" separation and distinctiveness, instead of the differential unification between poetry and thinking.

Heidegger's stress on the differentiation between poetry and thinking is sometimes seen as an effort to preserve the singularity of poetry. Yet, it should be noted that for him their distance is not on equal footing, but of a hierarchical order. Between them, originary thinking is primordial. Although poetry springs from originary thinking, it falls short of being thinking *propre*. It can be seen that Heidegger accords poetry a lower status than thinking.

In the poem "Winke" composed in 1941, Heidegger suggests that poetic language remains too tethered to images (that is, to beings) to free thought to enter into Ereignis [1941b, 33]. What he pursues is a thinking that is beyond even poetic language. This thinking, unlike poetic language, is imageless, and has no point of departure in beings. It can be argued that, instead of trying to preserve the singularity of poetry, Heidegger is using poetry to occasion a variation on the theme of the unconcealment of Being. As Véronique Fóti rightly observes, Heidegger "constrains the poetry [of his chosen poets] to fit the exigencies of an *essen*tial if always 'polemic' (or differential) unification" (1992, xix; em. or.).

Indeed, what Heidegger attaches importance to is not poetry as it is. His mind is fixated upon "genuine and great poetry" (*IM* 28/28). Similarly, what concerns him is not any poet in his own right, but those whom he considers as the great poets in an age of poverty, such as Rilke, Trakl and Hölderlin. Among them Heidegger regards Hölderlin as the poet of poets, the precursor of poets in a destitute time, whom no other poet of this world era can overtake. In his own words, Hölderlin is "our greatest *poet* . . . our most adventive [*zukünftiges*] thinker" ([1934/35, 6]; em. or.). Heidegger suggests that Hölderlin's poetry is futural and historic (*CP* 90/129), that "he arrives from [the future] in such a way that in the advent [*Ankunft*] of his words alone the future [*Zukunft*] presences" [1946c, 240/320]. In another place, he stresses that Hölderlin is "*the* poet of the other beginning of our futural history" ([1937/38b, 377]; em. or.).

Heidegger sharply distinguishes his reading of Hölderlin from those in literary studies or aesthetics. In a preface written in 1971 to the *Elucidations of Hölderlin's Poetry*, he states, "The present *Elucidations* do not claim to be contributions to research in the history of literature or to aesthetics. They spring from a necessity of thought" (*EHP* 21/7; em. or.). For Heidegger, the appearance of aesthetics is consequent upon the original forgottenness of the ontological difference between Being and beings. It is derived from the practice of carving out a specific object domain for the investigations of particular beings. Previous studies of Hölderlin's poetry have been dominated by this kind of orientation toward beings and the empirical, and suffer from the lack of deep concern. In opposition to this unessential approach, Heidegger insists that his lectures on this poet are neither mere commentaries (*Anmerkungen*) nor explanations (*Erklärungen*), but elucidations (*Erläuterungen*). He claims that his elucidations stem from a dialogue of his thinking (*Denken*) with Hölderlin's poetizing (*Dichten*), from the necessity of thinking. The historic uniqueness of poetry can never be proved by the history of literature, but can only be "pointed out by the dialogue with thinking" (*EHP* 21/7).

THE JOURNEY ABROAD

Heidegger's estimation of Hölderlin's poetry as world-historic is to a large extent associated with the latter's poetizing on Greece. He reads into his poetry a concern with the destiny of the world, where the history of Being is at stake. In the "Letter on Humanism," Heidegger writes,

> As the destiny that sends truth, Being remains concealed. But the destiny of the world is heralded in poetry, without yet becoming manifest as the history of Being. The world-historical thinking of Hölderlin that speaks out in the poem "Remembrance" is therefore essentially more primordial and thus more significant for the future than the mere cosmopolitanism of Goethe. For the same reason Hölderlin's relation to Greek civilization is something essentially other than humanism. (*LH* 258/339)

Heralded in Hölderlin's poetry is the history of Being as concealed in the destiny of the world. Therefore, his thinking is world-historic, and is more originary and essential for the future than that of any other literary figure. Heidegger attributes to Hölderlin's poetry a special relation with the Greek world. In this connection, he discerns a tripartite thematic of homeland (*Heimat*), the journey abroad (*Wanderschaft in die Fremde*), and homecoming (*Heimkunft*) in the latter's verses and expound it in the way in which it sits well with his concern with the history of Being.

Homeland

In his lectures *Hölderlins Hymnen „Germanien" und „der Rhein,"* Heidegger puts forward the following "definition" of *Heimat*,

> *Heimat*—neither merely the place of birth, nor the familiar countryside, but the *power of the earth,* on which the human being at a given moment according to his historical Dasein "dwells poetically" ([1934/35, 88]; em, or.)

Heidegger often uses *Heimat* with a view to man's "dwelling poetically"—that is, originally being at home in the abode of Being in correspondence to Being's call.[1] In an essay entitled "Language and Homeland," after citing the remark by the poet J. P. Hebel that "*regional poetry, written in regional dialect,* allows language *to reveal itself in its structure and texture*" [1960, 158],[2] Heidegger observes:

> Language is because of its poetising essence, the most hidden and therefore most adequate, emphatically bestowing bringing forth of homeland. In this way the title "Sprache und Heimat" gets its appropriate determination. It can now sound as it should sound; not only Language and Homeland, but:
>
> Language *as* Homeland. ([1960, 180]; em. or.)

In this place, Heidegger connects the homeland with the poetizing nature of language. The nature of language resides in bringing forth the homeland, in letting what is hidden to become unconcealed. Heidegger continues to state that the nearness of Being is called the "homeland," whereas homelessness is the symptom of oblivion of Being. Homelessness means the same as the abandonment of Being by beings. For Heidegger, homelessness is man's basic state of being. In another place, he relates homelessness to the spirit of the age, that is, extreme industrialization and calculative thinking [1955b].

   In the context of elucidating Hölderlin's poem "Homecoming/To Kindred Ones" [1943d], Heidegger identifies the homeland with "the German," which *prima facie* sounds to be something ontic. Hölderlin composed this poem on a trip back home in 1801, leaving a village near Constance in Switzerland and traveling back across Lake Constance to his Swabian homeland. As Heidegger reads it, this poem does not convey anything like joy at coming home. There is a sense of estrangement with the description of the arrival on the home shore, in that the people and the things of the homeland appear to be familiar, but actually they are not quite so. The "homecoming" is not accomplished by arrival on the shore of one's birthplace. As the poet states,

> What you seek, it is near, already comes to meet you. (*EHP* 32/13)

One cannot reach one's homeland by simply arriving there. The homeland is difficult to win, in spite of its nearness, in spite of its having already come. So one still needs to seek. If "find" means to appropriate it as a possession, then one has not yet found what one seeks:

> But the best, the real find, which lies beneath the rainbow
> Of holy peace, is reserved for young and old.

Later, Hölderlin replaced these two verses with the following (*EHP* 33/14),

But the treasure, the German, which lies beneath the rainbow
Of holy peace, is still reserved.

After drawing attention to this significant change, Heidegger speaks of the homeland and the German almost in the same breath. The German (*das Deutsche*) is "the homeland's very own peculiar character [*das Eigenste*]" (*EHP* 33/14). The nature of the homeland is a gift of destiny (*Geschick*) or history (*Geschichte*). This destiny has not yet conveyed (*übereignet*) what is most distinctive (*das Eigene*) of itself. What properly belongs to destiny is still held back and needs to be found. Yet what is unique of the homeland was already granted (*zugeschickt*) to those living in the land of their birth. This ambiguity Heidegger describes as "reserved" (*das Gesparte*). What is given as a gift is reserved because the residents are not yet prepared to receive "the homeland's very own peculiar character, 'the German,' as their own possession [*Eigentum*]" (33/14). Heidegger goes on,

> Therefore what constitutes the homecoming is that the countrymen must first become at home in the still withheld essence [*Wesen*] of their homeland—indeed, even prior to this, that the "dear ones" at home must first learn to become at home. (*EHP* 33/14)

In Heidegger's view, properly speaking, it is the German who are the people of the homeland. They belong to the homeland's very own peculiar character. In a preparatory remark on another version of his lecture on "Homecoming/To Kindred Ones," Heidegger emphasizes, "The innermost core [*das Innerste*] of the poem is concealed in line 42 [the line where "the German" occurs], which mentions the people of the country."[3]

When interpreting Hölderlin's hymn "Der Ister," Heidegger identifies the homeland with Europe:

> We know today that the Anglo-Saxon world of Americanism has resolved to annihilate Europe, that is, the homeland, and that means: the commencement of the Western world. (*HHI* 54/67)

While providing the homeland with "ontic" references such as "Europe" and "the German," Heidegger relates it to what he calls "the origin" and the history of Being, and in this way attributes ontological significance to it. He writes,

> What is most characteristic of the homeland, what is best in it, consists solely in its being this nearness to the origin—and nothing else

except this. That is why in this homeland, too, faithfulness to the origin
is inborn. . . . Homecoming is the return to the nearness to the origin.
(*HHI* 42/51; tr. m.)

For Heidegger, the homeland is the nearness to the origin.[4] The word "origin" does not refer to a substantial entity or a universal essence. As the origin,
it consists not only in giving forth its waters but also in concealing and with-
drawing. The original flow of the source goes back to its ground. The origin
tends to conceal or withdraw itself (*EHP* 106/79).

In the context of elaborating on the theme of homecoming, Heidegger
refers to the German as well: "homecoming is the future of the historical
being of the German people," who are "the people of poetry *and* of thought"
(*EHP* 48/30; em. or.). The people who are involved in the necessity of making the journey abroad and achieving homecoming are not any people arbitrarily. As Pöggeler points out, "the essential ground of man's historicality"
is "certainly not 'of man in general' or 'universal humanity' but of Western
man" (1987b, 180).

Peter Trawny provides a list of the motifs in Heidegger's interpretation
of Hölderlin, which according to him are borrowed from the ideas of the poet
Stefan George and Norbert von Hellingrath, principle editor of the collected
works of Hölderlin Heidegger consulted. These motifs are: 1. Europe finds its
beginning in Greece; 2. Hölderlin's poetry is the sign of the unique relation of
Germany and Greece that goes closer than the intimate relation of the Greek
and German languages;[5] 3. Hölderlin's hymns do not present the "public"
Germany, but a "secret Germany." This secret Germany, as distinguished from
a geopolitical entity, has a special role to play in the reflection on and thinking of (*zudenken*) another *Morgenland*. It is a destiny that withdraws itself in
its coming (2004, 75f). Trawny argues that it is in the sense of the third motif
that Heidegger's "abendländische Gespräch" (the title of an essay on Hölderlin) [1946–48] is a dialogue with Greece through Hölderlin's verses. Trawny
has pointed out some of the key assumptions at work in Heidegger's attention
to Hölderlin. The phrase "secret Germany" indicates the ontological significance that has been integrated with any literal reference to Germany.

After the Second World War, attention to the German became less pervasive and less obvious in Heidegger's writings (but this is not the case with
his attention to Greece). On some occasions, he seems to attempt to pre-
empt possible criticisms by accentuating that the homeland and the German
cannot be crudely regarded as fixated ontic references to determinate entities, but should be understood in terms of the ontological. In the "Letter on
Humanism," Heidegger writes,

> The word [homeland] is thought here in an essential sense, not patriotically or nationalistically, but in terms of the history of Being. . . . when Hölderlin composed "Homecoming" he is concerned that his "countrymen" find their essence. He does not at all seek that essence in an egoism of his people. He sees it rather in the context of a belongingness to the destiny of the West. . . . "German" is not spoken to the world so that the world might be reformed through the German essence; rather, it is spoken to the Germans so that from a destinal belongingness to other peoples they might become world-historical along with them . . . The homeland of this historical dwelling is nearness to Being. (*LH* 257/338)

In this place, Heidegger stresses that the appeal to the German is not meant to promote national egoism, nor to proselytize the whole world;[6] instead, it articulates the expectation that the Germans live up to the German essence, and thereby become world-historic along with, presumably, the Greek people. In the same vein, the appeal to the homeland is grounded in the history of Being, and hence cannot be reduced to superficial patriotism or nationalism.

The Journey Abroad and Homecoming

In his interpretation of Hölderlin's poems "Remembrance" and "The Ister," Heidegger discusses at length "the journey abroad to the foreign" together with the theme of "homeland" and "homecoming."[7] "Remembrance" appears on the first page of Hölderlin's river poem entitled "The Ister." It originates from the poet's trip to southern France. A superficial interpretation would take it to be a reflection of Hölderlin's journey. For Heidegger, this is a simplistic reduction of the richness of this poem by means of identification of its empirical subject matter.

According to Heidegger, remembrance (*Andenken*) is a "thinking of [*Denken an*] what is yet to come" (109/83). As a thinking of what is yet to come, this thinking can only be a thinking of what has been. What has been does not mean something simply past. It refers to "what is still coming into presence from afar" (109/83). Remembrance must "think of what has been as something *which is not yet unfolded*," as something which is coming to us as futural in one's experience of it (123/100; em. ad.). Remembrance of what has been makes it possible for one to possess its own nature.

In thematizing on the journey abroad, Heidegger draws inspiration from Hölderlin's verses (*EHP* 114/89; tr. m):[8]

For the spirit is not at home
Neither at the beginning, nor at the source. The homeland preys upon it.

According to Heidegger, the spirit is the "knowing will of the origin" (116/92), with origin referring to the homeland. In this context, "will" does not mean egoistic compulsion or calculative desire. Will signifies "the knowing readiness for belonging to the destiny" (111/87; tr. m.). There is a dialectical relation between the will and what it only wills, which is what is coming. What the will only wills has addressed the spirit and offered it the promise of becoming at home. Once again Heidegger connects being-at-home with the nearness to the source: "being-at-home . . . is constituted by the poetic spirit's abiding in the nearness *to the source*" (116/92; em. or.).

However, the spirit is not at the source from the very beginning. Because the origin tends to conceal and withdraw itself, the spirit cannot grasp it immediately. In his eagerness to find the homeland in the homelike, the spirit is banished from the homeland into a futile search for the homeland. It gets lost amidst what is homelike (*das Heimische*) but is in fact not the nearness of the homeland. While the homeland is withdrawn in its essence, it preys on the spirit, and endangers the spirit in that it may consume and exhaust its powers because of its will to be at home (*zu Hauß*) in the own (*im eigenen*). Although lost amidst the homelike, the spirit remains oriented toward the homeland (116/92). As Karin de Boer states succinctly in this connection, home "arises only from within homelessness as a future possibility" (2000, 165).

The will is awakened in the spirit to search for what is not homelike (*das Unheimischsein*). Here Heidegger is playing with the double meaning of *unheimisch:* the normal meaning of "uncanny" and the literal meaning of "not homelike." What is not homelike can bring near the homeland that is concealed. This is because what is not homelike (that is, the foreign) will turn out to be where the homeland resides. On the other hand, "That which essentially grants the state of not being-at-home" is the foreign (*EHP* 116/93). The foreign makes one think of the homeland. The spirit turns toward what is not homelike only for the sake of the homeland.

For the poet, "the journey abroad to the foreign remain[s] essential for the return home" (108/83; tr. m.). The journey abroad is necessary for becoming at home. As Heidegger writes, "Becoming homely demands a going away into the foreign" (*HHI* 142/178). There is an intrinsic connection between the "foreign" (*die Fremde*) and the "own" (*das Eigene*). When interpreting Hölderlin's "The Ister," Heidegger remarks,

The essence of the own is so mysterious [*geheimnisvoll*] that it unfolds its ownmost essential wealth only from out of a supremely thoughtful acknowledgement of the foreign. (*HHI* 55/69; tr. m.)

Only by acknowledgement of the foreign can the essence of the own reveal itself. The essence of the own entails one's initial not-being-at-home and the necessity of going through the foreign in order to be at home. Heidegger accentuates the importance of the foreign,

[W]here it remains only a matter of refuting, or even of annihilating the foreign, what necessarily gets lost is the possibility of a passage through the foreign, and thereby the possibility of a return home into the own, and thereby the own itself.[9] (*HHI* 54/68; tr. m.)

The law of going abroad and homecoming is at the same time the law of poetry and the law of history. Heidegger claims, "The historical character of history has its essence in the return [*Rückkehr*] to the own, a return that can only be made as a journey out into the foreign" (*EHP* 118/95; tr. m.). Furthermore, this law is also the law of reversal from the forgottenness of Being to the unconcealment of Being in its essential concealment. The essence of homecoming is not to create a new home out of nothing, but to come to be aware of one's belongingness to the destiny of Being, to realize that the homeland has been prepared. As John Sallis comments when discussing the theme of homecoming, "What is at issue is not that a new rootedness be *established* but rather that it be *granted*" (1970, 142; em. or.).

Heidegger regards the journey to the foreign as an unavoidable process for coming-to-be-at-home. It should be noted that the foreign does not refer to random geographical places, nor to what is not the own in general. Heidegger remarks,

That foreign, of course, through which the return home journeys, is not some arbitrary "foreign" in the sense of whatever is merely and indeterminately not one's own. The *foreign* that relates to the return home, that is, is one with it, is the provenance of such return and is that which has been at the commencement with regard to what is one's own and the homely. (*HHI* 54/67; em. or.)

The foreign is not something contingent or indeterminate, but instead has a definite and determinate reference. It belongs to the realm of the homecoming and is present at the source of the own and of the homeland. As Pöggeler observes, the foreign to which Hölderlin turns is not something arbitrary, but rather "the seminal element of one's own which has been, [i.e.] Geek culture" (1987b, 180).

In Heidegger's view, Hölderlin apportions a special place to the Greek and the German in his verses touching on the theme of the journey abroad and the homecoming.[10] The ontologically necessary process of not-being-at-home, passing-through-the-foreign, and becoming-at-home, is specifically related to the intrinsic link between the Greek and German Dasein. He quotes Hölderlin's observation in a letter that the people of southern France "made him more familiar with the authentic essence of the Greek" (*EHP* 107/82; 183/157), and that this experience makes him become aware of a higher truth, that is, to think of the land of the Greek. Hölderlin's reflection (*Andenken*), Heidegger comments, is a "fundamental trait [*Grundzug*] of the poiesis of this poet" (108/83).

For Hölderlin, the Greek world is the foreign in relation to the historic humankind (that is, the Germans) [1943a, 54]. Heidegger refutes the suggestion that at a certain time Hölderlin turned away from Greekness (calling it *morgenländisch*) toward a nationalistic German *Abendland*. According to him, Hölderlin's new relation to Greekness constitutes a more essential and originary *Auseinandersetzung* that aims at going back to Greekness [1941/42, 140–1]. With respect to the nature of the relation between the German and the Greek world, Heidegger argues that for Hölderlin this is not a matter of identifying the German with the Greek, nor of assimilating the German to the Greek. The Greek world is not taken to be the measure for human perfection. Neither is the Greek romantically conceived as the ideal state where the German should return. This view, however, does not loosen Hölderlin's tie with the Greek, but rather makes it more intimate (*HHI* 54/67).[11] Heidegger explains,

> For only where the foreign is known and acknowledged in its essential oppositional character does there exist the possibility of a genuine relationship, that is, of a uniting that is not a confused missing but a conjoining in distinction. (*HHI* 54/68)

The relation of the German Dasein to the Greek Dasein (that is, what is the foreign), is one of "conjoining in distinction." The Greek world represents the commencement of Western historicality. Only in and through the Greek could the essence of the homeland unfold; and the German is to be united with the Greek. This does not mean a simplistic return to the Greek. Rather, the German, as the embodiment of Western historicality, has to pass through the Greek as the foreign to them, and to strive for a homecoming in not-being-at-home. It is only when the foreign is recognized in its oppositional nature that a genuine relationship of conjoining between the Greek and the German could be established.[12] My last comment is: Stressing that the distinction between the German Dasein and the Greek Dasein is to be retained implies that the journey to the foreign is always underway.

The Journey Abroad and Interculturality

A few scholars have attempted to draw implications for intercultural dialogue from Heidegger's lectures on Hölderlin. Among them, Florian Vetsch (1992) has developed the most systematic argument concerning "Heidegger's beginning of intercultural confrontation," as the title of his monograph suggests (*Martin Heideggers Anfang der interkulturellen Auseinandersetzung*). On the basis of his reading of Heidegger's lectures on Hölderlin's poetry, especially with respect to the theme of the journey abroad, he constructs on behalf of Heidegger a "structure of intercultural *Auseinandersetzung*" (68–90). According to him, this structure can be applied to various phenomena: the process of a conversation, the reading of a text in a foreign language, the evolvement of an individual's life, the historical development of a people, and more importantly, the foundation of East-West dialogue. This structure of intercultural *Auseinandersetzung* consists in "two-and-a-half" steps, which can be summarized as follows,

1. Before setting upon the journey abroad, the wanderer remains caught in his own (*im Eigenen*). In the contemporary age, one may not even be able to achieve the first step, since one has become homeless. Modern modes of transportation, tourism, and exoticism may incur the danger that home be dissolved and deteriorated (*verfällt*).
2. The journey abroad is initiated, and the wanderer meets the foreign. The experience of the foreign awakens remembrance of one's own.
3. The wanderer returns, but remains in a state of thinking the foreign through which something new shows itself. Because one always remains underway, the third step is strictly speaking a half step. One must constantly take care of one's experience with the foreign, and bring it into conversation with the present.

Vetsch has advanced a sophisticated account of intercultural dialogue on the basis of generalizing the theme of the journey abroad. He rightly perceives that for Heidegger homecoming is a possibility, rather than an actuality, and that the interaction with the "foreign" is a necessary and ceaseless undertaking for the homecoming. As de Boer states, "In the going homeward that concerns Heidegger, all that takes place is the affirmation of the impossibility of actually being at home. To turn homeward is nothing but to dwell in the journeying itself" (165).

However, Vetsch has ignored the fact that the foreign refers to the Greek, and the homeland to the German. The dialectic of the homecoming is confined to the emergence of another dawning of the Morning-Land (that is, Greece). Vetsch misconstrues Heidegger's concern when he identifies the foreign with "other cultures." He neutralizes and generalizes the dialectic of the homecoming, and thus makes it applicable to intercultural dialogue. In speaking of the journey to the foreign, Heidegger stresses,

> This remembrance that is now bestowed, which thinks ahead toward the path to the source, again allows *what is merely alien* [*Nur-Fremde*] in the foreign to be forgotten, so that *only that foreign that is to be transformed through the own is preserved.* (*EHP* 164/142; em. ad.; tr. m.)

Heidegger clearly distinguishes between what is merely alien from the authentic, proper foreign. The former will be forgotten, whereas only the latter will sustain. The "foreign" in the context of Heidegger's elucidation of Hölderlin's poetry cannot be simplistically identified with non-Western cultures.

In addition, Vetsch has missed the subtle relation between the "own" and the "foreign." With Heidegger, the foreign is at the source of the own; the own can only unfold by encountering the foreign. Man starts where the own originates without being able to realize the own as truly the own. Man meets the foreign and tries to truly possess what is the own. The foreign is offered a privileged status, which has nothing to do with non-Western cultures. Historically speaking, it is the foreign that bestows the own. The own and the foreign are the two sides of the same coin. The journey to the foreign is not a forward progression, but a backward retrieval, albeit claimed to be futuristic in nature.

It is worth noting that in "The Way to Language" (1959), Heidegger relates the own with Ereignis. He writes,

> *The moving force in Showing of Saying is Owning [das Eignen].*
>
> It is what brings all present and absent beings each into their own, from where they show themselves in what they are, and where they abide according to their kind. This owning which brings them there, and which moves Saying as Showing in its showing we call Ereignis. (*OWL* 127/258; em. or.)

The English translator renders *das Eignen* as the gerund form of the verb "to own." This rightly captures the sense of movement of the own as consonant with that of Ereignis. It can be said that the own is in essence a transformative movement in which the Western tradition is to retrieve its source, where the foreign, i.e. the Greek world, is present.

In section 38 "falling and thrownness" in *Being and Time,* Heidegger refers to "the most alien cultures" in relation to the "own":

> With special regard to the interpretation of Dasein, the opinion may now arise that understanding the most alien cultures [*fremdesten Kulturen*] and the "synthesis" of these with the own [*eigenen*] leads to Dasein's for the first time complete and genuine enlightenment about itself. Versatile curiosity and restlessly "knowing it all" masquerade as a universal understanding of Dasein. But at ground-level it remains indefinite and unquestioned *what* is really to be understood; it has not been understood that understanding itself is a potentiality-for-Being, which must be made free only in the *ownmost* [*eigensten*] Dasein. (*BT* 222/178; em. or.; tr. m.)

The English translators of *Being and Time* have added "one's" before *eigenen* and *eigensten* respectively. This may mislead the reader to take Heidegger's discourse on Dasein to be neutral and general, and thus applicable to the self-understanding of other cultures. However, for Heidegger, Dasein is essentially singular; and the "own" of Dasein is not just one among others, but is *the* matter that calls for thinking. The English translators of *Elucidations of Hölderlin's Poetry* have done the same. This results in an interpretation of the own as something neutral and potentially plural.

It is recognizable that Heidegger's attitude is completely different when he turns to "the most alien cultures," which can be more convincingly related to non-Western cultures than the "foreign." The foreign refers to Greece, the proper *other* to the Western tradition. Heidegger distains interest and erudition in other cultures and regards it as superficial curiosity. Furthermore, this is a symptom of not-being-at-home, and exhibits pretensions to a universalistic stance. Knowledge of other cultures will not and cannot touch upon the *own*, the matter of thinking. To achieve genuine self-understanding, Dasein should focus on what is ownmost to itself.

In trying to bring Heidegger's writings to bear upon intercultural dialogue, one cannot completely ignore the original meaning of his terminology and relevant aspects of his thinking.

THE *MORGENLAND* AND THE *ORIENT*

In the preceding sections, it has become clear that the "foreign" refers to Greece. We should notice that, in the context of Heidegger's interpretation of Hölderlin's poetry, the words *Morgenland, Orient* and *Asien* in most cases refer to Greece as well, and cannot be identified with Asia, East Asia, or the East in general. Confusions are exacerbated when *Morgenland* is translated into English as "Orient" or "antiquity."[13] In the nineteenth century, *Morgenland* (Morning-Land) signifies everything indeterminate that is not part of Germany, which is the *Abendland* (Evening-Land). Nietzsche remarks that the Greeks provided the synthesis of everything *morgenländischen* and "the *beginning* of the European soul."[14] This convention may be what Heidegger and Hölderlin have in mind in calling ancient Greece the *Morgenland*.

In the context of elucidating Hölderlin's poems, Heidegger is using not only *Morgenland* but also *Asien* as a label for Greece. This is obvious in the following passage from his essay "Hölderlin's Poetry: a Destiny,"

> The foreign, however, is in the first place, as it is for all essential poets from the Abendland, Greece. Hölderlin often says "Asia." . . . The rising water, the mouth, which calls,—that [is what] the source follows. To the East *and back*. From there the Donau, homely stream; "Der Ister." From Asia to Europe, from Morgenland to the Abendland, "from land to land" . . . ([1945–46, 357]; em. or.)

It is clear that, *Asien* in Heidegger's usage does not refer to Asia in the contemporary cultural-geographical sense, but refers to Greece. On a few occasions, *Asien* refers to the Middle East, or "the Indies" (but certainly not East Asia), insofar as their historical relation to Greece is concerned.

Heidegger refers to Greece as *das Morgenländische* or the *Orient* as well. This is manifest in his lecture "Hölderlin's Earth and Heaven" (1959), where he contrasts European-occidental with Greece, *das Morgenländische* (*EHP* 200–1/176–7). "Morgenland" (or the "Orient") is ascribed ontological significance. It signifies the origin from which the Western destiny and philosophical tradition derive. For instance, in *Parmenides*, Heidegger states,

> According to this essential origination of ἀλήθεια, the Evening-Land [*Abendland*] is the not yet decided or delimited landscape of the earth upon which an evening [*Abend*] is descending, which as evening essentially takes its beginning from the dawn and therefore harbours in itself the morning of this landscape. [1942/43, 147/219]

The Evening-Land (the West) embodies in itself the Morning-land; therefore both have a world-historic sense.

In his essay "Anaximander's Saying" written in 1946, Heidegger raises the following question,

> Will this Evening-Land [*Abend-Land*] rising above [*über*] Occident and Orient and transcending the European, become the place of the coming, more primordially destined, history?[15] [1946a, 245/326]

What the "Orient" refers to is crucial to an adequate understanding of this passage. J. L. Mehta draws on this text to account for what he calls Heidegger's "planetary thinking." The alleged "planetary thinking" seeks "a new beginning of thought . . . beyond Orient and Occident, and [is] for the first time truly world-historical" (Mehta 1970, 312).

> [This thinking is] not unaware of the preciousness of similar resources within other traditions and languages which have developed independently, differently, and presumably without having undergone the kind of alienation from the wellsprings of life which has been the Western destiny. (Mehta 1970, 312)

For Mehta, Heidegger's project of planetary construction provides a ground on which different traditions can find their own justification, and enter into dialogue with each other. However, Heidegger makes the relevant remark in the context of reflecting upon the nature of the West from out of the nature of history. The Evening-Land is the historic *topos* where Anaximander's saying is heard, which is "the dawn of the Land of the Evening." One cannot take for granted that the "Orient" in the cited passage refers literally to Asia. The Orient in this context most probably refers to Greece; while the Occident seems to be distinct from the Orient in terms of a different kind of comportment toward Being. When it retraces its origin and truth, the Occident will find itself belonging essentially and historically to both the Orient (Greece) and the Evening-Land (the West), which is the nearness to the source.

The Evening-Land (which has become Europe in the present epoch), in achieving homecoming through a journey to the Morning-Land (that is, Greece), is the place where, hopefully, the newly commenced Morning-Land will emerge. Only the Evening-Land enjoys a "historic nearness" (*geschichtliche Nähe*), as concealed in chronological remoteness, to what is spoken in the early saying of Anaximander, which will speak out in that which is coming. Compare another passage from "Hölderlin's Poetry: a Destiny":

> *We,* the poets; the word, that which destiny has sent us, that which is *to be said says,* that which unifies Asia and Europe, *Morgen-* and *Abendland,* while it "is" "over" them [*weil es «über» sie « ist »*], only [thus] supporting and enabling their hidden historic essence. ([1945–46, 357–58]; em. or.)

It is obvious that in this context Asia does not refer to what is usually considered to be Asia, but to Greece. That the word is "over" Asia and Europe, over *Morgenland* and *Abendland,* is similar to the saying in the preceding passage with respect to the Evening-Land being "over" Occident and Orient. The incipient word in the dawning of philosophy is what unites Asia (that is, Greece) and Europe; at the same time, it is over both of them. This means that there is something inexhaustible with the word, and with Greece and Europe. This inexhaustible something is what constitutes the historic essence of the latter two.

Taking *Morgenland* and *Orient* to be Asia in the customary sense has given rise to inadequate interpretations of Heidegger's view of East-West dialogue. Similarly, on the basis of taking "the few other great beginnings" to be a referent to non-Western traditions, a grand conclusion is drawn with respect to Heidegger's connection with intercultural dialogue. Now I turn to this complex issue.

THE FEW OTHER GREAT BEGINNINGS

In a lecture entitled "Hölderlin's Earth and Heaven" delivered at the meeting of the Hölderlin Society in Munich on 6 June 1959, Heidegger makes a remark in which he uses the phrase "the few other great beginnings"

> The great beginning becomes present, as that which awaits us, only in its coming to the humble [*zum Geringen*]. But the humble can no longer abide in its occidental isolation. It is opening itself up to the few other great beginnings [*den wenigen anderen grossen Anfängen*] that belong, with their ownness [*ihren Eigenen*], in the sameness [*das Selbe*] of the beginning of the in-finite relation in which the earth is contained. (*EHP* 201/177; tr. m.)

Almost all the scholars who have touched on the question of Heidegger's relation to East Asian thinking or of his thinking on intercultural dialogue in general have attached great importance to this remark. Mehta is perhaps the first scholar who commented on it (1976, 469). In recent years, Parkes called attention to this passage and his observation has been the most influential.

He discerns in it a positive attitude toward East-West dialogue. To cite his own words, "The opening anticipated here must at the very least be an opening to the 'great beginning' of East Asian thought, wherever one locates it" (1996, 104). Obviously, he considers that "the few other great beginnings" refers to other philosophical traditions, in particular East Asian traditions.

Vetsch claims that this passage has "central significance" for the subject of his book. In his view, it speaks of "the necessity of the intercultural encounter for the other beginning" (1992, 28–29). Thurnher thus comments on the same text,

> Heidegger seemed to think that only in the dialogue of reflecting thought with non-Western ways of thinking, would the possibility appear of founding a changed destiny of the world. (1993, 138–39)

According to Hartig, in making the relevant remark in "Hölderlin's Earth and Heaven," Heidegger is articulating "his vision of a thinking dialogue [*Zwiesprache*] of the Western world with the few other great beginnings (i.e. the Indian and Sino-Japanese world)" (1997, 19). Hartig tries to strengthen his point by adding, "The call for this dialogue of the great beginnings with each other could not be formulated more explicitly" (19).

Other scholars who provide similar readings of this passage include, Beaufret (1977, 18), Strolz (1984, 84, 89), and May (1996, 47–48). More recently, Trawny argues that an "other great beginning" is "possibly the 'Asiatic'" (2004, 186). Blocker and Starling (2001) seem to be following Parkes' interpretation. In quoting Heidegger's relevant text from the English version of May's monograph, they explain the meaning of "the few other great beginnings" in terms of the "multiplicity of philosophical beginnings," and regard Heidegger's remark as unequivocal evidence that he is emphasizing "the importance of the transcultural" (170–171).

In his monograph *Martin Heidegger's Path of Thinking,* Pöggeler does not explicitly identify "the few other great beginnings" with East Asian traditions (1987b, 186), but elsewhere he speaks of "the beginnings [Heidegger] finds for the West in ancient Greece and for the Far East in Lao-tzu" (1987a, 68; cf. 56). Bernasconi is perhaps the only scholar who has expressed serious doubts concerning the reference of "the few other great beginnings." He senses that

> [the suggestion that this phrase represents a plurality of beginnings] is not readily reconciled with any of the prominent interpretations of Heidegger's other texts, leaving the question as to how to construe it as

anything more than an anomaly, particularly given his repeated claim that the technological world can only be addressed by the European tradition, because only it has the same source and vocation. (1995b, 250)

Nevertheless, Bernasconi has not attempted to offer a reasonable and convincing explication of this perplexing passage from "Hölderlin's Earth and Heaven." In the following pages, I provide an analysis of this text. It should be noted that this is the only passage among Heidegger's writings where he uses the phrase "the other few great beginnings." When we read his essay carefully, it becomes clear that this phrase does not refer to other philosophical traditions such as East Asian thought.

"Hölderlin's Earth and Heaven" is a lecture in which Heidegger offers his elucidation of Hölderlin's poem "Greece." This poem derives from the same trip to Southern France as "Remembrance" does. As the title of Heidegger's lecture indicates, he is primarily concerned with the rich connection between heaven and earth about which he hears Hölderlin speaking. Citing Hölderlin's statement in a letter, "all the holy places of the earth are together around one place, and the philosophical light around my window is now my joy," Heidegger provides a highly speculative thematization of earth and heaven:

> Through the place in which the poet now dwells, the earth becomes for him earth in a new way. The earth, as the structure of the heavenly ones, shelters and supports the holy, the sphere of the god. The earth is earth only as the earth of heaven; the heaven is heaven only insofar as it acts downward upon the earth. (*EHP* 186/161)

Earth and heaven have an inherent relation. They belong together in a rich relation in which they receive determination. Heidegger associates the phrase "philosophical light" in Hölderlin's verse with Greece, because for him the name φιλοσοφία discloses that the "philosophical" arises out of Greece. "Greece itself approaches [the poet] in the shining of earth and heaven, in the holy which conceals the god, in the poetizing-thinking being of man" (187/162). In this statement, Greece is inherently related to earth, heaven, god and man. On the basis of Hölderlin's writings, Heidegger defines the term "whole relation" as one in which earth and heaven and their connection belong to the "more tender in-finite relation" (187–88/163). This means that earth, heaven, god and man are held together integrally from out of the center of the full blooming relation of these four. It is important to notice already in this place that, first, the four of earth, heaven, god and man belong together in a whole relation; second, the four has an intimate relation with Greece.

Although the number four is not explicitly mentioned by Hölderlin, Heidegger comments that earth, heaven, god and man are first "caught sight of out of the intimacy of their togetherness," and that "[t]hey are already *numbered* in the originary sense of the tale of the 'old (scarcely heard) saying' of their togetherness" (195/170; em. ad.). The number four has nothing to do with a calculative sum. Rather, it refers to the self-unifying form of the in-finite relation of the voices of destiny. As Heidegger states, "The destiny would presumably be 'the center' which centers, that is, mediates, insofar as the center first determines the four in their belonging-together, sends them into their togetherness. The sending of destiny gathers the four to itself, into its center" (195/170). It can be seen that the number four as connected with earth, heaven, god and man has to be understood in an ontological sense. It is determined as the four in the belonging-together of the four, and in their being gathered into the center, that is, the destiny.

Heidegger relates the terms "destiny" and "center" to the term "beginning." The term "beginning" does not mean an ordinary event or happening that takes place at a definite time on a definite location. It describes an originary event in which something comes forth. Heidegger writes,

> But in what manner *is* a beginning? A beginning is present, insofar as it remains in its coming. For the mediation that gathers the four into the center of their intimacy is a first coming. Beginning remains as advent. The beginning remains all the more, the closer it keeps itself within the possibility that it can come, and in its coming brings and sends that which it keeps to itself: the in-finite relation. (*EHP* 195/171; em. or.)

The word "beginning" delineates a mode of coming and gathering. It preserves and gathers the in-finite relation of the four to itself. Using the copula "is," Heidegger explicitly identifies "destiny" and "center" with "beginning": "As the center of the whole relation, destiny is the all-gathering beginning. As the ringing out of the great destiny, the center is *the great beginning*" (195/171; em. ad.). A couple of pages later, Heidegger states, "The center is the joint of the relation of the four" (203/179). Since "center" is identified as "the great beginning," and it grounds the intimate relation of belonging-together between earth, heaven, god and man, it is reasonable to attribute a connection between "the great beginning" and a plural form of it (beginnings) in the ontological, non-calculative sense. In the meantime, it is consistent with the major line of development of Heidegger's text to treat "the few other great beginnings" as an alternative expression of the four of earth, heaven, god and man, which are closely related to Greece, and gathered together in the center. In this light, it is consonant with the concern and focus of this essay (beginning, center, the four: the center is the joint of the relation of the four; and the center is the great beginning) to regard "the few other great beginnings" as a plural form of "the great beginning." Let us read Heidegger's text further.

Another claim Heidegger makes is that there must be something great to correspond to the coming of the great beginning. This great something should be able to grasp greatly the coming of the great beginning, or to wait for it greatly. The occidental, that is, the humble (*das Geringe*), is exactly this great something which becomes great in becoming that to which the great beginning can come. Heidegger contrasts the occidental with the oriental, which is nothing else but Greece.

> The humble is the occidental. Greece, however, *the oriental* [*das Morgen-*
> *ländische*] is the great beginning that *may* possibly come. The humble is,
> however, only insofar as it becomes that to which the great beginning
> can come. (*EHP* 201/177; em. ad.)

Note that in this passage, Greece is labeled "the oriental" and described as *the great beginning that may possibly come*. With the domination of technology and industry, earth, heaven, god and man, which appeared in the occidental history as the bounded in-finite relation, have been displaced and their appearance has been denied. Following these statements, Heidegger quotes from a letter by Paul Valéry under the title "The Crisis of the Spirit," in which two questions are posed:

> This Europe, will it become *what it is in reality* (*en réalité*), that is, a
> small cape of the Asiatic continent? Or will this Europe, rather, remain
> *as what it appears to be* (*ce qu'elle parait*), that is, the precious part of the
> whole earth, the pearl of the globe, the brain of a specious body? (*EHP*
> 201/177; em. or.)

Heidegger comments that both of Valéry's descriptions suit the situation of contemporary Europe. While it is a mere cape, it is also the brain of the globe that participates in the technological-industrial calculation. Heidegger says that a third question should be raised, "Must Europe, as this cape and brain, first become a land of an evening from which another morning of world-destiny prepares its rise?" (201/177) He emphasizes that "[o]ur question does not pass over and beyond Europe, but back into its beginning," and that it has its ground in "an essential fact" (*Wesenstatsache*) on the one hand, and in "an essential supposition" (*Wesensvermutung*) on the other (201/177). In the following paragraph, Heidegger elaborates on what the essential fact and supposition consist in. This is where the phrase "the other few great beginnings" appears.

> The fact consists in this: In its essential beginning, which can never be lost, the present planetary-interstellar world condition is thoroughly European-occidental-grecian. However, the supposition reflects on this: What changes can do so only out of the reserved greatness of its beginning. Accordingly, the present world condition can receive an essential change or, for that matter, preparation for it, only from its beginning, which fatefully determines our age. It is the great beginning. There is, of course, no return to it. The great beginning becomes present, as that which awaits us, only in its' coming to the humble [*zum Geringen*]. But the humble can no longer abide in its occidental isolation. It is opening itself up to those few other great beginnings [*den wenigen anderen grossen Anfängen*] that belong, with their ownness [*ihren Eigenen*], in the sameness [*das Selbe*] of the beginning of the in-finite relation in which the earth is contained. (*EHP* 201/177; tr. m.)

For Heidegger, there is an undeniable intrinsic relation between Greece, the occidental, and Europe. This is indicated by the phrase "European-occidental-grecian" in the beginning of the passage cited above.[16] That the first great beginning occurs in Greece is an indisputable essential fact. Because of their inner bond, the contemporary Europe can receive from this first beginning an essential change, or a preparation for the change. Since there cannot be a simplistic return to the first beginning, a re-initiation of the great beginning remains to be a supposition. The great beginning is coming to Europe, the humble. With respect to Heidegger's saying: "But the humble can no longer abide in its occidental isolation," it should be noted that the term "occidental" is not used in contrast with the Eastern world, not to mention the East Asian world; rather, it is used in relation to the "oriental," which denotes nothing else than Greece. Heidegger continues, the humble "is opening itself to those few other great beginnings that belong, with their ownness [*ihren Eigenen*], in the sameness of the beginning of the in-finite relation in which the earth is contained."

To understand the phrase "the few other great beginnings," we need to keep in mind Heidegger's characterization of earth, heaven, god and man, that is, they belong together essentially in the in-finite relation of the four. Since a beginning is a coming to be, and that "what comes is not the god by himself alone [or any other member of this belonging relation]," but "*the whole in-finite relation in which, along with god and mankind, earth and heaven belong*" (200/175; em. ad.), it is most probable that in speaking of "the few other great beginnings," Heidegger is using the expression "great beginning" in the plural form with reference to the four of earth, heaven, god and man. Among the four, earth is highlighted. This is because in this lecture, earth, in its pairing relation to heaven, is conceived as the dwelling place for the poet, as what shelters and supports the holy.

In the paragraph immediately following the remark in which the expression "the few other great beginnings" occurs, Heidegger writes, "Yet we men of this age are presumably not even within the humbleness and neediness of that need from which *the four of the in-finite relation* call to each other" (201–202/177; em. ad.). It is justifiable to conclude that "the four of the in-finite relation" mentioned here refers back to "the few other great beginnings *that belong, with their ownness, in the sameness of the beginning of the in-finite relation* in which the earth is contained." Half a page later, Heidegger applies the plural form to the term "voice of destiny" in depicting the gloomy contemporary situation. He states, "The provocation to such making-available orders everything into a single design, the making of which levels the harmony of the in-finite relation. The togetherness of the four 'voices of destiny' no longer rings out" (202/178). Heidegger's lamentation on the fact that "[t]he togetherness of the four 'voices of destiny' no longer rings out" follows immediately the description that the harmony of the in-finite relation is leveled. It is evident that the four implies precisely earth, heaven, god and man, the four whose togetherness makes up the in-finite relation.

Through this study of Heidegger's text, it becomes clear that the expression "the few other great beginnings" is completely embedded in his thinking on the four of earth, heaven, god and man, which together constitute the in-finite relation. The four is inseparably related to Greece, where philosophy originated in the first beginning. Since the in-finite relation refers to the four of earth, heaven, god and man in their essential belonging-together and self-unifying, the "few other great beginnings" can be reasonably regarded as these four with the numeral words "few" and "four" taken in the originary sense, that is, they are not numbers in the ordinary calculative sense, but are intrinsically connected with the belonging-together and self-unifying of the in-finite relation.

A central concern of the lecture "Hölderlin's Earth and Heaven" is with present world situation. As Heidegger states, "we are bound to listen to the poem in terms of that which concerns us in the present age" (182/156). According to him, the occidental that has become Europe is characterized by technological-industrial domination. The earth has become an object at man's disposal. Earth and heaven as depicted in Hölderlin's poem have vanished. The in-finite relation of the four has been destroyed (200/176). Because of the inherent link between Greece, the occidental and Europe, the present planetary-interstellar world condition is brought about precisely by the denial of the in-finite relation. A change, or a preparation for a change, can only be made possible from within the originary great beginning. Since there cannot be a simplistic return to it, the humble must open up to the great beginning which becomes present in its coming to the humble. In the coming of the great beginning, which is constituted by the in-finite relation, earth and heaven are built up and receive determination from the rich in-finite relation.

Heidegger's reflection proceeds in accordance with his reflection on the *Ge-stell* and on the transition into the other beginning. What makes my exposition more convincing is Heidegger's use of the word *Ge-stell* in one of his prefaces to this lecture. In that place, he stresses that, in listening to Hölderlin's poem, there must be the "transformation into the thinking experience of the center of the in-finite relation—out of the enframing [*Ge-stell*] as the self-dissimulating event [Ereignis] of the four-fold" (*EHP* 176/153). Here the *Ge-stell* is explicitly associated with the four-fold. It is Heidegger's view that one needs to think from within the *Ge-stell,* the present planetary world that is in a dissimulated relation with the four-fold, toward the infinite relation of the four, that is, "the few other great beginnings," which appeared in early Greece.

In any case, the phrase "the few other great beginnings" has nothing to do with other philosophical traditions like East Asian thought. It is mistaken to ascribe to the relevant remark a concern with the issue of intercultural dialogue. For sure, my point is not to totally deny any concern with East Asian traditions to Heidegger, but to demonstrate that the importance that has been ascribed to "the few other great beginnings" has no textual basis at all.

Chapter Five
The Early Greeks' Confrontation with the Asiatic

In the 1930s, Heidegger remarks in a militant tone on the confrontation of early Greek thinking with the Asiatic [1934/35, 134; 1936c, 146; 1937b, 21]. These remarks may be shocking to commentators who propose favourable interpretations of Heidegger's Asian connection. It is difficult to clarify the precise connotation of the word "Asiatic." Charles Bambach claims with reference to these speeches,

> [Asia] stands as a name for the barbaric, the rootless, the allochthonic—those whose roots are not indigenous but who come from another place. For Heidegger, Asia comes to signify pure alterity, the otherness that threatens the preservation of the homeland. (2003, 177)

It seems, as will be shown in this chapter, that Heidegger is not totally blind to the historical concreteness of this word in the context of the early Greeks' confrontation with the Asiatic. Therefore, the "Asiatic" is not simply an abstract label for pure alterity. However, Heidegger may have deliberately left the designation of the Asiatic vague and thus creates room for drawing implications for the contemporary world situation from that historical event of overcoming the Asiatic. When Heidegger remarks on the early Greeks' confrontation with the Asiatic on his first trip to Greece in 1962 [1962a, 228], the militant tone has been softened. In the following pages, I examine these enigmatic remarks. As a contrast, I investigate his thoughts on the confrontation with French thinking.

THE MEANING OF *AUSEINANDERSETZUNG*

The German word *Auseinandersetzung* literally means setting out (*Setzung*) from (*aus*) one another (*einander*). Its connotation ranges between two opposite poles. On one side is the positive meaning of "conversation" or "dialogue." On the other side is the negative meaning of "struggle," "contest," or "controversy." Gregory Fried (2000) claims that the notion *Auseinandersetzung* is a thread going through multiple strands of Heidegger's thought. This claim reveals his assumption that *Auseinandersetzung* has a stable and consistent meaning.

In my view, this word has different emphases in different contexts of Heidegger's philosophizing. When used to translate the Greek word πόλεμος, it describes a fundamental mode of Being's unconcealment. The emphasis falls upon an ontological holding-sway in spite of the existence of strife between two parties. When used to characterize interpretations of philosophy and philosophers, it stresses the sense of interpretation as leading toward what is primary and originary. Admittedly, these two kinds of usage overlap each other. Beaufret (1977) identifies the struggle of confrontation as one between the power of beings and the truth of Being. This explanation is right insofar as it concerns the ontological. However, it should be noted that the latter assumes priority over the former. The truth of Being is not one party versus the other, it occurs in the originary holding-sway that lets beings come forth.

In the *Introduction to Metaphysics,* Heidegger frequently uses the word "confrontation" (*Auseinandersetzung*) and *polemos* (πόλεμος) to illustrate Being's unconcealment. With reference to Heraclitus' well-known fragment 53, he writes:

> Confrontation is indeed for all (that comes to presence) the sire (who lets emerge), but (also) for all the preserver that holds sway. For it lets some appear as gods, others as human beings, some it produces (sets forth) as slaves, but others as the free. (*IM* 65/66; brackets original)

Heidegger explains,

> The πόλεμος named here is a strife that holds sway before everything divine and human, not war in the human sense. As Heraclitus thinks it, struggle first and foremost allows what essentially unfolds to step apart in opposition, first allows position and status and rank to establish themselves in coming to presence. In such a stepping apart, clefts, intervals, distances and joints open themselves up. In confrontation, world comes to be. [Confrontation does not divide unity, much less destroy it. It builds unity; it is the gathering (λόγος). Πόλεμο and λόγος are the same.][1] (*IM* 65/66)

In this explanation, Heidegger tries to downplay traditional interpretations of πόλεμος as war and struggle. He allows this word to have a sense of

strife; nevertheless, this sense should be understood at the ontological, originary level. Rather than designating the conflicts and oppositions as found
in real life, confrontation refers to the fundamental mode which holds sway
and makes possible the arising and standing-forth of the world with different ranks and positions in it. Heidegger stresses in particular that instead of
destroying or dividing unity, confrontation builds unity.

On the other hand, when the word *Auseinandersetzung* is used in the
sense of interpretation, Heidegger emphasizes that confrontation is aimed at
the guiding, original source. For instance, in *On the Essence of Human Freedom*, he expounds,

> [*Auseinandersetzung*] is a bringing the other and thereby also oneself to
> what is primary and originary. This is the essence of the matter and is
> automatically the common cause of both parties, so we do not need to
> make up afterwards or aim at a subsequent alliance. *Philosophical confron-
> tation is interpretation as destruction.* ([1930a, 198/292]; em. or.; tr. m.]

Here confrontation is described as an engagement whose ultimate purpose is
to lead both sides to "what is primary and originary," which is most probably
the unconcealment of Being. This is not a free, arbitrary engagement. The
ultimate aim at the unconcealment of truth exerts a necessity upon the event
of confrontation. Sharing the same cause normally suggests an implicit alliance. However, Heidegger notes that the two parties involved in the confrontation do not need to make up afterward or to aim at achieving an alliance.
This points toward the negative meaning of *Auseinandersetzung* as struggle
or controversy. The phrase under emphasis: "interpretation as destruction,"
echoes Heidegger's concern with carrying out a project of destructuring
Western philosophical tradition. Confrontation, as Fried explains, is "not a
naked attempt to impose meaning or dominion; confrontation expects and
indeed demands resistance as the catalyst for understanding" (11).

When Heidegger uses "confrontation" with respect to the interpretation of Western philosophers, he accentuates strongly the guidance of what is
primary and originary. For example, he comments, "If, in Nietzsche's thinking, the prior tradition of Western thought is gathered and completed in a
decisive respect, then the confrontation with Nietzsche becomes one with all
Western thought hitherto" [1936/37, 4/5]. Confrontation with past thinkers
is to be guided by what is primary and originary, that is, the truth of Being.

These two senses are absent in the context of confrontation with the
Asiatic. In the lecture course on Nietzsche given in 1936/37, Heidegger
states, "Confrontation does not express itself in 'polemic,' but in the manner

of *interpretative construction,* of setting in place the antagonist, and rather in his highest power and dangerousness" [1936/37, /279; em. ad.]. The diction "setting in place the antagonist in his highest power and dangerousness" in this remark shows affinity with the characterization of the Asiatic as the "most foreign and most difficult" (see below) in Heidegger's discussion of the early Greek's confrontation with the Asiatic. However, the emphasis in the former case falls on the constructive, or one could say destructive, side of confrontation. The ultimate purpose is to bring out what is at stake in each other with respect to what is originary. In the latter case, the Asiatic mainly assumes a negative function in the birth of Greek thinking in all its splendor.

I suggest that we should distinguish at least three meanings of *Auseinandersetzung* in Heidegger's usage. When confrontation concerns the originary mode of unconcealment, the stress falls on its role of preserving, gathering and unifying. When it connects with interpretation, this sense retreats to the background. Instead, the accent is placed on the two sides as orientated to the original source. The relation between the two is one of opposing and resisting each other. In the context of confrontation with the Asiatic, confrontation takes on a different meaning. This will become clear in the following sections.

HISTORICAL BACKGROUND

Until the middle of the eighteenth century, it had been a prevalent assumption in Europe that the wisdom of the Greeks owed an enormous debt to non-Western traditions. For example, Joanne Ernesto Schubert's *Historia Philosophiae* (pars prima) of 1742 began with the philosophy of the Chaldeans, the Persians, the Phoenicians, the Arabs, the Jews, the Indians, the Chinese, the Egyptians, the Ethiopians, the Druids or Celts, the Scythians, the early Romans and the Etruscans. Only after recounting all these traditions did Schubert turn to the Greeks.[2] The story of philosophy as a single-handed product of Greece began to take hold at the end of the eighteenth century. The restriction of the history of philosophy to its alleged origin in Greece emerged with the restriction of the conception of philosophy to rationalistic systems, when rationalism arose in modern philosophy. According to Bernasconi, this process of restriction paved the way for Heidegger to explicitly exclude other traditions from the contemporary Western conception of philosophy (1997, 221). Although Heidegger was not the first to claim that ancient Greece is the sole and authentic birthplace of philosophy, his work has played the most crucial role in promoting the popularity this idea has come to enjoy.

In the nineteenth century the discussion continued concerning the early Greeks' involvement with what was called "the Asiatic." According to Scheiffele (1991), Nietzsche strongly believed that the Greek culture, in having incorporated "the living culture of other peoples," is *not* "autochthonous." It is a quintessentially Greek practice "not to create forms, but to borrow them from abroad and transform them in the fairest appearance of beauty."[3] The well-known historian Jacob Burckhardt shared Nietzsche's view of the relationship of Greek culture and cultures of Asia. However, Scheiffele seems to have placed too much emphasis on Nietzsche's occasional positive remarks on Egyptian, Persian, and other "Asian" cultures. In *Philosophy in the Tragic Age of the Greeks,* Nietzsche does say that "it is doubtless true that [the Greeks] picked up much there [i.e. the Orient]" and that "[t]heir skill in the art of fruitful learning is admirable" (1962, 29–30). However, in spite of his compliments for Asiatic civilizations, Nietzsche has always emphasized the uniqueness and supreme importance of Greek culture. He does not recommend looking for "true beginnings," because "the way to the beginnings leads to barbarism" (30).

According to Heidegger, we do not need to take into account "empirical" matters, because what is truly historic should be adjudicated on the basis of relevance to Being, instead of empirical scrutiny. Paying attention to miscellaneous historical facts amounts to a reduction of true history to an "objective" theory of science. In *Being and Time,* Heidegger quotes from letters of Count Yorck several times, in which the latter illustrates his idea of history. One quotation is as follows,

> We must keep wholly aloof from all such rubbish, for instance, as how often Plato was in Magna Graecia or Syracuse. On this nothing vital depends. This superficial affectation which I have seen through critically, winds up at last with a big question-mark and is put to shame by the great realities of Homer, Plato, and the New Testament.[4]

After quoting various such remarks, Heidegger makes positive comments on Yorck's ideas,

> Yorck gained his clear insight into the basic character of history as "virtuality" from his knowledge of the character of the Being which human Dasein itself possesses, not from the objects of historical study, as a theory of science would demand. (*BT* 453/401)

In agreement with Count Yorck, Heidegger does not attach importance to such stories as Plato once being in Syracuse. He refuses to explore the historical and symbolic significance of these stories, as told by the Greeks themselves, about how their sages traveled abroad, especially to Egypt, to learn wisdom. These stories that tell against the unilateral story about the uniqueness of Western philosophy with its unique origin with the early Greek thinkers, for Heidegger, should be treated as trivial anecdotes that would become pale by the side of those great figures from Greek civilization.

THE ASIATIC *FATUM* AND THE MYTHICAL

The earliest remark on the "confrontation with the Asiatic" occurs in Heidegger's lecture course on Hölderlin's poem "Germania" delivered in 1934/35. This is Heidegger's first series of lectures on Hölderlin. In one lecture, Heidegger claims that Hegel's thinking was fuelled by a new creative and repetitive execution of the originary thoughts (*Urgedanken*) of Heraclitus. As Hegel is, Hölderlin, Nietzsche and Meister Eckhardt are also under the sway of the power (*Macht*) of Heraclitus' thought. Following these claims, Heidegger makes a remark containing a terse reference to the "confrontation with the Asiatic,"

> The name Heraclitus is not the title of Greek philosophy in days long past; no more than it is the formula of the history of "everybody's humanity." Instead it is the name of the originary power [*Urmacht*] of Western-Germanic historical *Dasein,* more particularly in their first confrontation with the Asiatic. [1934/35, 134]

The first thing that concerns Heidegger is that Greek philosophy as symbolized by Heraclitus is not something past and dead. Rather, in the name Heraclitus resides the originary creative power of the destiny of the West. Here the word "Western" is juxtaposed with "Germanic."

After making these observations, Heidegger elaborates on the confrontation with Heraclitus' thought, from whose originary power Western thinkers cannot withdraw or be exonerated. This confrontation is not a useless game of scholarly comparison between contemporary and bygone beliefs, but a genuine and necessary questioning. Only this questioning will open up a historic spiritual space. A couple of pages further, when claiming that Hölderlin does not think the German word *Schicksal* (destiny) in terms of *Fatum,* or *Fatalität,* Heidegger makes another remark which contains two references to the Asiatic:

> This, as we might say, Asiatic imagery of destiny [*asiatische Vorstellung von Schicksal*], has been overcome in Hölderlin's creative thought. A first,

and of its kind unrepeatable overcoming of this Asiatic fate [*Fatum*], was achieved by the Greeks, and, in fact, it was at one with the poetic-intellectual-stately development of these people. [1934/35, 173]

In his philosophical corpus, Heidegger normally uses the two words *Schicksal* and *Geschick* to refer to destiny or fate. Both these words come from *schicken*, which means "to send, to arrange, to order, to prepare, to dispatch." In *Being and Time*, *Schicksal* is connected with an individual's self-chosen fate; while *Geschick* implies collective destiny as composed of individual fates. After *Being and Time*, Heidegger uses these two words interchangeably. He speaks of the *Schicksal* of the Germans, the Western *Schicksal*, and the *Geschick* of an individual. Gradually, *Geschick* becomes more important than *Schicksal*.[5] As we have seen in Chapter three, in the context of elucidating the essence of technology, Heidegger defines technology as the destiny of unconcealing (*Geschick der Entbergung*), and states that technology is something like a providential blessing sent to man by Being. In stating this, he sets himself against the trend that views technology as the *Schicksal* of the present age, with *Schicksal* meaning the "inevitableness of an unalterable course" (*QT* 330/26).

Heidegger has never used the word *Fatum* in relation to the West. Etymologically speaking, *Fatum* comes from the Latin word *fari*, which means "to express, to make known." It originally refers to the decree of a deity. Following his remark on the Greeks' overcoming of the Asiatic idea of *Fatum* as cited above, Heidegger explains *Fatum* as

> [a] Beying that is represented in the sense of a will-less and ignorant chasing thither of an obtuse distressing fate rolling forwards inside the totality of beings locked up in themselves. [1934/35, 173]

The Asiatic notion of *Fatum*, as Heidegger sees it, is confined within the inwardness of the totality of beings. It is a blind and restless force chasing around. Unable to grant room to the work of free will, *Fatum* is will-less and closed up in itself. It is insulated from the possibility of *alêtheia*, or from the revealing of the transcending Being [1934/35, 173]. In contrast, destiny (*Geschick*) is one of the ways in which Being discloses itself.[6] We will see that the distinction between *Geschick*, the true destiny that is the law of history, and *fatum*, the arbitrary and irrational force, displays affinity with Heidegger's distinction between the authentic and inauthentic mystical.

Heidegger's characterization of *Fatum* may well have been under the influence of Hegel, though Hegel ascribes this notion to the Greek religion, one of the determinate religions as contrasted with the absolute religion—Christianity. A look at how Hegel accounts for *Fatum* may help understand what Heidegger means in terms of the "Asiatic *Fatum.*" *Fatum* is an explanation the Greek people provide for themselves in terms of external necessity. Hegel characterizes *Fatum* as "the cold necessity lacking all determinateness" (1982, 388). It stands for abstract, blind, unintelligible power that is devoid of purpose and concept (*Begriff*). In resorting to the notion of fate, man remains related to the world externally. Hegel explains,

> When confronted by fate [*Fatum*], it is only by self-denying submission that human beings can save their freedom—so that although fate conquers them externally, it does not do so inwardly. Because outward existence is not in harmony with *their* purpose, they abandon *all* purpose—this is an abstract freedom. The viewpoint of the absolute religion is that even misfortune yields an absolute content, so that the negative turns into the affirmative once more. But the Greek spirit had still no absolute content to oppose to this external necessity. (1982, 756; em. or.)

Since fate lacks internal determinations and presides over and above people, the relation between adverse happenings and people is conceived externally. The way in which people who hold on to this notion of fate attempt to achieve freedom against adverse happenings, as Hegel describes, is to renounce their own purpose and power. When this is done, because nothing inside them goes against the outside world, they attain a sort of inward freedom, though externally remaining in the grip of fate. Hegel claims that this freedom is abstract freedom, not true freedom. What is abstract cannot be comprehended properly. With absolute religion, in contrast, adverse happenings people encounter are not things external and coldly resistant to understanding; they have concrete determinations and relate to man in an internal, rather than external, manner. What is adverse bears in itself an absolute content that turns the negative into the positive. For Hegel, only what is rational is comprehensible, because it is inwardly concrete and determinate.

A la Hegel, Heidegger attributes to *Fatum* a connection with an incomprehensible, ruthless and unruly force. Contra Hegel, Heidegger does not embrace the idea that a "higher" notion of fate, or destiny, can be derived dialectically from a lower one. He does not perceive an internal mediation between the higher and the lower notions. For him, grecian-occidental thought is not just higher, but is unique. It does not evolve internally from the presumably lower-staged Asiatic traditions. Rather its birth is accompanied by a radical opposition against Asiatic traditions. It is by overcoming the Asiatic *Fatum* that is brought about the all-round development of the Greek people, poetic, intellectual, and political.

Heidegger's characterization of Asiatic thought in terms of a particular notion of fate bears affinity with his description of it as the mythical (*das Mythische*). In the lecture course on Schelling's *Treatise on the Essence of Human Freedom* delivered in 1936, Heidegger remarks,

> In philosophy we can no more go back to Greek philosophy by means of a leap than we can eliminate the advent of Christianity into Western history and thus into philosophy by means of a command. The only possibility is to transform history, that is, truly to bring about the hidden necessity of history into which neither knowledge nor deed reach, and transformation truly brought about is the essence of the creative. For the great beginning of Western philosophy, too, did not come out of nothing. Rather, it became great because it had to overcome its greatest opposite, the mythical [*das Mythische*] in general and the Asiatic in particular, that is, it had to bring it to the jointure [*Gefüge*] of a truth of Beyng, and was able to do this. [1936c, 145–46/252]

These observations occur in the context of exploring the notions of evil and sin, and the role of Christianity. One cannot go back to Greek philosophy in a literal sense, nor can one dismiss Christianity's historical influence on Western philosophy. What matters is a creative transformation. Heidegger admits that, historically speaking, the great beginning of Western philosophy was not immune from such heterogeneous elements as the Asiatic traditions. The saying that it "did not come out of nothing" (which can be interpreted as "it was not created *ex nihilo*") may lend itself to a favorable reading with respect to Heidegger's conception of the role of the Asiatic. However, in defining the Asiatic as the "greatest opposite" of Western philosophy, Heidegger does not even attribute an internal developmental connection to these two antipodes, as Hegel tends to do. Rather, their connection is portrayed as extrinsic, in that the Asiatic seems to be an obstacle that was overcome without leaving a trace in what has overcome it. That which is not "nothing" (*nihilo*) (that is, the something out of which "the great beginning of Western philosophy" arises) does not refer to Asiatic traditions; rather, it refers to the *event* of the early Greeks' overcoming of the Asiatic. This event accords with the event (that is, the occurrence) of the essence of true creation.

It is notable that in this passage Heidegger uses *das Mythische* to characterize the Asiatic civilizations. In view of the attention he pays to the mythical in his philosophical corpus, would this be an indication of his acknowledgment of the role of the Asiatic traditions as characterized by the mythical? In *What is Called Thinking?*, Heidegger observes that the early Greek thinkers employ μῦθος (*mythos*) and λόγος (*logos*) in the same sense: "μῦθος and λόγος become separated and opposed only at the point where neither μῦθος nor λόγος can keep to its originary nature [*anfängliches Wesen*]" (*WCT* 10/7). The μῦθος that belongs to the truth of Beyng is to be radically distinguished from the μῦθος (if one should use the same word for it) that is separated from and opposed to λόγος. The latter inauthentic μῦθος has only a misleading surface resemblance to the authentic μῦθος that is of originary nature. In essence, they are completely different.

When Heidegger asserts, "Philosophy does not arise from myth. It arises solely from thinking, and in thinking" ([1946a, 265/352]; tr. m.), he is going against inauthentic myth. In *Parmenides,* Heidegger states that the Greeks distinguish themselves from other peoples and call them barbarians, and that barbarism is opposed to "dwelling within μῦθος and λόγος" [1942/43, 70/103]. From this perspective, inauthentic myth can be seen as analogous to barbarism. In the passage cited from Heidegger's lectures on Schelling's *Treatise,* insofar as the "mythical" is said to be the Greeks' "greatest opposite," it cannot be the authentic μῦθος that is inextricably entangled with λόγος. When the inauthentic mythical is brought to the "jointure of a truth of Beyng," it is completely overcome and transformed.

The point Heidegger wants to accentuate by referring to the Asiatic in the context of discussing the role of Christianity in Schelling's *Treatise* resides in the following: In spite of the recognized extent to which the commencement of Western philosophy was exposed to extrinsic influences from the Asiatic, which is characterized by inauthentic μῦθος, it achieved radical, unique, and absolute beginning of Western historicity by corresponding to the claim of Beyng. Likewise, despite the strong influence of Christianity on Western philosophical traditions, Western man can eliminate this influence and go back to Greek philosophy by originarily engaging into dialogue with the early Greek thinkers, by placing himself within the call of Beyng, and thus entering into the other beginning.

AUSEINANDERSETZUNG WITH THE FRENCH

In the essay "Ways toward Discussion" (*Wege zur Aussprache*) written in 1937, which contains a reference to the early Greeks' confrontation with the Asiatic, Heidegger discusses at length the confrontation of the German and French people. An examination of this essay may help us better appreciate what is at stake in Heidegger's thought regarding confrontation with the Asiatic.

Heidegger's article starts with the intriguing relation between the German and the French people. Although they are neighbors, they have great difficulty understanding one another. This is surprising because both they together played "the most essential part in the historical-cultural formation of the *Abendland*" [1937b, 15]. Because in the present world epoch the mission of the history-creating Western people (*abendländische Völkern*) is to save the *Abendland*, it is important for the German and French people to achieve a proper understanding between one another. Such an *Auseinandersetzung* must commence and sustain in the face of the "impending uprooting of the West, an uprooting whose overcoming demands the commitment of every people with the strength for creation" [1937b, 20].

The devastating world age calls urgently for creative dialogical exchange between the German and French people, who alone bear the historic mission of saving the West. Any creative understanding presupposes genuine pride of these peoples. They should have the courage to work toward their own destiny. Trying to achieve an understanding of the other is not an indication of weakness. Heidegger claims,

> The grounding form of *Auseinandersetzung* is the actual creative dialogue (*wirkliche Wechselgespräch*) between the creators (*Schaffenden*) themselves in a neighbourly encounter. [1937b, 20]

It is clear that Heidegger attaches special importance to the *Auseinandersetzung* between the German and French in defining it as the "actual creative dialogue" between the creators. This *Auseinandersetzung* plays the crucial role for the future of the West. It also sets the two historical people into their own.

These considerations find testimony in Beaufret's comments on "Ways toward Discussion." According to Beaufret, this essay is a message to both the French and German people. The Greek beginning, which raised the question of Being, is the first epoch of a whole history, which is the history of the German and French people. Beaufret concludes, "the relation of your [Heidegger's] thinking to France and the French is an essential matter, much *more essential than other European or world-wide encounters*" (1977, 20; em. ad.). These comments convey Heidegger's concern very well. What is essential and incomparably important is the re-enactment of the other beginning of Western thinking. It is against this background that one should understand Heidegger's caution against questionable syntheses and assimilations in contemporary East-West encounters in "A Dialogue" (*DL* 3/87).[7]

In the next to last paragraph in "Ways towards Discussion," Heidegger mentions confrontation with the Asiatic by way of setting the historic background for the German and French people:

> When we reflect on the possible greatness and the standards set by Western "culture," we immediately remember the historical world of early Greece. And at the same time we as easily forget that the Greeks did not become what they always already are by being enclosed in their "space." It is only on the strength of the sharpest but creative confrontation with the most foreign and most difficult—the Asiatic—that this nation grew up in the short course of its historic uniqueness [*Einmaligkeit*] and greatness. [1937b, 21]

Obviously, Heidegger's portrayal of the essential bond between the German and French people and of the mode of their confrontation contrasts markedly with his account for the early Greeks' confrontation with the Asiatic. In the latter case, the emphasis falls on the uniqueness and greatness of Greek thought that attains maturity out of confrontation with the Asiatic, and on the Asiatic being the "greatest opposite" to Greek thought. Although the same word *Auseinandersetzung* is used for both the historical involvement of the Greek world with what is called the Asiatic, and the engagement of the German and the French, it is evidently used in very different senses. The modes of confrontation in these two cases differ in the following respects.

In Heidegger's eyes, the German and French people share an innate bond. They are neighbors not only in the geographic sense, but also, and more importantly, in the sense of intellectual kinship. These two peoples are the kernel constituents of the *Abendland,* in terms of its historic, cultural formation. Therefore, they share the same historic mission of salvaging the *Abendland.* This is what makes their creative understanding of each other significant and necessary. In contrast, as I have already pointed out, the Asiatic under Heidegger's pen is the "greatest opposite" to Western philosophy, or "the most foreign and most difficult," which held on to an incomprehensible and irrational notion of fate (*Fatum*).

Heidegger describes the confrontation with the French people as "the actual creative dialogue of the creators themselves in a neighbourly encounter" [1937b, 20]. This confrontation sets these two peoples into what is their ownmost. To arrive at genuine understanding between them, there need be earnest listening to one another and the courage for self-determination. In addition, this confrontation is of historic necessity and urgency for the sake of transforming the destiny of the West.[8]

In the case of the confrontation with the Asiatic, the interaction has never been described as "the actual creative dialogue." The West unilaterally overcomes the opposition of Asiatic mystic thinking. How the encounter with the Greek affects the Asiatic side is left unthought. In a certain sense, the creative dialogue between the German and the French can also be said to be unilateral insofar as the emphasis is on their dialogue being guided by the historic beginning of the West. However, in the case of the Asiatic, the confrontation is conceived as unilateral overcoming.[9]

In speaking of the early Greeks' confrontation with the Asiatic in a militant tone, Heidegger may have in mind the threat to Europe posed by Russia in the 1930s. In the beginning of a lecture delivered on 8 April 1936 at the Hertziana Library of the Kaiser-Wilhelm Institute in Rome, entitled "Europe and the German Philosophy," Heidegger remarks,

> Our historic Dasein experiences with increasing urgency and clarity that its future is facing a stark either-or salvation of Europe, or [alternatively] its own destruction. But the possibility of salvation requires two things:
>
> 1. The shielding [*Bewahrung*] of European people from the Asiatic.[10]
>
> 2. The overcoming of its own rootlessness and disintegration.
>
> Without this overcoming that shielding will not succeed. However, both require, in order to cope, a transformation of Dasein out of the final grounds applying the highest standards. Such a transformation of historical Dasein, however, can never happen as a blind pushing forward into an undetermined future, but only as a creative confrontation [*Auseinandersetzung*] with the whole of history up to now—its essential configurations [*Gestalten*] and eras. [1936b, 31]

In this remark, Heidegger urges that Europe keep away from the Asiatic because it needs to achieve its self-overcoming in the first place so as to ascend to an advantageous position to deal with the Asiatic. Its self-overcoming requires confrontation with all the essential configurations and eras of the whole of Western history. After the First World War, Russia was often regarded as the Eastern world on the rise. In the *Introduction to Metaphysics* [1935], Heidegger mentions Russia as a cultural-political power exerting menace upon Europe, "This Europe, in its unholy blindness always on the point of cutting its own throat, lies today in the great pincers between Russia on the one side and America on the other" (*IM* 40/28). The lecture "Europe and the German Philosophy" was given one year after the lecture course on *Introduction to Metaphysics*. From this perspective, it is highly probable that the Asiatic conceived as a peril to Europe in the phrase "shielding of European people from the Asiatic" refers to Russia.

It is not unreasonable to presume that whatever sense of animosity or militancy is involved in Heidegger's remarks on the early Greeks' confrontation with the Asiatic, he bears Russia in mind. [11]

THE MYSTERIOUS RELATIONS TO THE EAST

Heidegger's phrase "mysterious relations to the East" (*geheimnisvolle Bezüge zum Osten*) has often been taken to bear on East Asian thinking. It appears in the "Letter on Humanism" (1946), where Heidegger writes, "We have still scarcely begun to think of the mysterious relations to the East that found expression in Hölderlin's poetry" (*LH* 257/338). In a footnote, he gives the reference to Hölderlin's hymns "The Ister" and "The Journey." In speaking of the "mysterious relations to the East," Heidegger obviously bears in mind such phrases as "East," "the Indies," and "the journey to the foreign," which appear in Hölderlin's poems.

In my view, Heidegger's attention to such phrases is primarily involved with their relation to the Greek. One cannot unequivocally identify his concern in this context as one with the relation between the contemporary West with the contemporary East. Of course, just as in the case of the Asiatic, he may have deliberately left these references to the East vague so as to give space for a reflection on the contemporary situation.

In "The Ister," Hölderlin sings,

He [the Ister] appears, however, almost
To go backwards and
I presume he must come
From the East [*Osten*]. (*HHI* 4/3)

In addition, in both "The Ister" and "Remembrance" Hölderlin mentions "the Indies."[12] In the beginning of his elucidation of Hölderlin's "Remembrance," Heidegger makes a connection between "coming from the East" with a seemingly empirical observation. He notes the fact that near to its source the Danube river sometimes stops and even goes back, forming whirlpools. On this basis, he imagines that the river Ister comes from the place where it flows into the "foreign sea" and that it "belongs to the foreign land of the East" (*in die Fremde des Ostens gehört*) (*EHP* 106/79).

In the meantime, Heidegger observes that Hölderlin's journey abroad did not come to an end with his trip to "the southern land" [1943c, 108/83]. Instead, in the beginning of the concluding stanza of "Remembrance," Hölderlin "points beyond Greece toward the more distant East, toward the people of India" (*EHP* 108 /83). Heidegger comments, "If '*remembrance*' is already a thinking back, then it thinks of the *rivers* of the Indians and the Greeks" (108/83; em. or.). He notices that the first stanza of "The Ister" sings,

> But we sing from the Indus,
> Arrived from afar, and
> From the Alpheus, . . . (*HHI* 10/10)

As Heidegger notes, "Indus" and "Alpheus" are names of rivers and streams, one belonging to the land of the Indians, the other to the land of the Greeks. In his commentary on "Remembrance," Heidegger states that at the commencement of their history, the Greeks are not at home. By "pass[ing] through what is foreign to them," by learning from poetry, thinking and art from the foreign, they are enabled to collect themselves, to appropriate what is their own and thus to become at home (*EHP* 112/87). Although Heidegger does not use the word "Asiatic" or the "East," from the context one can see that the reference to passing through the foreign is related to the historical episode of the early Greeks' confrontation with the Asiatic. Therefore, if the East in Heidegger's phrase "mysterious relations to the East" should bear on places beyond Greece, the mysterious relations do not extend beyond the confrontation between the early Greeks and the "Asiatic."

In "Hyperion," Hölderlin sings,

> . . . In the
> depths of Asia there is supposed to be concealed a people
> of rare perfection; it is there that
> his hope drove him further. (*EHP* 162/140)

Heidegger comments,

> The distance of this further has meanwhile lost the indefiniteness of what was simply surmised. This "further" does not mean here the mere expansion of an adventurous journey into a still greater expanse. What is the most distant of all distant things is the *beginning of the parents'* origin. It is where the Indies are that the journey turns from the foreign back toward home. Where the journey turns itself toward "Germania," it brings the

journey abroad to its decisive site. But in this manner the southern land, which stands for Greece, becomes the departure place for the journey to the location of the journey's turn. That is why the poet must now not just name the place of this departure in general. With the emphasized word there, he must expressly confess the necessity of departing from the splendid foreign land as well. (*EHP* 162/140; em. or.)

The "distant East" serves as a reminder that the "further" is nothing indefinite. The journey to the foreign is not an arbitrary adventurous journey into an indeterminate distance. To the contrary, "the most distant of all distant things" (that is, what is the proper "foreign") is "the *beginning of the parents' origin*," that is, Greece. In the same manner, the place of departure cannot be named in general either. It is out of necessity that Greece becomes the place of departure.

It is important to pay attention to the fact that, according to Heidegger, where the Indies are, the journey turns back toward the homeland, that is, toward Germania. At this decisive point, Greece, as symbolized by the southern land, becomes the place of departure. This means two things. One is that the mysterious relation to the East involves a journey that starts from Greece and takes a turn with the Indies. This is a historical journey in which Greece as the homeland was trying to recover what is its own. Another implication is that the references to the "depths of Asia," to the Indies, serve as a reminder that Greece is "the *beginning of the parents' origin*," and "the most distant of all distant things." This accords with what has been explicated in Chapter four, that is, the "own" and the "foreign" are actually the two sides of the same coin, and the journey to the foreign is not a forward progression, but a backward retrieval. The mysterious relation to the East reminds one that Greece is not only the proper foreign, but also the beginning of Western historicality.[13]

In any case, what prefigures in the mysterious relation to the East is the importance of Greece. The distant East is involved insofar as the early Greeks' confrontation with the Asiatic is concerned, and insofar as it serves to remind us that it is with Greece that Western historicality begins and unfolds. In addition, this is also one of the reasons why Heidegger considers that the conditions for the contemporary West to engage with (East) Asia can only be prepared through first engaging the Greek and accomplishing the authentic becoming at home. Western historicality begins with Greece, and it is through overcoming the Asiatic that Greece achieves its maturity. Therefore, any possible engagement with the East of the contemporary West presupposes engagement with Greek thinking.

Heidegger writes,

> [T]he poet knows that each place that must become a place of rest dur-
> ing the departure abroad is an essential place, through whose location
> the journey is more decisively, i.e., more originally, granted its begin-
> ning as its own. That is why the poet can never place too high a value on
> one place in favour of the other. Nevertheless, the land of the Greeks, in
> distinction to one's own homeland, remains the first to be greeted and,
> in the departure of the journey to the turning place of the journey, also
> the last to be greeted. (*EHP* 163/141)

In Heidegger's mind, Greece assumes the most important place in the journey to the foreign. Greece is the medium through which alone can the West
possibly encounter the East in the future. A dialogue with the East necessarily has to take the detour via Greece.

THE JOURNEY TO GREECE

When visiting Greece, the birthplace of philosophy, for the first time in the
spring of 1962, Heidegger remarks once again on the "confrontation with
the Asiatic." During his visit, Heidegger took retrospect on the history of the
origin of Western philosophy and historicity. As Petzet states, "[Heidegger]
sought what is simple and found therein the fullness and richness of what
has the character of a beginning. . . . It was Hölderlin's ode that gave him
his lead" (164). In refusing to use something like a guidebook for a trip to
Greece, such as the one written by Peter Bamm, Heidegger states,

> [This book] is written as a secondary text and . . . actually mixes what is
> Greek with Roman and Hebraic elements. The success of the book obvi-
> ously rests on this mixture. Preparation for the trip consists in bracket-
> ing out all preconceptions and in keeping oneself ready for that which
> is there—in Greek terms, for that which, unconcealed, emerges [*anwest*]
> in the light.[14]

During and after this trip, Heidegger composed *Aufenthalte* (*Sojourns*),
a kind of "travel story," which had remained inaccessible to outsiders until
its publication in 1989 [1962a]. It consists in descriptions of places which
he visited, and in the thoughts occurring to him while traveling there. When
the ship reached Rhodes Island which is under the coast of Asia Minor, the
following thoughts came to Heidegger,

Are we farther away from Greece? Or are we already within the domain of its destiny, which was structured through its confrontation with the Asiatic, by transforming the wild and reconciling the passion with something "greater," that remained great for the mortals and so it granted them the place for reverend awe?

. . . the confrontation [*Auseinandersetzung*] with the Asiatic was a fruitful necessity for the Greek *Dasein*. For us today, and in an entirely different way and to a far greater extent, it is the decision about the destiny [*Schicksal*] of Europe, and that, which calls itself Western world [*westliche Welt*]. . . .

With the hourly changing blueness of heaven and sea the thought arose whether for us the Orient might be a sun-rising of light and enlightenment, whether rather only historically fabricated [*hergestellten*] and artificially sustained lights are deluding [us] with false hopes of the appearance of a revelation coming from there.

Once the Asiatic brought the Greeks a dark fire, whose flames joined [*fügten*] brightness and measure to their poetizing and thinking. . . . ([1962a, 25–27/228–29]; tr. m.)

Notice that Heidegger does not use the more common word *Abendland*, but *westliche Welt*. Heidegger's juxtaposition of Europe and "what calls itself *westliche Welt*" suggests the idea that Europe, into which the *Abendland* has submerged itself, has as its main constituents the German and the French traditions, whereas the Anglo-American world, which calls itself the Western world, is in fact derivative compared with Europe. Europe directly originated from the birth of the Greek world. The technological Anglo-American world, on the other hand, stays on the margin of Europe, the *Abendland*.

In the meantime, Heidegger finds it difficult to carry out an evaluation of the role the Orient has played. He asks whether the Orient has brought light and enlightenment, or whether there is a lot of fabrication and artificiality involved in the stories about the Orient. The phrase "dark fire" recalls a common conception of the Eastern tradition as oriented toward the nothing, non-being, or the irrational, as reflected in Heidegger's others locutions such as "*Fatum*," "mystical," and "the most foreign and most difficult."

However, on further analysis, the characterization of "dark fire" may entail something more than negative. There are frequent references to the image of fire in Hölderlin's poetry. For example, "A fire has been kindled in the souls of the poets" (*EHP* 71/49), "And hence the sons of the earth now drink/Heavenly fire without danger" (73/50). In his elucidation of these verses, Heidegger connects fire with φύσις, one of the grounding words at the beginning of Western thought. Φύσις signifies a rising into the open, into the clearing. It is the place of light whose illumination belongs to fire. Fire affords brightness and the open for what appears. Thus, as the illuminating-blazing light, fire is the open, that which comes to presence in everything that emerges and goes away within the open (79/56–57).

When commenting on Hölderlin's hymn "Remembrance," Heidegger writes,

> What is proper to the Greeks is the fire of heaven. The light and the blaze which guarantee them the arrival and the nearness of the gods is their home. But at the beginning of their history, they are not really at home in this fire. In order to appropriate this proper character, they must pass through what is foreign to them. . . . They must first be astonished and seized by it, in order to enlist its aid in bringing the fire into the serene splendor of its ordained brightness. (*EHP* 112/88)

It may not be possible for Heidegger to consider the Asiatic "dark fire" to be the "fire of heaven." However, the suggestion that the flames of the dark fire gave "brightness and measure" to the poetizing and thinking of the Greeks discloses a slightly different evaluation of the role of the Asiatic than do characterizations such as "*Fatum*," "mystical," and "the most foreign and most difficult." The suggestion that the "confrontation with the Asiatic" was a "fruitful necessity for the Greek Dasein" that determines the destiny of Europe and the contemporary world situation also shows a positive attitude. It seems that in the 1960s, Heidegger has softened his militant tone in the 1930s.

Chapter Six
Heidegger's Encounter with the *Daodejing*

This chapter is devoted to Heidegger's connection with Daoist thinking. First I inquire into his reference to the word *dao* in "The Nature of Language" (1957/58) and "The Principle of Identity" (1957). I argue that, only when interpreted in the particular manner, or thought in the nature as Heidegger has prescribed, can *dao* be said to refer to *Weg* (way). *Weg* is the standard against which *dao* is measured. This is because *Weg* is the primary and grounding word-thing in Heidegger's thought. Heidegger's involvement with Hsiao Shih-yi in an attempt at translating the *Daodejing* has been a matter of controversy. I defer my survey of this event to the Chapter seven.

The main body of this chapter consists in careful studies of Heidegger's citations from the *Daodejing*. I locate them in the immediate textual context as well as against the broad background of the fundamental presuppositions and orientations of Heidegger and Laozi's thinking. According to my archival and textual investigation, Heidegger has cited from five chapters of the *Daodejing* (chapters 9, 11, 15, 28, 47) in six pieces of his writings: the lecture "Basic Principles of Thinking" (1957), the essay "The Uniqueness of the Poet" (1943), and the address "To the Seventieth Birthday of Siegfried Bröse on 8 August 1965" (the latter two pieces have remained unpublished until 2000), the letter to Ernst Jünger on 29 May 1965, the letter to Hsiao Shih-yi on 9 October 1947, and the letter to Andrea von Harbou on 6 August 1965. The last-mentioned letter is a new archival discovery concerning Heidegger's connection with the *Daodejing*. In addition, in his letter to Erhart Kästner on 30 July 1973, Heidegger makes a comment on chapter 15 of the *Daodejing* without quoting the verses. My investigation of Heidegger's citations from the *Daodejing* has gathered together all the relevant materials discovered so far.

Despite apparent affinities between their locutions, there are crucial differences between Heidegger and Laozi's concerns and orientations, some of which I sketch in connection with Heidegger's citation from chapter 28 of the *Daodejing*. In his letter to Jünger, Heidegger treats chapter 47 as an aid for his severe criticism against what are for him alien and exotic things. From his citation of chapter 11, one can see Heidegger's heavy-handed modifications of Laozi's verses in order to suit them to his central concern with Being. His most innovative modification is to use *Sein* four times to translate the original *yong* character. In adding the phrase *ins Sein zu bringen* to the verses from chapter 15, he grafts a concern with Being to this scripture. Heidegger's anxiety about the *Ge-stell* leads him to consider the possibility that ancient Chinese thought might have something to contribute. For this purpose, he revises the thought embodied in chapter 9 so that his citation can fit well into his pre-conceived scheme of thought.

THE *DAODEJING*

The *Daodejing* was composed during the period 350–250 BC. Because of traditional attribution of its authorship to the legendary and later deified sage Laozi, it is also called the *Laozi*.[1] Later it became the most important scripture in Daoist religious and philosophical tradition. There are hundreds of editions of the *Laozi*, among which the Wang Bi version has been most commonly consulted for almost two thousand years by commentators in China. It is also the version used for translations into Western languages. After the archaeological discovery of the Mawangdui texts (transcribed on silk, two versions) in 1973 and of the Guodian texts (transcribed on bamboo scrolls) in 1993, new exegeses and interpretations have appeared.

In modern times, the *Daodejing* is the Asian classic with the greatest number of translations. The earliest European translation was a Latin version produced by Jesuit missionaries to China, which was presented to the British Royal Society in 1788. The Jesuit missionaries aimed to search for ideas corresponding to Western religious tradition in the *Daodejing* in order to demonstrate that "the Mysteries of the Most Holy Trinity and of the Incarnate God were anciently known to the Chinese nation."[2] In addition to the efforts by missionaries, the early researches of the *Daodejing* by Western scholars were mainly carried out at institutions for comparative studies of religion or at departments of Oriental studies in various universities.

In the twentieth century, scholars began to consider the *Daodejing* in its own right. Arthur Waley's *The Way and its Power* (1934), in which he translated *dao* as "Way," marked the beginning of a widespread understanding of the *Daodejing* as an embodiment and edification of the value of a particular way of life. Chan Wing-tsit translated *dao* as "Way" in his *The Way of Lao Tzu* (*Tao te ching*) as well. As Chan sees it, "the chief subject of the book is how to live, including ethics, government, and diplomacy" and its "main objective . . . is the cultivation of virtue or *te* [德]" (Chan 1963, 10, 11).[3]

In recent decades, a variety of philosophical schools, such as hermeneutics, pragmatism, analytic philosophy, and feminist theories, came to inform studies of Chinese philosophy. In two monographs *Language and Logic in Ancient China* (1983a) and *A Daoist Theory of Chinese Thought: A Philosophical Interpretation* (1992), Chad Hansen attempts to expose the theory of language that has shaped ancient Chinese ways of reasoning and to shed light on ancient Chinese philosophy with this very understanding. He puts forward a systematic theory concerning the role of *dao*. According to him, the objective of early Chinese schools of thought is to find a constant form of discourse. Against this trend, the *Daodejing* claims that it is impossible to have such a constant guiding discourse. Instead, one can only discuss the plurality of ways in which *daos* shape and mould our behaviour: "Daoism is a *dao* about *dao;* it discourses about discourse, prescribes about prescription. It is a series of theories about *daos*" (1992, 210). The word *dao* refers to a "form of discourse" that reliably guides behaviour (5). One can speak of "a *dao*, any *dao*, some *daos* or *daos*" (215, 402n26)."[4]

Almost all English translations add a definite article to the word *dao* in the opening verse of the *Daodejing:* "The way that can be spoken of / Is not the constant way" (Lau 1982, 3).[5] Hansen claims that "the *Dao*" implies that *dao* is an ineffable, nameless and transcendent metaphysical entity. This is a mistaken construal. He suggests that it is less misleading to place an indefinite article before *dao*. In this way, the first verse of the *Daodejing* means, "any prescriptive system put into words gives inconstant guidance" (Hansen 1992, 216).[6]

The German translations to which Heidegger had access are four in total: Victor von Strauss (1874), Alexander Ular (1903), Richard Wilhelm (1911), and Jan Ulenbrook (1962). Von Strauss was a Sinologist with numerous scholarly publications. Ular claimed that his version was based on a close reading of the components of Chinese characters. According to him, this is the only way in which one could gain access to the meaning of this ancient work. Wilhelm was a protestant minister and missionary to China. Ulenbrook offered two translations: a character-by-character literal version and an interpretative version. All these four translations went through several reprints. By present academic standards, the translation by Ulenbrook is the most professional. The translations by von Strauss and Wilhelm suffer from

"theologoumena." Wilhelm's version has made the greatest impact, constitut-
ing fifteen percent of the fifty German translations of the *Daodejing* sold in
the twentieth century.

In addition to these four German translations, I have consulted the following texts in my study of Heidegger's citations from the *Daodejing:* Mawangdui A and B versions, the Wang Bi edition;[7] bilingual Chinese/English
editions of the Wang Bi version by Paul Carus and D.T. Suzuki (1898) and
D.C. Lau (1982); bilingual Chinese/English editions of the Mawangdui versions by Lau (1982) and Henricks (1989); the Chinese/English edition of
the Guodian version by Henricks (2000); and finally, the version by Ames
and Hall (2003), which is based on a comparison and collation of the Wang
Bi, Mawangdui, and Guodian versions.

Before embarking on his encounter with the *Daodejing,* a brief note
on Heidegger's connection with the *Zhuangzi* is due.[8] As early as 1930, Heidegger recited the story of the happiness of the fish from Buber's abridged
translation after delivering a lecture on the essence of truth at Bremen.[9] During a discussion on modern art in 1960 again at Bremen, Heidegger mentioned Zhuangzi's parable of the wooden bell stand (*Glockenspielständer*) to
make a point concerning the connection of word and image.[10]

In the context of reflecting upon the nature of technology, language
and tradition in his lecture "Traditional Language and Technical Language"
delivered in 1962, Heidegger invites the audience to "listen to a text from
the writer Dschuang-Dsï, one of Lao-Tse's students" [1962b, 131/8]. In stating that reflection (*Besinnung*) means "to awaken the sense [*Sinn*] for the
useless," he cites Zhuangzi's story of the useless tree to illustrate his idea of
the useless. This is the only occurrence in Heidegger's published writings in
which he explicitly refers to the *Zhuangzi.* He gives the reference to Wilhelm's
version.[11] After this digression, Heidegger returns to the topic at hand: reflections on such notions as technology, language, and tradition yield nothing
directly useful. This parable suits his purpose of reminding us that the useless
may have its own greatness. The way in which Heidegger appropriates this
parable is very similar to his appropriation of passages from the *Daodejing.*[12]

IS *DAO* A GUIDEWORD FOR HEIDEGGER?

"The Nature of Language," where Heidegger's famous reference to *dao*
appears, consists of three lectures he delivered at the University of Freiburg
in 1957 and 1958. These lectures are concerned with how to bring man to
undergo an experience with language. As Heidegger explains, "to experience something means to attain it along the way, by going on a way" (*OWL*

73/177). The first lecture tries to achieve this by focusing on Stefan George's poem "The word." It moves in the neighborhood of poetry and thinking. The second lecture contrasts method with way. *Weg* (way) belongs in the region (*Gegend*) that is the freeing and sheltering clearing. This freeing-sheltering is a kind of way-making (*Be-wëgung*), in which ways that belong to the region are generated. *Weg* is that which allows man to reach what concerns and summons them. Heidegger does not conform to the common view according to which method is connected with scientific instruments or tools. For him, method is more primary than those. It is generated from *Weg* (74/178).

The third lecture elaborates on the guideword (*Leitwort*) that accompanies the region of clearing, that is, "The being [*Wesen*] of language: the language of being" (94/200). Language is proper to what moves all things, and what moves all things moves in that it speaks. What concerns man as language "receives its definition from Saying as that which moves all things" (95/202). *Weg* is concerned with the way in which man undergoes an experience with Saying, that is, with the nature of language.

Heidegger's meditation on *dao* appears in the beginning of the third lecture when he is summarizing the second one. In explaining that the word *Be-wëgung* should be understood in relation to the idea of "to be the original giver and founder of ways" (92/198), Heidegger provides a gloss on the etymological connections and usage in the Swabian dialect of the verb *bewegen* and its cognates.[13] Following this, he inserts a discussion consisting of two paragraphs in which the word *dao* appears five times. For the convenience of discussion, I quote these two paragraphs one by one. The first one runs,

> The word "way" probably is a primal word [*Urwort*] of language that speaks to the reflective mind of man. The guideword [*Leitwort*] in Laotse's poetic thinking is Tao, which "properly speaking" [*eigentlich*] refers to [*bedeutet*] way. But because we are prone to think of "way" superficially, as a stretch connecting two places, our word "way" has all too rashly been considered unfit to name what Tao says. Tao is then translated as reason [*Vernunft*], spirit [*Geist*], raison [*Raison*], meaning [*Sinn*], logos. (*OWL* 92/198; tr. m.; em. or.)

In this passage, Heidegger notes that *Weg* is probably an *Urwort*, and that *dao*, the *Leitwort* of Laozi's "poetic thinking," "properly speaking," refers to *Weg*. Then he regrets that *Weg* is often understood as a path stretching from one place to another, so it has been regarded as unsuitable for translating *dao*. Consequently, *dao* has been rendered as *Vernunft, Geist, Raison,*

Sinn, Logos. Heidegger's observation may be partially based on Hegel's explanation of *dao.* The following are three comments on *dao* by Hegel:

> Dao-dao: Direction, law of reason. . . . Abel Résumat says that the best
> way it [that is, *dao*] might be expressed is by the Greek word λόγος.
> (*Lectures on the History of Philosophy*)

> Dao is generally called the way [*Weg*], the right way of spirit, that is,
> "reason." (*Lectures on the Philosophy of Religion*)

> The principle [of Chinese thought] is *Vernunft, dao,* this everything
> underlying essence, which moves [*bewirkt*] everything. (*Lectures on the
> Philosophy of History*) [14]

Note that Hegel is already using *Weg* to explain the meaning of *dao,*
though he seems to equate *Weg* with the notions of *Geist* and *Vernunft.* One
may presume that Heidegger has borrowed Hegel's word *bewirkt.* Hence, it
is somewhat surprising that Heidegger claims that the word *Weg* has been
"considered unfit to name what *dao* says." In making such a claim, Heidegger
does not seem to be concerned with the question how *dao* should be translated; rather, his purpose is to enhance the unique sense he ascribes to his
notion of *Weg.*
   Checking the four German versions of the *Daodejing* that Heidegger
has quoted from or consulted, one finds that von Strauss (1874) leaves *dao*
untranslated, but adds in a note on the first page that *dao* should not be
translated as *Weg, Wort* or *Vernunft,* but as God. Ular (1903) translates *dao*
as *Bahn* (way, course). Wilhelm (1911) renders *dao* as *Sinn,* alluding to the
beginning of St. John's Gospel where *logos* is often translated as *Sinn.* Heidegger may have this in mind when he includes *Sinn* into his list of translations. Ulenbrook (1962) translates *dao* as *Weg* (his translation was published
after Heidegger delivered the lectures "The Nature of Language"). Other
German translations of *dao* in the first half of the twentieth century include
"the unfathomable" (*das Unergründliche*) and "the essence" (*das Wesen*). The
contemporary versions either translate *dao* as *Weg* or leave it untranslated. [15]
   The second paragraph in which Heidegger discusses *dao* runs,

> Yet *Tao* could be the way that gives all ways [*der alles be-wëgende Weg*],
> that which makes possible our power to think what reason, mind, mean-
> ing [*Sinn*], *logos* may say properly, that is, by their proper nature. Perhaps
> the mystery of mysteries of thoughtful Saying [*denkenden Sagens*] conceals

itself in the word *Weg, Tao,* if only we will let these names return to what they leave unspoken, if only we are capable of this, to allow them to do so. Perhaps the enigmatic power of today's reign of method also, and indeed preeminently, stems from the fact that the methods, notwithstanding their efficiency, are after all merely the drainage of a great hidden stream which moves [*be-wëgt*] all things along its track-drawing way [*seine Bahn reißen-den Weges*]. All is way. (*OWL* 92/198; tr. m.)

In this place, Heidegger suggests that *dao could* be the *Weg* that gives all ways, as that which makes possible for man to think through what "reason, mind, meaning, and *logos*" may say out of their nature. In the second sentence, Heidegger *seems* to treat *Weg* and *dao* as near-synonyms in saying that "[p]erhaps the mystery of mysteries of thoughtful saying conceals itself in the word *Weg, Tao.*" However, he is not suggesting that these two words are completely identical. The final remark, "All is way" follows up what is asserted in the preceding. Methods are the drainage of *Weg* that moves all things. *Weg* is that from which all the variety of methods arise in various forms. It is in this sense that Heidegger says, "All is way." [16] After this assertion, the fleeting reference to *dao* has faded away from Heidegger's text. In any case, it is the word *Weg* to which Heidegger attributes significance, and his mention of *dao* is subordinate to this primary intention. One should not be confused and misled by the *apparent* semantic affinity between these two words.

In the lecture series on Parmenides [1942/43], one can find a few discussions of the Greek word for way (ὁδός) that are strikingly similar to the remarks in "The Nature of Language." In Parmenides' "didactic poem," the goddess greets the thinker arriving on a "way." She reveals to him that it is his destiny to have to go along an extraordinary way outside of the trodden path [1942/43, 9/14]. Heidegger ascribes an essential connection to the essence of the goddess' ἀλήθεια (*alētheia*) and the way leading to her home. In opening up a perspective, the way provides disclosure, and belongs within the realm of ἀλήθεια. Conversely, ἀλήθεια and its holding sway require the way.

In connection with this idea, Heidegger observes that the ordinary Greek word for way (ὁδός) has a connotation of per-spect and pro-spect.

Weg is not "stretch" in the sense of the remoteness or distance between two points and so itself a multiplicity of points. The perspective and prospective essence of the way, which itself leads to the unconcealed, that is, the essence of the course, is determined on the basis of unconcealedness and on the basis of a going straightway toward the unconcealed. [1942/43, 59/87]

That *Weg* is not "stretch" in the sense of distance between two points is very similar to the saying in "The Nature of Language" that we are inclined to consider *Weg* to be a stretch connecting two places (but instead it is not). Heidegger continues his discussion in the *Parmenides*: *Weg* is essentially connected with unconcealedness. From the word ὁδός derives μέθοδος (method), which means "to-be-on-the-way, namely on a way not thought of as a 'method' man devises but a way that already exists, arising from the very things themselves, as they show themselves through and through" [1942/43, 59/87]. Heidegger stresses that "method" in its original meaning in Greek should not be confused with method in the contemporary sense. It does not have a procedure of an inquiry with the aid of which man undertakes an assault on objects with his investigations and research. Rather, it is inquiry itself as a remaining-on-the-way. Heidegger's remark on "method" is again strikingly similar to that in the second lecture of "The Nature of Language."

A possibility suggests itself. As Heidegger mentions in his letter to Jaspers dated 12 August 1949, Hisao Shih-yi, the Chinese scholar who collaborated with him in translating the *Daodejing*, attended his lectures on Heraclitus and Parmenides in 1943–44, and found resonances with Eastern thinking in Heidegger's ideas (*HJC* 172/181).[17] It is quite possible that Heidegger's elaboration on *Weg* reminded Hsiao of the Chinese word *dao*. His suggestion about this similarity may have motivated Heidegger to know a bit more about the word *dao* and to consider whether it can be used as support for his thinking on *Weg*.

Another reference to the word *dao* occurs in "The Principle of Identity" (originally delivered as a lecture in 1957),

> The word *Ereignis*, thought in terms of the matter indicated, should now speak as a guideword (*Leitwort*) in the service of thinking. As such a guideword, it can no more be translated than the Greek λόγος or the Chinese *Tao*. (*ID* 36/101)

This fleeting reference to *dao* has been ascribed a great deal of importance. In relation to it, Cho claims that *dao* can be called "an other way" (*ein anderer Gang*) and that *dao* is the *Leitwort* of Heidegger's thinking (1993, 150).[18]

Cho's claim does not seem to be well-grounded. As a matter of fact, it is *Ereignis* that Heidegger says should speak as a *Leitwort* of thinking. *Ereignis* can no more be translated than the Chinese *dao*. This juxtaposition seems to be of too slim basis to support Cho's extravagant claim that Heidegger has adopted *dao* as the *Leitwort* of his thinking (or, thinking as such). That *Ereignis* can no more be translated than the Chinese *dao* at most means that, to the same degree in which *Ereignis* speaks as a *Leitwort* of thinking, *dao* speaks as the *Leitwort* of ancient Chinese thinking. Heidegger leaves unaddressed whether and how *Ereignis* can be *related* to *dao*. Immediately after the remark cited above, Heidegger stresses the uniqueness and singularity of *Ereignis*. He writes,

> The term *Ereignis* here no longer means what we would otherwise call a happening [*Geschehnis*], an occurrence [*Vorkommnis*]. It now is used as a *singulare tantum*. What it indicates happens only in the singular, no, not in any number, but uniquely [*einzig*]. (*ID* 36/101)

I would like to use Frege's (1892) terminology of sense (*Sinn*) and reference (*Bedeutung*) in order to elucidate the nature of the relation between *Weg* and *dao* in Heidegger's writings, in particular in the two paragraphs in "The Nature of Language." First of all, as a guideword of Laozi's thinking, *dao* is untranslatable. Yet, "properly speaking" (*eigentlich*), *dao* refers to (*bedeutet*) *Weg*. Therefore, *Weg* can be said to be the *Bedeutung* of *dao*. However, *dao* cannot be said to be identical or freely interchangeable with *Weg*; it does not share the same *Sinn* as *Weg*.

The ambiguous relation between *Weg* and *dao* gives rise to both universalist and relativist readings of Heidegger's writings. A universalist reading considers that *Weg* and *dao* share the same reference, but have different senses. That is the basis on which *Weg* and *dao* could enter into dialogue. A relativist reading presupposes that *Weg* and *dao* have different sets of reference and sense. Therefore, there cannot be an intelligible dialogue between them.

In my view, both universalist and relativist readings neglect the fact that Heidegger does not treat *Weg* as merely a linguistic sign that refers to an object through the mediation of a certain sense. As the proper *Urwort*, *Weg* is a special entity. *Weg* has a kind of givenness or grantedness in spite of its appearance as a word. In other words, its sense and reference are not external, but internal. Both universalist and relativist readings fail to recognize the uniqueness of *Weg*, whose reference and sense are not on the same par as that of other words. *Weg* is what makes possible the experience of the nature of language; it is that in which the thoughtful Saying of language conceals itself. In this light, it would be more appropriate to describe *Weg* as the primary and grounding *word-thing*, rather than as an ordinary word among others.

It is only "properly speaking" (*eigentlich*) that *dao* can be said to refer to *Weg*. This means that only when interpreted in the particular manner, or thought in the nature as Heidegger has prescribed, can *dao* come into relation with *Weg*. *Weg* is the standard against which *dao* is measured. The same consideration applies to the relation between *Ereignis* and *dao*. In fact, Heidegger has characterized *Weg* in the same way as *Ereignis*. Like *Ereignis*, *Weg* is associated with a sense of movement. Heidegger coins a word *bewëgen* on the basis of *bewegen*, and speaks of *Weg* as that which moves all things.[19] As a special word-thing, *Weg* conveys a similar movement as *Ereignis*, a movement of reversal by means of which both man and language are returned to their proper nature.

Heidegger does not grant *dao* the same status as *Weg* or *Ereignis* without qualification, nor does he assert that *Weg* is no more than a translation of *dao*. It is *Weg*, not *dao*, that is properly Heidegger's guideword.

CITING THE *DAODEJING*

Light and Darkness—Chapter 28

In the lecture "Basic Principles of Thinking" delivered in 1957, Heidegger quotes a verse from chapter 28 of the *Daodejing*. The basic principles of thinking in Western philosophical tradition are: the law of identity, the law of contradiction, and the law of excluded middle. According to Heidegger, it is with Fichte and Hegel (on the basis prepared by Kant) that these laws are seriously examined for the first time. They have brought the laws of thinking to a higher dimension of possibility in that thinking has become essentially dialectical. Heidegger distinguishes between dimension in the ordinary sense and dimension in the world-historic (*weltgeschichtlicher*) sense. The dimension with which he is concerned is the latter one.

Heidegger points out that our ordinary thinking does not follow those "fundamental" laws of thinking but contradicts them. Such a contradiction is the root of all movements and liveliness. Citing Hölderlin's verse "life is death, and death is also life," Heidegger claims that here contradiction unfolds itself as "that which unites and abides" (*das Einigende und Währende*) [1957a, 51/87]. Invoking Novalis' remark that "to deny the logical law of contradiction is perhaps the highest task of logic," Heidegger comments that this remark says exactly what Hegel is thinking, that is, one has to deny the law of contradiction in order to save contradiction as the law of the reality of the real (52/88).

For Heidegger, the origin of the basic principles of thinking and the place of thinking these principles are the same thing. Both of them remain concealed (*bleibt gehüllt*) in the darkness (*Dunkel*), which is the secret of light (*Geheimnis des Lichten*). Darkness keeps light within it; and light belongs to darkness. In this context, Heidegger cites from Hölderlin's hymn "Remembrance":

But it passes,
full of dark light,
to me the fragrant cup

Heidegger explains, "light is not *Lichtung* any more, if light is merely
brightness, 'brighter than one thousand suns.' It remains difficult to safeguard the purity of darkness. That is to say, we have to keep far away the
intermixing of inappropriate brightness in order to find the light that goes
with darkness" (56/93). At this point, Heidegger cites from the *Daodejing,*

> Laozi says (chapter 28, translated by V. v. Strauss): "Who knows his light,
> will remain covered in his darkness" [*Wer seine Helle kennt, sich in sein Dun-
> kel hüllt.*] To this we add the truth which we all know but few are capable
> of: mortal thinking has to go into the depth of a well in order to see the
> stars. This is difficult. It is even more difficult to protect the purity of dark-
> ness, which is being interfered by a light that will only shine. That which
> only shines, does not give light. The scholastic presentation of the doctrine
> of laws of thinking just shines in such a way, as if the content of these laws
> and their absolute validity become clear at once to everyone. (56/93) [20]

What Heidegger quotes is from von Strauss' translation (140).[21] The Chinese original of this verse and my English translation is:

知其白，守其黑   *zhi qi bai, shou qi hei*
In knowing the white, one needs to safeguard the black.

The import of the original verse primarily concerns the relation between
polarities. In quoting this verse, Heidegger shifts away from this concern.[22]
His focus does not fall on the relation between white and black, or between
light and darkness, but on a different kind of light that he is seeking.

According to Heidegger, Western philosophical tradition has been
searching for inappropriate brightness. This is manifest in the presumption
that the basic principles of thinking are clear and distinct without ambiguity
or opaqueness. For Heidegger, this kind of light is not *Lichtung.* It is pure
brightness without proper sophistication. One needs to keep away from this
simplistic notion of brightness and look for the appropriate brightness that
goes well with darkness. True light lies concealed in the darkness that is both
the origin of the basic principles of thinking and the place of considering
these principles. Similarly, true darkness is not complete darkness without
any light. It is pregnant with genuine light.

From this perspective of thinking, Heidegger may have found Laozi's verse concerning the dialectic relation between white (light) and black (darkness) well-serving his purpose of delineating another kind of light, which is a deeper and more concealed origin of thinking.[23] He adapts this verse to what he is trying to say in this context.

Heidegger's characterization of the origin of the basic principles of thinking in terms of true light concealed in true darkness resembles his reflection on truth (and of Being). To him, truth resides in ἀλήθεια. It is unconcealment with reserved concealment. Concealment is a fundamental dimension of truth. Truth lies in the movement toward unconcealedness that is continuously challenged, if not thwarted, by the power of concealment.[24] With Heidegger, the dynamic relation between unconcealment and concealment, between light and darkness, is one in which each member of a relevant pair of contraries is indispensable. This bears similarity with Laozi's idea of contraries as reflected in chapter 28.

However, the following difference sets Heidegger away from Laozi. According to Heidegger's characterization of unconcealment and concealment, of light and darkness, neither member of the pair of contraries has a determinate external reference. They represent internal mediation achieved by a movement called ἀλήθεια. Although Heidegger's interpreters have often ascribed an essential openness to this movement, one should notice that ἀλήθεια is not a neutral arbitrary movement. What can be unconcealed is already unconcealed partially in the first beginning of Western historicality. Unconcealment is a movement that possesses historic necessity. With Laozi, the opposites are externally recognizable and determinable. The distinction between the opposites is not logical, but concrete.[25] The white and the black in the verse "know the white, yet safeguard the black" do not constitute two internal sides of a certain logical or historical unity. They refer to concrete whiteness and blackness, or concrete light and darkness.

Sages Do Not Travel?—Chapter 47

In a letter to Ernst Jünger (dated 29 May 1965), just before Jünger set upon a journey to East Asia, Heidegger quotes the whole of chapter 47 of the *Daodejing*, which is as follows,[26]

> Nicht zum Tor hinausgehen
> und die Welt kennen,
> Nicht zum Fenster hinausspähen
> und den Himmel ganz sehen:

Geht man sehr weit hinaus,
   weiss man sehr wenig.

Darum der Weise:
   nicht reist er,
      doch er kennt,
   nicht guckt er,
      doch er rühmt,
   nicht handelt er,
      doch er vollendet.[27]

   Heidegger is rather critical of exoticist interest in and adventure to alien cultures. Once he speaks disparagingly of "whatever is merely foreign in the sense of the alien and exotic, that which the adventurer sets out in search of in order to settle his conscience" (*HHI* 131/164). For him, Jünger is a prime example of thoughtless attending to alien cultures.[28] In citing chapter 47 from the *Daodejing* in his letter to Jünger before his journey, it seems that Heidegger is using Laozi to make his point that one needs to concentrate on what belongs to one's own world, instead of pursuing distant and strange things outside. Would this be what Laozi is edifying in these verses? Below is the Chinese original and my English translation of this chapter.

不出於戶，	One does not need to go beyond one's house
以知天下。	To know the world;
不窺於牖，	One does not need to look outside one's window
以知天道。	To know the dao of heaven;
其出彌遠，	The farther one goes,
其知彌少。	The less one knows.
是以聖人	For this reason, sages know:
不行而知，	Without going anywhere out of the necessary,
不見而明，	Understand without seeing anything out of the necessary,
弗為而成。	And get things done without doing anything out of the necessary.

   Laozi does say something to the effect that one does not need to bother about the outer world in order to acquire better knowledge and have more achievements. This is an idea which Heidegger may have found catering to his heart. However, Laozi does not claim that not going outward constitutes the necessary condition for knowing and practice. His point is that one needs to concentrate on what is within access, instead of chasing after superfluous things impertinent to what is at issue. This holds true in Laozi's times, when frequent wars brought about chaotic conditions and travelling was almost equal to emigration or exile. Laozi may be criticizing those political strategists who travelled to various states with the purpose of obtaining power and position by persuading the kings to instigate wars.

As Ames and Hall point out, the commonly consulted Wang Bi version of the *Daodejing* has for the last line *bu wei er cheng* (不為而成) which literally means, "And gets things done without doing"; whereas both Mawangdui A and B texts have *fu wei er cheng* (弗為而成), which literally means, "And gets things done without doing something." Since the two lines preceding this one are missing in the Mawangdui texts, one can extrapolate this sentence structure starting with the word *fu* to them, and assume that both these lines have *fu* and thus a similar meaning. Because *fu* 弗 is a negation word which entails an object after the verb it negates, while *bu* 不 does not, Ames and Hall translate the last three lines as (2003, 150),

> It is for this reason that sages know without going anywhere out of the ordinary,
> Understand without seeing anything out of the ordinary,
> And get things done without doing anything out of the ordinary.

Their point is that Laozi is expressing a localistic view of knowledge. That is, knowledge is obtained through "responsive and efficacious participation in one's environments, and through one's full contribution at home in the local and the focal relationships that, in sum, make one who one is" (150). Ames and Hall have made an important contribution to revealing the sentence meaning of the last three verses, and they rightly stress the role of participation in the constitution of knowledge. However, to state Laozi's view exclusively in terms of localism (or contextualism) may risk taking the local to be something immutable and self-evident. Ames and Hall place such a strong emphasis on the local that, for them, leaving home seems to necessarily endanger one's defining roles and relationships. They regard concentrating on local life as a necessary condition for knowing the world (151).[29] This interpretation is suggestive of deterministic ideas that do not accord with Laozi's insight that there are many ways of going about in the world.

In my view, what Laozi stresses is not that knowledge is definitely acquired through focusing on the local and the ordinary, but that, to obtain knowledge, or *dao,* one does not need to be concerned with impertinent matters. The negation word *fu* 弗 entails an object for the verb *wei* 為. On this ground, the misunderstanding that the sages do not need to do anything can be cleared up. The point is that they do not need to do unnecessary things. I follow Ames and Hall's exegesis about the sentence meaning of the last three lines based on the findings from the Mawangdui texts, but disagree with the interpretation they ascribe to it.

In Heidegger's times, convenient means for travelling and transportation makes going beyond one's dwelling place much easier and even necessary. It can be said that one's dwelling place has been significantly broadened and become more complex. Often necessity arises for one to travel afar, which was not possible in ancient times. Heidegger's awareness of this is shown in what he writes in the beginning of the essay "The Thing,"

> All distances in time and space are shrinking. Man now reaches overnight, by plane, places which formerly took weeks and months of travel. He now receives instant information, by radio, of events which he formerly learned about only years later, if at all. [1950b, 163/165]

In Heidegger's eyes, the fact that distant sites have become accessible in a heretofore-unprecedented way is necessarily complicit with forms of inauthenticity. He is worried that apparent nearness of formerly far-off events and people would cause confusion and alienation such that one cannot concentrate on and preserve what properly belongs to oneself. This conviction could account for the seemingly-contingent fact that during his lifetime, Heidegger never travelled further than France and Greece, which for him are the only two places belonging to the same lineage as Germany. In a letter of 1955, he cannot help express irritation at being invited to go to Japan.[30]

Heidegger feels fully justified in viewing things in such a way. However, in the contemporary world one can no longer make sense of one's dwelling place without paying attention to other places that have also become part of one's own world. In addition, one's defining role is open to change and multiplicity. This in some cases may bring a new lease on life, rather than necessarily leading to loss. Laozi's succinct verses may lend themselves for Heidegger to make his case. Nevertheless, in light of a contextualized analysis, chapter 47 of the *Daodejing* does not fully support his case.

YOU *AND* WU —*CHAPTER 11*

In an essay entitled "The Uniqueness of the Poet" ("Die Einzigkeit des Dichters") [1943b], Heidegger cites the whole of chapter 11 from the

Daodejing. In this essay, he addresses the question where the uniqueness of the poet resides. Two ready approaches offer themselves. One approach is historical, which assumes that one can discover the poet's singularity through a comparative study of poets in the history of literature. Another approach is unhistorical, which believes that one can find the distinctive characteristics of poets in accordance with the nature (or measure) of poetry. In the eyes of Heidegger, these two approaches, and their combination, fail to provide an adequate answer to the question at issue. Because they are both separated from the originary event (Ereignis) that makes a poet poet, a poem poem, these approaches are arbitrary, external, and superficial.

In accordance with his distinction between *Historie* and *Geschichte*, Heidegger claims that poetry can only originate in and be determined by *Geschichte*. He writes, "Were the poet to have to compose the complete essence of poetry in particular, with this essence understood as *Geschichte*, that is, what is coming (*Kommendes*), then . . . the uniqueness of the poet enters into light immediately" [1943b, 36–37]. The unique poet Heidegger has in mind is no other than Hölderlin, since his poetry takes its origin in the coming time.

"What is coming," the future, characterizes the essence of time. It is intermingled with what is past and what is present. The uniqueness of Hölderlin is sent by destiny (*Schickung*). His poetry is post-saying and at the same time pre-saying (*nach-sagenden Vorsagen*) in response to the call (or the word) of Being. Hölderlin's poetry says (*dichtet*) "that and how Beyng appropriates itself and is sent only in appropriation and that is called destiny [*Geschichte*]" (37).

Now the question is whether man remains inattentive to the uniqueness of the poet and to what is always coming (that is, the authentic time), or attempts to learn attentiveness, out of which we learn the originary remembrance of what is to be thought. This is the unique historic decision man has to make. Heidegger continues,

> How do we *learn* attentiveness, we, the late-born ones during centuries of inattentiveness?
>
> We learn attentiveness, in that we see the unseemingly simpleness [*das unscheinbare Einfache*], which we appropriate originarily ever and ever, and *before* [*vor*] which we become more and more awesome.[31]
>
> Already the unnoticeable simplicity of simple things brings to us what we call, according to old habit of thinking, Being [*Sein*] in its distinction from beings [*Seiende*].

Being in *this* distinction is spoken of by Lao-Tse in the eleventh saying [*Spruch*] of his *Tao-Te-King.* (42; em. or.)

At this point, Heidegger cites the whole of chapter 11 of the *Daodejing.*

Dreißig Speichen treffen die Nabe,
Aber das *Leere zwischen* ihnen gewährt das SEIN des Rades.
Aus dem Ton ent-stehen die Gefäße,
Aber das *Leere* in ihnen gewährt das SEIN des Gefäßes.
Mauern und Fenster und Türen stellen das Haus dar,
Aber das *Leere zwischen* ihnen gewährt das SEIN des Hauses.
Das Seiende ergibt die Brauchbarkeit.
Das Nicht-Seiende gewährt das SEIN. (43; em. ad.)

Heidegger's version is the closest to Ular's translation among the four to
which Heidegger has access, which is as follows,

Dreißig Speichen treffen die Nabe,
aber das *Leere* zwischen ihnen <u>erwirkt</u> das WESEN des Rades;
Aus Ton entstehen Töpfe,
aber das *Leere* in ihnen <u>wirkt</u> das WESEN des Topfes;
Mauern mit Fenstern und Türen bilden das Haus,
aber das *Leere* in ihnen <u>erwirkt</u> das WESEN des Hauses.
Grundsätzlich:
Das Stoffliche birgt Nutzbarkeit;
Das Unstoffliche <u>wirkt</u> WESENHEIT. (Ular, 17; em. ad.)

Heidegger's text differs from Ular's translation in several places. He
changes both *erwirkt* and *wirkt* (both of which occur twice) into *gewährt,*
and places a hyphen within the word *entstehen,* and thus writes *ent-stehen.*
He replaces Ular's word *Töpfe* (*qi* 器) with *Gefäße,* and modifies *birgt* in the
next to last sentence as *ergibt.* He uses *zwischen* twice, once more than Ular
does, and replaces Ular's *Stoffliche* with *Seiende,* and *Unstoffliche* with *Nicht-
Seiende* correspondingly. The most important change is his replacement of
Ular's word *Wesenheit* (*yong* 用) with *Sein.*[32] In the meantime, Heidegger follows Ular in rendering *wu* (無) as *Leere.*[33]

Below I provide a Chinese version as well as my paraphrasing translation of chapter 11. I give the *pinyin* after the Chinese characters in order to
make it easier for the reader to locate the relevant characters.

卅幅共一轂   *sa fu gong yi gu*
Thirty spokes unite around a nave.

當其無有，車之用也   *dang qi wu you, che zhi yong ye*
Adapting the space between the spokes [*wu*] and the spokes themselves
[*you*], one uses it as a cart.

埏埴而為器   *shan zhi er wei qi*
Molding clay to make a vessel,

當其無有，器之用也   *dang qi wu you, qi zhi yong ye*
Adapting the void within the vessel [*wu*] and the shape of the vessel itself
[*you*], one uses it as a vessel.

鑿戶牖而為室   *zao hu you er wei shi*
Cutting out doors and windows out of walls to make a room.

當其無有，室之用也   *dang qi wu you, shi zhi yong ye*
Adapting the space of the doors and windows [*wu*] and the walls that
stand on the ground [*you*], one uses it as a room.

有之以為利   *you zhi yi wei li*
Where something is present [*you zhi*], it makes a basis for adaptation.

無之以為用   *wu zhi yi wei yong*
Where nothing is present [*wu zhi*], it lends space to an actual use.

The lack of a definite system of periodization in classical Chinese writings gives rise to multiple possibilities of reading. One of the things important
for understanding chapter 11 concerns whether the three *you* characters should
go with the *wu* character preceding them, or with the following words to form
such phrases as "*you . . . zhi yong ye.*" Most translators or interpreters have read
this text in the latter way. Accordingly one obtains the three phrases: *you che zhi
yong* (there comes the use of a cart), *you qi zhi yong* (there comes the use of a
vessel), *you shi zhi yong* (there comes the use of a room). In James Legge's bilingual version, the *you* characters are listed in the former way. That is, they follow
the *wu* characters. However, Legge does not seem to have considered seriously
whether *you* here is functioning differently from what is commonly assumed.
The common way of reading chapter 11 makes it easier to isolate *wu* from the
particular context and interpret it as an abstract notion.

I suggest that the first way of reading *you* is more adequate. That is,
you immediately follows *wu*. The word *you* literally means "to have," "there
exists," as contrary to *wu*, which means "not to be present," or "not to be
around." In the three cases that involve a particular use of a certain object
(a cart, a vessel, a room), it is more convincing to attribute what make such

a use possible to *both* the space or void where there is nothing (*wu*) and the concrete tangible materials that make the space or void what it is (*you*) than only to the former (*wu*). That is, *wu* is not an abstract philosophical notion. It refers to the particular space. In the penultimate line, *you* appears as a word in itself, followed by the word *zhi.* The word *zhi* is used here as a pronoun to represent the things that are said to be present in the previous cases: the thirty spokes, the clay shape of the vessel, the walls of a room. In this light, it is rather incredible to explain away the role *you* plays in the earlier occurrence by taking it as a word that forms the phrases "there comes the use of a cart," "there comes the use of a vessel" and "there comes the use of a room." A. C. Graham's reading supports my explanation. According to him,

> [this chapter deals] not with Nothing in general, but with the parts of the wheel, vessel or house which do not exist (*qi wu*). Each is a combination of something and nothing; the hole in the wheel which takes the axle, the empty space inside the vessel, doors and windows in the house, are nothing yet belong to the things which could not be used without them. (Graham 1990, 346) [34]

The point of my discussion about the meaning of *wuyou* resides in the following. Treating the word *wu* as unrelated to *you* and translating it as "nothing," or "Leere" as Heidegger does, enhances the tendency to regarding it as a metaphysical term. For example, Lin Yutang's translation is, "From their not-being (loss of their individuality) / Arises the utility of the wheel" (1976). D. C. Lau's is, "Adapt the nothing therein to the purpose in hand, / and you will have the use of the cart" (1982). Victor Mair pays attention to the concreteness of *wu*, "but it is the empty hole in the middle which makes a cart possible" (1990). However, he renders the word *wu* in the last verse as an abstract notion: "Therefore, while benefits may be derived from something, / it is in EMPTY NOTHING that we find usefulness" (em. or.).

I adhere to current established interpretation of *you* and *wu*. According to this view, classical Western metaphysical notion of Being is generally conceived as ontological ground or reality behind appearance, while Non-Being is negation of Being. In traditional Chinese thought, the word *you* overlaps with the sense of "having." It has nothing to do with "Being" or existence. The word *wu* does not indicate strict opposition or contradiction, but absence. While *you* means "to be present" or "to be around," *wu* means "to not be present" or "to not be around." Thus, the *you-wu* distinction suggests contrast in the sense of presence or absence of x rather than assertion about the existence or non-existence of x. What the words *you* and *wu* signify should not be treated as ontological categories with a load of metaphysical implications, but as interdependent explanatory categories of "something" and "nothing," of "presence and absence." As early as the third century, Pei Wei has argued that nothing is merely the absence of something in reaction to the Daoist mystification of nothing and doing nothing.[35]

Heidegger may have found the word *Leere* (which translates *wu*) in Ular's version very interesting inasmuch as it corresponds to his way of philosophizing.[36] As already mentioned in the section on Heidegger and Daoism in Chapter one, in the essay "The Thing" written in 1950, he speaks at length of the *Leere* (emptiness, void) of the jug. This point of apparent Daoist connection has been noticed by quite a few scholars without being aware that elsewhere Heidegger quoted the whole of chapter 11 that contains important verses bearing on *wu*. In "A Dialogue on Language," Heidegger talks about the "sameness" between the Japanese notion of *Leere* (*kū* 空) and his idea of Nothing (*DL* 19/108). However, the implication of the word "sameness" in Heidegger's pairing of *Leere* as a Japanese notion and his idea of Nothing is not the same as "same" in its ordinary sense. These matters will be further discussed in chapters eight and nine.

Heidegger's translation of *yong* as *Sein*, in contrast with *Seiende* and *Nicht-Seiende* in the last two verses, indicates the extent to which he has taken liberty with Laozi's saying. It is as an exemplification of Being in distinction from beings that chapter 11 of the *Daodejing* is transplanted into Heidegger's text.

Paraphrasing Translations from Chapter 15

One year after their attempt at translating parts of the *Daodejing* in the summer of 1946, Heidegger sent Hsiao a short letter of greetings (dated 9 October 1947), in which he cites from chapter 15 of the *Daodejing*.[37]

"Wer kann still sein und aus der Stille durch sie auf den Weg bringen (be-wegen) etwas so, dass es zum Erscheinen kommt?"
[Wer vermag es, stillend etwas so ins Sein zu bringen?
Des Himmels Tao

"Who can be still and out of stillness and through it move something on to the Way so that it comes to shine forth?"
[Who is able through making still to bring something into Being?
The *tao* of heaven

It may have been through his collaboration with Hsiao that Heidegger was particularly impressed by these two verses. They were apparently dear to his heart, as he had requested Hsiao to explain the original Chinese words one by one, and to write them out in traditional Chinese calligraphy on a pair of vertical parchment rolls. Hsiao added a horizontal scroll with two characters, *tiandao* (天道 the *dao* of heaven), to form a standard set. This set of calligraphy hung in Heidegger's study (Petzet, 168). In Chinese the two relevant lines are, followed by an English translation:

> 孰能濁而靜之徐清   *shu neng zhuo yi jing zhi xu qing*
> Muddy water, when stilled, slowly becomes clear.
>
> 孰能安而動之徐生   *shu neng an yi dong zhi xu sheng*
> Something settled, when agitated, slowly comes to life.

The Wang Bi and the Guodian versions of the *Daodejing* have the words *shu neng* 孰能 at the beginning of both lines (which literally means "who could"); whereas the Mawangdui A and B versions do not contain these words. The English translation I choose dispenses with these two characters (Ames and Hall 2003, 98). This seems to be more consistent with the preceding verses, which are a series of descriptions of ancient dao masters. Von Strauss and Wilhelm's translations are, respectively, "Wer kann das Trübe, indem er es stillt, allmählich klären? Wer kann die Ruhe, in dem er sie verlängert, allmählich beleben?" (80) and "Wer kann (wie sie) das Trübe durch Stille allmählich klären/Wer kann (wie sie) die Ruhe durch Dauer allmählich erzeugen?" (17).[38] These two versions are very close to Hsiao's own German translation, "Wer kann das Trübe stillend allmählich klären? Wer kann die Ruhe bewegend allmählich beleben? (Hsiao 1977, 127).[39] An English translation of this is, "Who can, settling the muddy, gradually make it clear? Who can, stirring the tranquil, gradually bring it to life?" (Hsiao 1987, 100).

It can be seen, in comparison with these translations, that Heidegger has obviously found something bearing affinity to his way of saying. One example is the word *Stille* and its cognates. In von Strauss and Hsiao's German versions there occur the words *stillt* and *stillend,* both of which come from the verb *stillen,* meaning "to settle, to stop." Apart from *stillen,* Heidegger also uses the adjective *still,* meaning "quiet, secret," and the noun *Stille,* meaning "silence, quietness." He may have been inspired by Wilhelm's phrase *"durch Stille"* and may have derived the expression *"aus der Stille"* from it.

Heidegger's use of *Stille* as a technical notion has so far been rarely noted. As early as 1936–38, he employs this word in the *Contributions to*

Philosophy: "In and as *da-sein,* Beyng enowns the truth which it manifests as not-granting, as that domain of hinting and withdrawal—of stillness— wherein the arrival and flight of the last god are first determined" (*CP* 15/20). "Stillness" indicates the region which gives hints and at the same time withdraws itself. Toward the end of the essay "Language," almost two pages are devoted to *Stille.* It is delineated in the same manner as Ereignis [1950a, 205/29–30]. In "A Dialogue," *Stille* is used to characterize the Japanese notion *iki: "iki* is the breath of the stillness of luminous delight (*DL* 44/141). *Stille* and *Weite* (vastness) form the pairing mode in which Ereignis occurs (*DL* 53/153).

It remains difficult to decide whether Heidegger drew inspirations concerning *Stille* from his reading of German versions of the *Daodejing* before he met Hsiao, or he happened to find striking similarity of wording in Laozi's verses after he collaborated with Hsiao. In any case, it can be seen that certainly Heidegger is very fond of the image this word denotes in using it three times in his version of the verses.

An innovation Heidegger makes with the couplet is his use of the word *Weg,* which is neither in the original text nor in its translations. Furthermore, instead of the more or less literal translation of *klären* (*qing* 清) Heidegger uses the expression *"zum Erscheinen kommt"* (comes to shine forth). *Erscheinen,* signifying "appearance, phenomenon," is strongly suggestive of Heidegger's hermeneutic phenomenology.

According to Hsiao's report, Heidegger told him that one could extend some of the motives in these two sayings and consider the idea that "clarifying finally brings something to light, and subtle motion in the tranquil and still can bring something into being" (Hsiao 1987, 100). It is clear that Heidegger has changed the rather literal translation *beleben* (*sheng* 生, bring to life) in the second verse into the phrase *"ins Sein zu bringen"* (bring something into Being). This is completely Heidegger's own innovation. It seems that he will never fail to coin different phrases to express his concern with Being. In the meantime, Heidegger has completely neglected the words *Trübe* (*zhuo* 濁) and *allmählich* (*xu* 徐).

One could conclude that the alleged citation from chapter 15 of the *Daodejing* in Heidegger's letter is an integration of his own ideas with Laozi's saying. It is the result of ignoring irrelevant words while highlighting relevant ones. As May rightly explains, the verse in quotation marks is Heidegger's appropriated paraphrase on the basis of the collaboration with Hsiao; while the verse following the square bracket "can be ascribed to Heidegger alone" (May 1996, 2–3).

A Struggle between Technology and Art?—Chapters 9 and 15

On 7 August 1965, Heidegger gave a brief speech on the occasion of the seventieth birthday of Siegfried Bröse [1965b]. Bröse is one of Heidegger's friends, working with the Freiburg Art Society. He had organized an exhibition on Chinese art, which would open the day after Heidegger delivered his speech. Heidegger started his talk by saying that he wanted to hold on to "a word" (*ein Wort*) from Laozi's book "Vom Weg," which also spoke for Bröse. He quoted the translation by Ulenbrook of the following lines from chapter 9 of the *Daodejing*,[40]

> Dem Werk nachgehen,
> sich selbst entziehen,
> das ist des Himmels Weg.

Below is the Chinese version, followed by my translation:

功遂身退，天之道也   *gong sui sheng tui, tian zhi dao ye*
To withdraw when the work is done is the way of heaven.

Laozi's chapter 9 purports to draw an analogy between the way of heaven and the way of human conduct. When the vessel is filled to its brim, it will overturn;[41] when the blade is made too sharp, it will not hold its edge; when there is abundant treasure one may not be able to maintain it. Wealth and station may well incur calamity. Therefore, one should try to avoid excess or extremes and keep to a life of moderation and balance. To retreat when the deed is accomplished accords with the way of heaven.

Heidegger observes that artworks from a four-thousand-year old profound tradition constitute the thought from which the exhibition on Chinese art had sprung (*entsprungen*). This tradition entered the technological world-epoch in the last decade of the nineteenth century. Its artworks are presented at a moment when the power of scientific technology is dominating forms of experience. Heidegger suggests that instead of following the latest technical innovations, art should engage in a struggle (*Widerstreit*) between the restfulness of the work of art and the raging of technology. Following this, Heidegger remarks that the thinking of the ancient Chinese world may have pre-thought (*vorausgedacht*) this struggle in its own way [1965b, 618].

It can be seen that, in quoting the verse, "To withdraw when the work is done is the way of heaven," Heidegger has borrowed and at the same time revised the thought embodied in it. Originally, this saying concerns an analogy between the way of heaven and the way of humans. The implication is that one should not over-rely upon one's achievements, becoming dominated by them. Instead, it is better to let go off what was accomplished, rather than taking advantage of the benefits coming from the achievements. This rule resembles the cyclical patterns of nature in which one season gives way to the next, with the full range of natural forces playing their roles in due course. In this way, the environment always remains lively.

For Heidegger, "To withdraw when the work is done is the way of heaven" means something different from the above. He reads into this verse a depiction of the struggle between technology and art. Although he does not specify the details in which this should be understood, what he has in mind may be something like this: to stay in a triumphant and dominant position is the way of the *Ge-stell*. What needs to be cherished is the way of letting-be as manifest in art. The way of art is well depicted in the verses he cites.

In order to enhance his point, Heidegger also quotes from chapter 15 of the *Daodejing* [1965b, 618]:

Wer aber ist imstande, ein quirlend Wasser
durch die Behutsamkeit der Stille zu klären?
Wer aber ist imstande, die Ruhe
durch die Behutsamkeit dauernder Bewegung zu erzeugen?

These are exactly the same verses as covered in the previous section, where I have discussed Heidegger's own paraphrasing of them. On this occasion, he quotes from Ulenbrook's translation (published in 1962) without any modification. For him, the modes of *klären* (to clear—as of water) and *erzeugen* (to bring forth) represent something like the restful ways of art.

These four lines are the ones Heidegger cites the most often. Among Heidegger's *Nachlass*, there is a letter addressed to Andrea von Harbou dated 6 August 1965, one day before he delivered this lecture in relation to the exhibition on Chinese art. In this letter, he quotes exactly the same verses of chapter 15 as translated by Ulenbrook.[42] It seems that Heidegger was aware that his own version of these verses in the letter to Hsiao in 1947 diverged significantly from what is said in the original text. Thus, in quoting them on these two occasions, he deemed it suitable to use an existing translation. And he might have considered that Ulenbrook's translation surpassed the others or captured well what he wanted to express.

On reading a collection of essays by Erhart Kästner, Heidegger for the last time refers to this pair of verses in a letter to the author on 30 July 1973. In a short essay in that book entitled "Quirlwasser," Kästner discusses whether *Trübwasser* (turbid water) or *Quirlwasser* (whirling water) might be the best translation of the word *zhuo* 濁 in chapter 15 of the *Daodejing.* He concludes that it might be better not to decide for one or the other, but to keep both in view (Kästner 1973, 59–62). Heidegger comments that he finds Kästner's reading of chapter 15 "nice and convincing" [1986b, 122].

Chapter Seven

East-West Dialogue and the Question of Language

In a number of places, Heidegger suggests that language is the most central *topos* for the question of East-West dialogue. In "On the Question of Being," he speaks of "the realm of possible dialogue between . . . the language of Europe and that of East Asia" [1955a, 321/424]. In "A Dialogue on Language" [1953/54], he expresses his concern whether what he had been attempting to think of as the nature of language was "also" adequate for the nature of the East Asian language and whether there could be a nature of language that could initiate East-West dialogue [*DL* 8/93–4]. Below is a virtually unknown remark by Heidegger with respect to language and East-West dialogue,

> One theme appears to me to be inevitable: Speech and Writing; here become evident the essential questions of East-West dialogue; questions of signification and image in the widest sense can be brought into the open.[1]

This remark appeared in a letter dated 6 April 1955. It was addressed to Emil Pretorius, President of the Bavarian Academy of Fine Arts, who had invited Heidegger to give a lecture in a series with the title "Of Language."

It seems that Heidegger has seriously thought about relevant issues surrounding Asian languages. However, disparate strands of thoughts and considerations are entangled together in his claims. On the one hand, he suggests that there is a radical inaccessibility of these languages, and that it is impossible for him to engage with Asian thought because of linguistic differences. On the other hand, he makes inquires about words in these languages that might correspond to some of his key notions important for his project of re-enacting the other beginning of Western philosophy. These signs and gestures apparently point in opposite directions and entail irreconcilable implications.

This chapter aims to provide a balanced and convincing treatment so far as possible of Heidegger's reflection on Asian languages. I begin by examining his fleeting remarks bearing upon East Asian languages, several of which are scattered in a number of texts published in German and have rarely been brought into discussion.[2] Then I investigate Heidegger's attention to words from Asian languages. After surveying the often-cited attempt at translating the *Daodejing,* I introduce his discussion of Japanese words for art. This occurs at a colloquium on the theme "Art and Thinking" on 18 May 1958 at Freiburg. Last, I address his inquiry about Sanskrit words. Heidegger's direct contact with Indian thought has as yet not received attention.

AN ONTOLOGICAL BARRIER?

In a letter to the Swiss psychiatrist Medard Boss, dated 30 June 1955, Heidegger told him,[3]

> Today I am amazed that years ago I dared to give the lecture on language. The greatest omission belongs to the fact that the possibility for a *sufficient* [*zureichenden*] discussion about the East Asian languages is *lacking* [*fehlt*]. (*ZS* 251/316; em. Philosophia or.)

On this occasion, Heidegger seems to be expressing regret that his lecture on language had been inadequate because it had not been possible to discuss Asian languages.[4] He calls this the "greatest omission." What is *prima facie* bewildering is that, if Heidegger considers that a "sufficient" discussion of East Asian languages is of crucial importance, if he deems that East Asian thought can make important contributions to a thinking beyond traditional metaphysics, if he attaches importance to hearing things in their original tongue, why, instead of taking sufficient initiative to learn a bit more about these languages, for a long stretch of years, he reiterates from time to time his ignorance of the original East Asian languages? One of the reasons that could be invoked is that these languages are so formidably difficult to learn that most Western philosophers cannot gain access to them.[5] This is what Heidegger sometimes accentuates. In a letter on 20 June 1966 to Matsuo Keiklchi, Japanese translator of *Being and Time,*[6] Heidegger writes,

> Because we Europeans usually fail to have a command of the Japanese language, unfortunately the necessary mutual understanding comes from one side only. [1966b, 228]

Here Heidegger appears to be commenting on the empirical fact that most Europeans do not have a command of the Japanese language, and thus understanding between Europeans and Japanese is inevitably unilateral. He may well have in view the fact that numerous Japanese scholars are pursuing Western learning with enthusiasm, and as a result tend to approach their own tradition from the perspective of Western conceptual systems.[7] Therefore, their own understanding of Japanese tradition could also be said to be unilateral.

In his letter to the organizers of the symposium "Heidegger and Eastern Thought" held at the University of Hawai'i during 17–21 November 1969 (addressed to Prof. Borgmann), Heidegger again addresses the lack of command of Eastern languages,

> Again and again it has seemed urgent to me that a dialogue take place with the thinkers of what is to us the Eastern world. The greatest difficulty in this enterprise always lies, as far as I can see, in the fact that with few exceptions there is no command of the Eastern languages either in Europe or in the United States. . . . May your conference prove fruitful in spite of this precarious [*mißlichen*] circumstance. [1969b, 721–22]

With respect to the possibility of a dialogue with the "thinkers of what is to us the Eastern world," Heidegger attributes the "greatest difficulty" to the lack of command of Eastern languages in the West. In the context of such a conference, however, this suggestion seems to be somewhat out of place; because most participants of this conference were at home with both Asian and European languages. Heidegger's stress upon the inaccessibility of East Asian languages must be more than an empirical observation.

Before elaborating this point, I would like to supplement the background of Heidegger's letter. A large part of this letter was read out in the introduction address by Winfield E. Nagley (1970), chairman of the department of philosophy at the University of Hawai'i, and published under the title "Introduction to the symposium and reading of a letter from Martin Heidegger." This title is misleading. All the scholars whose relevant work I have consulted have assumed that this excerpt is the full text of the letter, for example, Denker (2000, 270, item 1969i), Elberfeld (2000, 158), Groth (2004, 163, n96, 260, item 72), May (1996, 5n20), and Parkes (1987, 12–13).[8] However, in checking the full text of Heidegger's letter, dated 4 July 1969, in volume 16 of Heidegger's *Gesamtausgabe*, which remained unpublished until the year 2000, one finds that the last paragraph of his letter was missing in what was published in *Philosophy East and West*. Probably, Nagley did not read it out to the conference participants either. In the last paragraph, Heidegger says,

Now in regard to the words of welcome and introduction for which you ask, I have to appeal to your kindness to excuse me for not honouring your request. From all sides I am receiving requests of this kind so that I have to refuse every one of them in order not to offend somebody. [1969b, 722]

Heidegger declined the invitation to write "the words of welcome and introduction" for the organizers. Probably because of this refusal, he was contacted again. In another letter to Borgmann, dated 29 October 1969, Heidegger agreed that his previous letter written on 4 July could be read out at the conference and printed as a message of "special greetings and thanks to the participants of the conference" [1969b, 722]. Nagley did not mention the second letter. It remains unknown whether this letter had already reached Nagley when he gave his speech on 17 November. It is clear that the previous well-known letter was initially not intended to be an address to the conference participants.[9]

Another striking remark on the inaccessibility of East Asian languages is made during Heidegger's conversation with Hellmuth Hecker on 30 August 1952. Hecker was professor of philosophy at the University of Hamburg and an important German scholar of Zen Buddhism. He recounted this conversation with Heidegger from memory in "A Walk with Heidegger."[10] The relevant conversation runs as follows:

Hecker: An important question: Have you engaged yourself with Eastern, that is, Indian and Chinese philosophy?

Heidegger: Hardly. The linguistic difficulties with the translations are insurmountable. I know what the difficulties are already with Greek; one has to start when young to penetrate in this language. To the Chinese and Japanese world I simply have no access. *Sein und Zeit* has been translated into Japanese, but about the "how" I cannot judge. With our logistic-grammatical conceptual apparatus there are many words [when translating] that we cannot grasp sharply. For example when I read the translations from Chinese by Richard Wilhelm, I see that he has approached the text completely in the framework of Kantian philosophy. (Hartig 1997, 269)

That one has to start early to learn a difficult foreign language seems to be a trivial empirical truism. However, this is not Heidegger's last word. In reiterating linguistic difficulty and the lack of access to East Asian languages, he invokes a non-trivial reason for the inaccessibility of East Asian languages.

This is related to the barrier that consists in the logistic framework of Western languages.

Heidegger has access to four German translations of the *Daodejing*, including that of Richard Wilhelm (Laozi 1911), as well as the latter's (1923) and Martin Buber's (1922) edition of the *Zhuangzi*. In Heidegger's eyes, Wilhelm has read Kantian ideas into the Laozi and Zhuangzi. In the following passage, quite probably Heidegger has Wilhelm in mind when he speaks of Laozi being made into a Kantian.

> "Thinking"–that is our Western thinking, is determined by and attuned to λόγος. Definitely this doesn't mean that the ancient world of the Indies, China and Japan remained without thought (*gedanken-los*). On the contrary the λόγος -character of Western thought demands from us that if we should dare to touch these alien worlds, we must first ask ourselves whether we are capable at all of hearing that which was thought there. This question becomes even more urgent, because European thinking is threatening to become planetary [*planetarisch*], in that contemporary Indians, Chinese and Japanese can usually bring to us what is experienced by them only through our European way of thinking. Thus from there and from here everything is stirred around in an enormous hodgepodge, in which one cannot distinguish any more whether the ancient Indians were English empiricists and Laotse a Kantian. [1957a, 145–46]

This excerpt comes from the lecture series "Principles of Thinking," where Heidegger shows concern about the "planetarization" of the world in relation to those "alien worlds." It is clear that the inaccessibility of Asian languages is not simply due to the fact that few Europeans enjoy mastery of these languages, but more fundamentally due to the logistic framework of Western thinking. The dualistic metaphysical system has prevented European people from being able to hear what was thought in the old traditions of India, China and Japan.

It need be noted that for Heidegger this awareness of linguistic restriction *itself* does not arise from outside of Western thinking. On the contrary, to consider the question whether "we are capable at all of hearing that which was thought there" is a demand precisely made by the λόγος character of Western thinking itself! Whenever European scholars should dare touch those alien worlds, they need to first ask themselves this question. Both the failure of the capacity to comprehend Asian thought and the demand for an awareness of this, come from the same source, the Western tradition itself.

Furthermore, in accordance with Heidegger's insight, the practice of making a Kantian out of Laozi cannot be attributed only to Wilhelm in particular and to Western Sinologists in general; contemporary Asian intellectuals are not exempt from it. Heidegger draws attention to the fact that the European way of thinking is becoming "planetary." This implies that the mode of experience and of thinking of contemporary Asian scholars is under strong European influences. The result is that their representation of Asian traditions is not pure and authentic. The dominance of a European framework of thinking leads to incautious identification or assimilation of Asian and European thought, such that Indian thinkers are described in analogy with English empiricists, and Laozi is represented as a Kantian. All this chaos is generated from the planetarization of European thinking.

In *Time and Being* (1962), Heidegger articulates similar considerations. He states,

> Being as presencing in the sense of calculable material . . . claims all the inhabitants of the earth in a uniform manner without the inhabitants of the non-European continents explicitly knowing this or even being able or wanting to know of the origin of this determination of Being. (*TB* 7/7)

For Heidegger, Being as presencing is essentially interrelated with the metaphysical mode of representation of European languages. Those people in the non-European continents are not excluded from the planetary expansion of this mode of determination of Being, even if they may not be aware of this, or have no intention to know anything about its origin. The matter is not just that European people have no access to Asian thought, but also that Asian people themselves, dominated by the planetary European mode of thinking, have no access to their own traditions either.

Now we are in a better position to understand Heidegger's saying in his conversation with Hecker, "*Sein und Zeit* has been translated into Japanese, but about the 'how' I cannot judge." As his lifelong friend Petzet records, in a conversation in his last years with a German scholar, Heidegger expressed skepticism about "what his Japanese friends made out of his philosophy," and said that he "has difficulty believing blindly that thoughts in a language so foreign would mean the same" (167). These utterances seem to imply a relativistic stance regarding the reverse side, that is, while European people have no access to Asian languages, Asian people (in this case, Japanese scholars) may not be able to gain adequate understanding of European thought because of linguistic barriers. However, with a view to what we have discussed in the foregoing, underlying Heidegger's comment on the Japanese translation of his work is something more complicated. It is most probably part of the suggestions of his remarks that, because of the domination of the European metaphysical dualistic framework of thinking over the Japanese mind, Japanese scholars may not be able to receive and convey the message from *Being and Time*. Inasmuch as European ways of thinking as determined by the logos character of their languages have become planetary, inasmuch as neither European nor Asian people have access to ancient Asian traditions, Heidegger describes the circumstances as "precarious" in his letter to the organizers of the Hawai'i conference.

The precondition for engaging with Asian languages is a dialogue with Greek thinkers. This is because the origin of Western metaphysical tradition resides in the first beginning initiated by Greek thinking and its language; at the same time, a possibility for reversal is also opened up. Despite occasional criticisms of Western languages, Heidegger has the conviction that only through these languages could one find possibilities of a true Saying. The other beginning of thinking is impossible without what is already present in what is said in the first beginning.[11] The way out of the dilemma where access to Asian traditions is lacking presupposes an engagement with the inceptual thinking of Greek thinkers and their language. As Heidegger clearly states in his lecture "Science and Reflection," "a dialogue with the Greek thinkers and their language . . . remains for us the precondition of the inevitable dialogue with the East Asian world" [1953b, 157/41].

Meanwhile, Heidegger seems to presuppose the existence of pure ancient traditions uncontaminated by a Western binary metaphysical framework of representation. In a letter to Hellmuth Hecker on 16 February 1955, Heidegger writes,

> That Buddhism and not less so Chinese and Japanese thought need a completely different interpretation, which is free from eighteenth and nineteenth century images, needs no further elucidation given my concerns about classic philosophy. However I lack the presuppositions for both.[12]

In saying this, Heidegger presupposes the existence of the other traditions uncontaminated by the *Ge-stell*. In suggesting that "Chinese and Japanese thought need a completely different interpretation" freed from eighteenth and nineteenth century images, Heidegger opposes himself radically against the Orientalist practice of selecting intellectual sources from Eastern tradition according to European interests and presenting them in conformity with European conceptual systems. However, Heidegger is not a simplistic anti-Orientalist.

What differentiates Heidegger from an anti-Orientalist is: for an anti-Orientalist, viewing things from the East in a limited European perspective represents a colonialist consciousness. Whether the Europeans are doomed world-historically to be relying on the Orientalist perspective remains unconsidered. In general, an anti-Orientalist would think that with the proper hindsight, it is possible and necessary to get rid of colonialist consciousness and understand other cultures in their own right. For Heidegger, the Orientalist attitude toward Asian traditions (for this matter) does not arise by accident, but world-historically out of the evolvement of the history of Being. It is a manifestation of the *Ge-stell*. Non-Western sources are not accessible in their true identity because of the *Ge-stell*.

Sometimes one can find in Heidegger's remarks the hint that the (empirical?) time will come when Eastern thought can be revealed to Western people in their authenticity. For example, in the conversation with Hecker on 30 August 1952, there is the following exchange:

Hecker: Surely, one can find important matters in oriental philosophy.

Heidegger: Certainly, but we have to develop the questions from (out of) our Western thinking. First our philosophy up to now has to become question-able. For the process of the encounter between West and East I estimate 300 years [will be needed]. (Hartig 1997, 269)

In insisting that a transformation has to be enacted from within Western thinking, because this is where the present problematic approach to Being has evolved, Heidegger seems to offer a crude un-Heideggerian estimation about the time span for the East to become available. It may not be completely a coincidence that the phrase "300 years" also occurs in the *Spiegel* interview in 1966. A digression on this episode may be helpful to grasp Heidegger's intent.

During that interview, a line of inquiry that the journalist is concerned to pursue is Heidegger's view on the relation between philosophy and the technological world, that is, whether the effectiveness of philosophy has come to an end, and whether philosophy, in particular Heidegger's new philosophy, has a bearing on social reality. Heidegger's reply is that there cannot be a direct transformation of the present situation of the world. His philosophy can only have an indirect effect on the world by means of awakening, clarifying and fortifying the readiness for the appearance of a god. In the context of this question, there is the following exchange:[13]

S: But you did not make clear in this conversation with the Buddhist monk just how this passing over into reality [*Verwirklichung*] takes place.

H: I cannot make this clear. I know nothing about how this thinking "has an effect [*wirkt*]." It may be that the path of thinking has today reached the point where silence is required to preserve thinking from being all jammed up just within a year. It may also be that it will take 300 years for it "to have an effect."

. . . . .

S: A clear answer. But can and may a thinker say: just wait and within the next 300 years something will occur to us?

H: It is not a matter simply of waiting until something occurs to man within the next 300 years, but of thinking ahead (without prophetic proclamations) into the time which is to come, of thinking from the standpoint of the fundamental traits of the present age, which have scarcely been thought through. [1966a, 109–110/675–76]

In response to the journalist's insistent pursuit of the question in what fashion philosophy, especially Heidegger's own thinking, can be of wholesome benefit to the modern world, Heidegger resorts to a suggestion of 300 years. When the journalist takes up the phrase 300 years to interrogate what he sees as an impoverishment in Heidegger's thinking, Heidegger sheds light on his speaking of 300 years. The underlying implication is that one needs to think in terms of the temporality that belongs to thinking and Being, to think from within the position of the essence of the present age. This means that one needs to think through the essence of the *Ge-stell;* simultaneously, one also needs to think ahead of the present age. From a futuristic perspective, one can see more clearly the urgency of excavating the untapped sources embedded in the Western tradition that constitute the other to the evolvement of this tradition, as well as the fact that this renovation should not be paralleled with a pre-mature interaction with non-Western traditions.

This clarification helps us better understand Heidegger's saying, "For the process of the encounter between West and East I estimate 300 years [will be needed]." In accordance with the structure of his account of temporality, what is to come is always yet to come; this is consistent with the statement that a thinker always remains on the way. Since it is indeterminate when the transformation of the Western tradition will be accomplished, it is also indeterminate when the time will come when European people can finally have access to non-Western sources. In this light, the presumption concerning the existence of these sources uncontaminated by the logos character of Western thinking is vague and vacuous. On the other hand, postponing East-West dialogue to an undeterminable future seems to offer him with justifications to evade addressing East-West dialogue in any detail. Still, as long as he keeps the guiding assumptions of his thought intact, even when an authentic East-West dialogue as he foresees should happen in the future, it would inevitably be visited by similar irreconcilable tensions and ambiguities. I will spell this point out in Chapter Nine.

In spite of all these problematics in Heidegger's general reflection on Asian languages, on various occasions he does encounter and approach concrete texts and words from Asian traditions. This is examined in the subsequent sections.

THE ATTEMPT AT TRANSLATING THE *DAODEJING*

One of the most well-known cases of Heidegger's engagement with ancient Chinese language was his collaboration with Paul Shih-Yi Hsiao (1911–1986), to translate some verses from the *Daodejing* in the summer of 1946.[14] Both the reality and significance of Heidegger's collaboration with Hisao have been a matter of controversy. Some insist that it is completely a fabrication, for example, Hermann Heidegger (Heidegger's son) and Cheung (1998). Some attribute abundant significance to this story and spare no efforts in reading Laozi's ideas into Heidegger's writings after this event, for example Cho (1993). In my view, this incident is not without any factual basis, since Heidegger himself mentions it in one of his letters to Jaspers in 1949 (see below).

According to Pöggeler, the reason why Heidegger's family members deny the factuality of this event might be that, if Heidegger should be said to have studied and commented on the *Laozi* (that is, the *Daodejing*) without knowing the relevant language, this might give rise to another scandal following the one concerning his involvement with the Nazis.[15] Furthermore, in denying the factuality of the translation attempt, Herman Heidegger is concerned to deny Heidegger's relation with Hsiao (Pöggeler 1999, 106). This is because, in his report on his collaboration with Heidegger, Hsiao mentions the rumor prevalent at Freiburg at that time that he avoided meeting Edith Stein, Husserl's student and assistant.[16] In my opinion, it is unreasonable to disown Heidegger's transitory attempt at translating the *Daodejing* on the basis of non-academic considerations. On the other hand, it may be far-fetched and unconvincing to make a Laozi out of Heidegger on the basis of the actuality of this event and a highly inventive interpretation of Heidegger's texts.[17]

According to Hsiao's report of his meeting with Heidegger, Hsiao studied psychology and Chinese philosophy while in China and then went to

Milan for further studies at the University of the Sacro Cuore. He attended
some seminars Heidegger was invited to give there in 1942. Already at that
time Hsiao presented Heidegger with parts of his Italian translation of the
Daodejing (Siao 1941). According to Heidegger's letter to Jaspers in August
1949 (see below), Hsiao attended his lectures on Heraclitus and Parmenides
in Freiburg in 1943–44. When he met Heidegger again at the Holzmarktplatz in Freiburg in the spring of 1946, Heidegger was still under the control
of the unpleasant process of de-Nazification. Believing that he was suffering
from injustice, Hsiao tried to console him with some words of Mencius.[18]
Seeming to be moved by these words, Heidegger suggested that they cooper-
ate in translating the *Daodejing* into German in his cabin at Todtnauberg in
that summer. After Hsiao left for other commitments when the summer of
1946 ended, this attempt was not followed up.[19]

Their translation started with the chapters concerning *dao*.[20] According
to Hsiao's account,

> Heidegger had essentially inquired—and asked penetratingly, tirelessly, and
> mercilessly—about every imaginable context of meaning in the mysterious
> interplay of the symbolic relations within the text. (Hsiao 1987, 98)

Heidegger was perhaps resorting to the same methods of attending to the
field and context of key words as in his close analysis of the writings by early
Greek thinkers. One can also explain his endeavour from the perspective of
his view of translation. According to Heidegger, translating (*übersetzen*) in
its ordinary sense is a passing-over into a foreign language with the help of
one's own language; in such a case, the emphasis falls upon *setzen,* to convey.
Translation in its originary sense is an "awakening, clarifying, and unfolding of one's own language by coming to grips [*Auseinandersetzung*] with the
foreign language" (*HHI* 65–66/80). In such a case, the emphasis falls upon
über. Authentic translating is a crossing-over (*über-setzen*) to another shore of
one's own mother tongue. It refers to re-appropriating and transmitting of
the forgotten or covered-up depth of the whole history of one's own language
by means of an encounter with a foreign language.

From the perspective of this idea of originary translation, it could be
presumed that Heidegger's interest in translating the *Daodejing* may not so
much reside in venturing into the ancient Chinese language than attempting
to encounter fresh stimulations of insights into his own language through a
creative understanding and interpretation of a foreign language, in particular, an ancient language with a sustained history. In other words, Heidegger
is probably less motivated to understand Laozi than to discover in it what he

had already contemplated himself, or to obtain inspirations for alternative expressions. Hsiao admits feeling "unsettled" with what Heidegger was doing with the *Daodejing*. He suspected that Heidegger's practice "might perhaps go beyond what is called for in a translation" (Hsiao 1987, 98).

Apart from Hsiao's record, Heidegger himself mentioned this event in a letter dated 12 August 1949, in response to Jaspers' saying in a previous letter that he (Jaspers) believes "to have perceived something of this in Asia" in a few recent writings by Heidegger. Heidegger writes,

> What you say about the Asiatic is exciting [*aufregend*]: a Chinese [that is, Hsiao] who came to my lectures on Heraclitus and Parmenides in 1943–44 (I gave at that time only one-hour interpretations of a few fragments) likewise found resonances with Eastern thinking. I remain sceptical where I am not at home in the language; I became even more sceptical when the Chinese, who is himself a Christian theologian and philosopher, translated with me a few words [*einige Worte*] of Lao Tze. Through questioning, I came to realise how alien the whole nature of language already is for us; we then gave up the attempt. (*HJC* 172/181; tr. m.)

This is the only occasion where Heidegger refers to the attempt of translation.[21] It is his realization that Chinese language is completely alien to his European understanding that led to the end of this attempt. In saying this, he almost diminishes any importance of his involvement with translating the *Daodejing*. According to Walter Biemel, Heidegger admitted to him that it was because of his different view of translation from Hsiao that he decided to give up their cooperation.[22] Heidegger paid attention to representing the originariness of the text, while Hsiao emphasized faithfulness to the original text, which, to Heidegger, was equal to forcing the original into the system of Western concepts. Biemel's account accords with the preceding discussion touching their different ideas about translation.

Of all the commentators, Pöggeler's position is the most balanced one. He affirms the positive influence that this encounter with the original Chinese text exerted on Heidegger's style of philosophizing (1987a, 52). However, he broke off his concern with Laozi and sought possibilities of the other beginning in Europe, for example, in the paintings of Paul Klee (Pöggeler 1989, 11n3). In a discussion at the conference held in München on 10–12 January 1989, Biemel supported Pöggeler's position that Heidegger soon gave up mediating on Laozi.[23] In 1999, Pöggeler re-affirms that the *Daodejing* provides "a temporary assistance on [Heidegger's] own path of thinking" (1999, 112). In the following, I offer my own analysis of what could be called a second Heidegger case.

In my view, two sides need to be taken into account as regards Heidegger's involvement with the Chinese language. One is that Heidegger does ponder over whether or not ancient Chinese language shares something similar with what he has been considering. Another occasion of his encounter with the Chinese language is reported by Chang Chung-yuan, who participated in the Hawai'i conference in Heidegger's honour in 1969. During their meeting on 18 August 1972, in reference to the idea of identity of language with Being, Heidegger asked him whether this also occurs in the ancient Chinese language. He also asks Chang how to say "this is a tree" and "this is an old tree" in Chinese. Using expressions steeped in Heidegger's thought, Chang responded that the latter expressions show that the being of the speaker and his utterance are totally identified, or "belong together" (1977c, 68).[24] Hartig provides a similar account of this meeting allegedly on the basis of a piece of manuscript in German from Heidegger's *Nachlass*. According to this account, Chang Chung-yuan and Heidegger talked about Chinese language, in which a sentence can be without subject and verb. Heidegger was pleased that in Chinese being and thinking (whose nature is similar to that of language) are identical, as with Parmenides (Hartig 1997, 151–52).[25]

Assuming that these records are reliable, Heidegger seems to be wondering about whether ancient Chinese language manifests certain features that he had been trying to articulate in terms of the nature of language. This may well have been in his mind when he engaged Hsiao with penetrating questions about Laozi's verses, and in particular about the word *dao*. However, one needs to be cautious about making any strong claim in terms of the importance Heidegger attaches to the Chinese language (and Asian languages in general). There is another side that should be taken into account in this connection.

In spite of occasional or improvisatory ponderings and explorations, in his letter to Jaspers, Heidegger confesses to be "sceptical" where he is "not at home in the language." It is through the attempt at translating "a few words" of Laozi that he came to the conclusion that "the whole nature" of Chinese language is extremely alien to his European understanding. In addition, in view of his emphasis on originary translation as a matter of re-appropriating the forgotten recesses of one's mother tongue, it is wrong-headed to claim that understanding the *Daodejing* in Laozi's own terms is the primary objective that Heidegger sets for himself in dipping into this ancient scripture.

Heidegger may have hoped that discussing and translating the *Daodejing* could be of help for reviving the worn-out metaphysical language.

However, insofar as his primary motivation in dealing with the *Daodejing* is concerned, he does not need to render his reflections on it into the form of a translation in the ordinary sense of the word. It would be sufficient to integrate the linguistic resources he could obtain into his philosophical essays.

This practice, even when he cites directly from the *Daodejing*, does not contradict Heidegger's claim that the nature of Chinese language is totally different, and that not being at home with this language, he lacks the requisites for addressing Chinese thought. This is because what is at stake is not so much what Laozi would really think, or whether Laozi would think otherwise, but the ways in which his verses could fit nicely into the whole textual and meditative space Heidegger creates in his writings. Therefore, appropriating verses from the *Daodejing* does not interrupt Heidegger's overall philosophical enterprise of thinking more radically of what remains unthought in the first beginning of philosophy in order to re-enact the other beginning.

To be fair to Heidegger, it need be mentioned that, following what has already been cited from his letter to Jaspers, he continues,

> Nevertheless, something exciting lies here and, as I believe, something essential for the future, when, after centuries, the devastation has been overcome. The resonances presumably have an entirely different root. (*HJC* 172/181; em. or.)

I have already analyzed what is at stake in Heidegger's postponing the possibility of truly grasping Asian ideas to an indeterminate future. This fleeting remark well reflects this idea. After this remark, Heidegger insists that the resonances with Asian ideas that some scholars allege to perceive in his thinking come from an entirely different root, that is, from Eckhardt, Parmenides, and other Greek thinkers.

IS THERE A JAPANESE WORD FOR ART?

Another major episode of Heidegger's involvement with Asian languages is a colloquium on the theme "Art and Thinking" that he co-held with Hisamatsu Shinichi at Freiburg on 18 May 1958.[26] Hisamatsu met Heidegger at Vienna where Heidegger presented his lecture "Poetry and Thinking" on 11 May 1958. When they met again at Freiburg, they held a colloquium on art and thinking. This meeting has rarely been noted and discussed. Through its investigation, we can obtain a clearer picture of Heidegger's attitude toward Asian languages.

The other participants included Hermann Gundert, Max Müller and Siegfried Bröse (these three from the University of Freiburg), Egon Vietta (from the University of Darmstadt), L. Alcopley, and an unidentified person referred to as Y. A record of this colloquium with the focus on Heidegger's contribution can be found in *Japan und Heidegger* (*KD* 211–15). The more detailed proceedings were edited by Alcopley and published in a slim tri-lingual (English, German, and Japanese) limited edition, entitled *Listening to Heidegger and Hisamatsu* (1963) with some pieces of Alcopley's Zen-inspired artwork.[27]

Heidegger opened the colloquium by saying, "We would like to, from our European standpoint, make an attempt to grasp certain characteristics of the nature [*Wesenszüge*] of art" (*KD* 211). After claiming that whether art still occupies a place in this age is a pressing question, he presented the opening question: "how that, which we call East Asian art, is understood in itself." As we well see below Heidegger's concern is with the existence of ancient (or at least pre-modern) Asian intellectual sources that are uncontaminated by Western influences. Heidegger probed further,

> In concrete terms we shall ask, keeping in mind the great variety within the East Asian world, whether it is at all possible to speak of art and art work in our sense [*Sinn*] of the word. Do you have a name [*Name*] for art in Japan?" (*KD* 211)

Heidegger seemed to be challenging the legitimacy of applying the terms art and artwork, which are of Western origin, to East Asian art; he seemed to be keen to excavate genuine characteristics of East Asian art as distinct from Western conceptual transplantations. However, Heidegger's focus swiftly moved to the inquiry whether there is a word in the Japanese language that corresponds to the Western word "art."

In response to Heidegger's inquiry, Gundert suggested a reversal of Heidegger's way of questioning. With this reversal, one does not take what are taken to be art and art work in the West as the absolute starting point. Instead, one considers whether objects or phenomena treated as art in the West would be accepted as such from the perspective of East Asian people. Gundert added that this is a matter of frequent disputation in Japan. At Gundert's contestation, Heidegger responded,

> To answer that question one would have to question the notion of art radically. We confine ourselves here to the preliminaries [*ein vorläufiges*]. Is there a Japanese word for what we call art? (*KD* 211)

Heidegger's way of inquiring is strikingly similar to that in "A Dialogue." Before the question about the Japanese word for language is brought forth, one reads,

> J: . . . How, then, could our reflection get out into the open?
>
> I: Most easily if from the very outset [*Anfang*] we do not demand too much. Thus I shall permit myself for the moment to put to you an altogether preliminary [*durchaus vorläufige*] question. (*DL* 23/113)

Heidegger's formulation of his questioning is,

> What does the Japanese world understand [*verstehen*] by language? Asked still more cautiously: Do you have in your language a word for what we call language? If not, how do you experience what with us is called language? (*DL* 23/113)

In asking these questions, Heidegger does not concern himself with the more primordial questions such as whether or not language is considered as central for life in Japanese thought. His inquiry consists of three interconnected questions. First, how language is understood in the Japanese world? This question assumes a certain determinate identity of language. The following two questions are relatively qualified: Is there a word in Japanese that names what the European people call language? If there is not such a word, how do the Japanese people experience what is called language?[28]

At the colloquium on art and thinking, it is in fact Gundert's proposal that comes nearest to breaking through the confines of Eurocentrism. Despite Heidegger's quasi-anti-Orientalist gestures, his practice of asking whether there is a Japanese word for what Europeans call art remains within the "European standpoint," which he presented as the general framework of questioning for this colloquium.

To Heidegger's repeated question, Hisamatsu replies that the Japanese word for art is *geijiz* (that is, *geijutsu*), a compound word: *gei* originally means capacity (*Können*) and skilfulness (*Kunstfertigkeit*). At the end of the nineteenth century, this compound word *geijiz* (*geijutsu*) was coined as a translation, or representation (*Wiedergabe*), of the Western aesthetic concept of art. The Japanese have adopted Western notions and rendered them with words taken from their own tradition. Concerned with the pre-modern form and the original experience of art, Heidegger interrogates searchingly,

> What preceded these adaptations? Was it a picture they saw in a work of art? Which was their original experience of art before the adoption of European concepts? This is the interesting point. (*KD* 212)

Heidegger seems to be very earnest in finding out the primitive word that is occluded from modern European influences. In response, Hisamatsu cites an older word for art, *geidō,* which he considers as lying beyond European influences. Literally, *geidō* means the way of *gei* (as elucidated above); *dō* is equivalent to the Chinese word *dao.* As Hisamatsu explains, *dō* has the connotation of way, or method. It also refers to nature and life. Given Heidegger's special interest in the Chinese word *dao,* it is surprising that he does not pursue the connection of the Japanese word for art with *dao.*

Heidegger's phrase "our sense of the word [art]" has to be understood with caution. It is well known that Heidegger opposes himself against the metaphysical conception of art as involving a subject-object relation, and proposes a view of art as what shelters truth, as "the letting happen of the advent of the truth of beings" [1935–36, 44/59]. In order to overcome the former misleading conception of art, understandably he is motivated to know how art is understood in the old Asian traditions, where, as he must have often been informed by his numerous Japanese visitors, is absent the dualistic metaphysical framework of representation. In these traditions, he may be able to find ideas about art that are distinct from metaphysical conceptions (and thus in a sense do not fit with current Western terminology of art and art work), and at the same time suit well his innovative notion of art, or lend an aid to his philosophizing. For example, as Heidegger mentioned in the same colloquium, East Asian art sees representation as a hindrance that will be removed once one has reached the source (*KD* 213). Also, the picture is neither a symbol nor visual imagery; rather, in painting or writing one sets in motion the movement toward the self.

However, it is Heidegger's deep-seated belief that, fundamentally speaking, overcoming metaphysics can only be achieved from within the Western philosophical tradition itself; a genuine questioning of a tradition can only come from within. Therefore, any inquiry about non-Western sources has to start from the European standpoint. To turn the inquiry the other way around, to set as the aim an examination how East Asian people would think of what is taken to be art in the West (as Gundert suggested), for Heidegger, would lead to putting the whole of Western tradition in question in an external way, that is, from the standpoint of East Asia.

This is why Heidegger insisted that the participants keep to what he calls the preliminaries by asking whether there is a word in Japanese for what is called art in Europe. It could be said that Heidegger's philosophical enterprise remains immanent in that radical questioning is always evaded. He is not ready to subject existing key notions and themes from the Western tradition to external challenges. This account of Heidegger' view holds true even when in the same colloquium Heidegger made two extraordinary favourable remarks about East Asian art: one is, ". . . what we have been searching for so far, is already in place in Japan—the Japanese actually have it" (*KD* 214); another remark is made in concluding the colloquium:

> It has become clear that we, with our preconceived ideas, namely, the conception of art as following a direct and steady path, cannot arrive at the point the Japanese have already reached. (*KD* 215)

The first remark suggests the existence of pure Japanese tradition uncontaminated by modernity. As I discussed in the previous section, this presupposition is inevitably vague and vacuous. The second remark is consistent with Heidegger's general attitude toward Asian languages: Contemporary (European) thinking is not yet mature enough to confront what is present in traditional Japanese thinking. A genuine understanding of East Asian traditions can only become possible after the West has renewed its tradition in the indeterminate future. Before that, it could be said either that because of linguistic difficulties these traditions are inaccessible, or that Europeans have not yet acquired the proper means for investigating these advanced questions.

ENCOUNTER WITH THE SANSKRIT LANGUAGE AND INDIAN THOUGHT

Despite the amount of comparative studies of Heidegger's philosophy and Indian traditions, there are very few references to Indian thought or language in his writings. In 1952, Heidegger mentioned Indian philosophy once, but only to point out that, together with Chinese philosophy, it is not philosophy (*WCT* 224/228). In the lecture series "Principles of Thinking," he made a charitable gesture in saying that the statement that (Western) thinking is determined by and attuned to *logos* does not imply that "the ancient world of the Indies, China and Japan remained without thought," and pointed to the situation where "the ancient Indians" were presented as English empiricists [1957a, 145]. In his commentary on Hölderlin's poems, he uses such phrases as "depths of Asia," "the Indies," "the rivers of the Indians and the Greeks."[29] According to J. L. Mehta (1987), a partial explanation of this neglect of Indian thought is Heidegger's critical attitude toward neo-Kantian presuppositions with which most of his older contemporaries approached Eastern thought; in addition, as an Indo-European language, Sanskrit also involves a subject-object structure that tends to promote metaphysical thinking.

In the 1960s, because of his contact with the Swiss psychiatrist Medard Boss (1903–1990), Heidegger develops a serious interest in Indian philosophy and the Sanskrit language. This is revealed mainly in the *Zollikon Seminars,* edited by Medard Boss. Boss' friendship with Heidegger started through correspondence in 1947, while Heidegger was still in a difficult situation. By the time of his death, Heidegger had sent Boss 256 letters and 50 greeting cards. From 1959 to the end of the 1960s, at Boss' invitation, Heidegger gave seminars to 50 to 70 psychiatrists or psychiatry students on a regular basis. Boss recorded these seminars as well as his conversations with Heidegger. In this collection Boss also includes edited versions of Heidegger's handwritten drafts for the seminars and letters addressed to him.[30]

Boss used Heidegger's philosophy to construct his own theory of medicine and psychiatry, which he called *Daseinsanalytik* as distinguished from psychoanalysis. He also took a strong interest in Indian thought. In 1956, as professor of psychotherapy at Zurich University, Boss was invited to work for five months as guest lecturer in a psychiatric clinic in India, and then at an Indonesian University for a further month. His second visit to India lasted three months in 1958. During his two trips to India, Boss underwent apprenticeship with a guru in Kashmir associated with the line of Kashmiri Shaivism. His knowledge of Indian thought was also deepened by means of intensive correspondence with his Indian friends. Boss' theory about dream is obviously influenced by Indian ideas.[31]

In a letter on 9 November 1959, probably commenting on his meeting with Boss a few days before, Heidegger said, "the talk about India showed me that my attempts do not remain totally isolated" (*ZS* 254/318). Probably, Boss had drawn his attention to affinities between his thinking and Indian philosophy. In another letter to Boss on 7 March 1960, Heidegger asked him to find out and share with him Sanskrit words for "ontological difference," that is, as Heidegger explained, for "Being" and "beings," and for "unconcealedness" (*Unverborgenheit*) and "forgetfulness" (*Vergessenheit*) (*ZS* 254/318–19). On 12 March Boss contacted his colleague and former student Erna M. Hoch, who was working in India.[32] In this letter, Boss mentioned that a few weeks before he wrote to Professor K. C. Pandey of Lucknow University, a Sanskrit scholar and also a philosopher,[33] to inquire about the Sanskrit equivalents of these terms; but failed to receive a reply. In this circumstance, he asked Hoch, who had visited Pandey previously, to make a face-to-face inquiry. It seems that Heidegger had already asked about the Sanskrit words before 7 March 1960. The letter on 7 March 1960 may well be a reminder of his special assignment.

The first time Hoch discussed her visits to Prof. Pandey in print was on the occasion of the eightieth birthday of Boss in October 1983. She wrote a paper in German on the basis of her notes in English typescript of 1960 when she was sent on special errands on behalf of Heidegger. This paper was published in the journal *Daseinsanalyse* in 1985.[34] In his letter to Hoch, Boss wrote:

> These days, when Heidegger comes to stay with me, he shows more and more interest in Indian thought. He regrets in particular that he has no knowledge of Sanskrit. He now has asked me to inquire what would be the Sanskrit of some fundamental terms and concepts. Above all, he wishes to know whether the Sanskrit language can distinguish between Being [*Sein*] and beings [*Seiendes*].[35]

Boss made a few preliminary suggestions about these words and reminded Hoch, for his own sake and for that of Heidegger, to pay attention to exploring the meaning of those words right down to the connotations of the Sanskrit roots (Hoch, 252–53).

Hoch visited Pandey on 20 March 1960 and reported back to Boss. On receiving Boss' reply on 10 April, with a long list of detailed questions regarding her notes of discussion with Pandey, Hoch visited Pandey on 15 May once again. According to Hoch's report, there are two different roots for being in the sense of the mode of being of individual beings: one is *as* from which only forms in the present tense can be derived, such as *sat, sattā*. It expresses the fact of being as such. Another is *bhū* from which can be derived verbal forms pertaining to the past and the future, such as *bhāvana*. It indicates change, transformation and development. The suffix *tā*, meaning "capacity, power, possibility," is normally added to nouns and adjectives to form abstract nouns; so *sattā*, being a noun, means the "possibility or power to be, being capable of being everything." The Sanskrit word for the highest Being is *Mahāsattā* (*mahā* meaning "great, big"). Literally it means "the absolute possibility of being." It is infinite, unlimited and unchanging.[36] Hoch concluded that Sanskrit thus gives expression to what Heidegger calls the ontological difference (285). Furthermore, the words for "concealedness" and "unconcealedness" are *āvṛtatva* and *anāvṛtatva* respectively. The root of these words is *vṛ*, or *var*, which means the original condition. Hoch commented that Indian philosophy knows these notions as well; however, it is difficult to establish relations of congruence with Heidegger's thought (287).

In a letter on 22 May 1960, Boss told Hoch that Heidegger was "extremely impressed" by the Indian view of Being and truth; yet, there is nothing more in terms of Heidegger's response than that (282). Following the foregoing reference to Heidegger, Boss immediately turned to his own view on the basis of Hoch's record. According to him, these inquiries reveal "the decisive difference" between ancient Indian thought and Heidegger's philosophy. This difference resides in the "fundamentally different thinking about the role of 'human being' within the total 'event' of 'Being'" (282). We will see this point again in a short while.

In view of the richness of Hoch's report, it is somewhat surprising that Heidegger has never commented in his writing or speech on the Sanskrit words he learned in this connection. In the seminar on Heraclitus held together with Eugen Fink in 1966–67, when discussing the nature of sleep in connection with Fragment 26 of Heraclitus, Heidegger commented, "For Indians the state of sleep is the supreme life."[37] This remark most probably has come from his acquaintance with Indian thought through Boss and Hoch. Involved in the latter's report are discussions of the state of deep sleep.[38]

On a few occasions in his discussion with Boss, Heidegger stresses that there is a fundamental difference between his philosophy and Eastern thought. In a conversation with Boss in the period 24 April—4 May 1963, during their vacation together in Taormina, Sicily, when Heidegger was talking about Being and Dasein, Boss spoke of how Indians would think about these issues, "Indian thought does not require a guardian for the clearing. There is clearing in and for itself. . . . " (*ZS* 178/224). Boss rightly saw that with Indians the human being does not assume such an important role as Heidegger ascribes to it, that is, as a guardian of Being. Heidegger concurred,

> In contrast, it is very important to me that the human being is a *human* being. In Indian thought, the point is "a giving up of being human" in the sense of Da-sein's self-transformation into the pure luminosity [of Being]. (*ZS* 178/224; em. or.)

In this place Heidegger put his finger on the right point. The role of human beings is in fact conceived very differently in Western and Eastern traditions. After Heidegger's lengthy elaboration of his own thoughts, Boss asked him in what ways his conception of the matter of Being was more adequate than Indian thought, which, as Boss repeated, does not need a guardian of clearedness. Heidegger responded:

> My conception is more adequate, insofar as I am proceeding from Dasein and from [its] understanding of being, and insofar as I limit myself

to what *can be experienced immediately.* Thus, I do not need assert anything about clearedness itself. . . . Above all, the above quoted Indian
insight cannot be assimilated into my thinking. (*ZS* 180/225; em. or.)

In spite of Heidegger's interest in Sanskrit words corresponding to his
key notions such as Being and beings, and unconcealedness, he knew very
well the important difference between his philosophy and Indian ideas and
insisted that his conception is more adequate. A staunch defender for Heidegger's special bond with the Chinese *dao* (such as Cho or Chang) would
possibly take to be trivial his saying that the relevant *Indian* insight cannot
be assimilated into his thinking. However, Chinese Daoist thinking is also
opposed to granting the human being the most supreme status and to setting
up an abysmal gap between the human being and other beings. Therefore,
Heidegger's disclaimer can very well be extended to Chinese Daoist thinking.
    In response to Heidegger's speech cited in the foregoing, Boss quoted
the Indian insight that not only the essence of the human being, but also the
essence of all other beings belong immediately to the clearedness in itself.
Heidegger reiterated the fundamental difference between humans and other
beings in reference to the criterion of whether or not they possessed language.
He explained that *hellen* (to clear) occurs originally as *hallen* (to resound), as
tone, and stressed that all other beings fall short of this grounding tone. Following this, he put forward a rhetorical question invoking his famous claim
about language, which concluded this conversation: "How close this is to
Indian insights into ultimate truths is best shown by my assertion: 'Language
is the house of being'" (*ZS* 181/226).
    The stress on the centrality of language is in a way a corollary of the
emphasis on the unique status of the human being. Again, this idea is lacking in the majority of Asian traditions. For example, as Weinmayr points
out, in Japanese thinking, language is regarded as a practice among other
ones. He characterizes this view as lococentrism. In contrast, logocentrism is
essential to European languages. In the latter case language is regarded as the
"one site of truth," and is separated from other practices (1989, 185).
    In this chapter I have revealed and assessed Heidegger's various remarks
on and approaches to Asian languages. How are we to understand the seemingly irreconcilable suggestions and implications of his comportment toward
Asian languages? Why does he insist on highlighting the fact that he has
no access to these languages while occasionally engaging with these alien
languages, such as, requesting information about the Japanese word for art,
about counterpart Sanskrit words for some of the key notions that he has
been concerned to develop, attempting at translating "a few words" from the

Daodejing, and assimilating Laozi's verses to his writings. Notwithstanding the latter, Heidegger has always held onto his fundamental tenets and orientation of thinking, that is, a reversal of the current situation, where Western dualistic metaphysical thinking has become planetary and ancient Asian inheritance remains inaccessible to either European or contemporary Asian intellectuals. This reversal or the "other beginning" can only be achieved from the very origin that gives rise to these "precarious" circumstances. In other words, the most urgent task is for the Western philosophical tradition to transform itself from within, to reconfigure what was said in the first beginning. Because of this historical necessity, in stating that anything "authentically" Asiatic is inaccessible, Heidegger is not simply articulating a matter of fact, but is observing a matter of normativity. The project of reversal has to proceed without any genuine challenge from the Asiatic.

Heidegger may have assimilated a few specific words and verses from Asian intellectual sources into some of his writings. On a positive note, it can be said that he has initiated a Heideggerian style of reading Asian classics and of interpreting Asian ideas analogous to his approach to Western classical thinkers. However, Heidegger's interest in Asian words and verses is limited to the motivation of finding support for his own preconceived ideas. Throughout all his inquiries about Asian words and encounter with Asian sources, Heidegger has never thought of modifying his central ideas in light of the insight from other traditions; for example, the idea that language is central for the notions of clearing and thinking, or the idea that the human being assumes an indispensable role as the guardian of Being. Because of the "preliminary" character of his queries, because of his insistence that those queries be made from a European perspective, requesting certain items of information about Asian languages neither conflict with nor detract from the central thrust of Heidegger's thinking.

Chapter Eight
Japanese Themes in "A Dialogue on Language"

Among Heidegger's writings "A Dialogue on Language: Between a Japanese and an Inquirer" is a highly complicated text. The heavy involvement of prominent Japanese themes in particular adds to its complexity. In the following I present the major contents of this essay in accordance with a six-section thematic partition.[1]

Section one (1–5:13) serves as the prelude to the whole essay, introducing Kuki and the Japanese aesthetic notion *iki*, and the "danger" involved in discussing *iki* in European languages. Since the language in which *iki* is explained shifts everything into European conceptual systems, the Inquirer fails to experience what is said in *iki*. At this point, the phrase "language is the house of Being" is invoked, from which is derived the saying that "a dialogue from house to house remains nearly impossible" (*DL* 5/90).

Section two (5:14–13:17) can be seen as an excursus of Heidegger's intellectual development, to which more is added in section four. The Inquirer's memoir is prompted by the question: what had motivated Kuki to study with him in Germany? He recalls the first time when he came across the question of Being as far back as 1907. The Inquirer makes the famous remark whether his reflection on the nature of language is "also" adequate for the nature of East Asian languages (8/94). Correspondingly, the Japanese raises the question about an authentic explanation of hermeneutics (11/98).

Section three (13:18–21:15) resumes the topic on the danger of explaining *iki* in European languages. Inquiries are made about the Japanese notions *iro* (*shiki*) and *kū*, the film *Rashōmon*, and the *Nō* play. When the discussion comes to the *Nō* play, a turn in the dialogue occurs. The stress on the inaccessibility of *iki* is toned down.

In section four (21:16–28:13) deliberations return concerning the phrase "language is the house of Being." While searching for a suitable word for the nature of language, or for hermeneutics, the Inquirer raises the question about the Japanese word for the nature of language. Admitting that such a word exists, the Japanese interlocutor nevertheless refrains from its immediate disclosing. This is because this word, as a hint, needs to have the possibility of "swinging widely" (27/119). In order for the space of swinging freely to be opened, the Inquirer suggests that they change roles: let the Japanese be the inquirer, and let himself answer the question about hermeneutics raised in section two. In this section, it is pronounced that there is a "kinship" (*Verwandtschaft*) between the suspended Japanese word for language and the Inquirer's phrase that language is the house of Being (24/114).

In section five (28:14–44:last line), the Inquirer describes his thinking on hermeneutics as the shining forth of Being and man's correspondence to Being's call. It is revealed that the two central questions of "A Dialogue," the one about hermeneutics and the one about the Japanese word for language, ask "the Same" (*das Selbe*) (30/123). At the end of this section, an explanation of *iki* is provided. This paves the way for the elucidation of the Japanese word for language.

Section six (45–54) is almost a monologue in the literal sense, with little differentiation between the two roles of the Japanese interlocutor and the Inquirer. The Japanese word for language (*kotoba*) is eventually disclosed (45/142), followed by "a more fitting word" for the nature of language: *die Sage* (47/145). The notion of dialogue is elaborated on the basis of the assumption that both *kotoba* and *die Sage* say the "Same" (52/151).

It can be seen that "A Dialogue" is interspersed with quite a few Japanese themes, namely, the aesthetic notion of *iki,* the Japanese word for language (*kotoba*), the film *Rashōmon* and the *Nō* play, as well as the Buddhist notions *shiki* and *kū.* In what follows, I consider these themes in relation to their broad background in Japanese culture, and show how they are broached and domesticated in Heidegger's essay. In the first section on *iki,* I reveal a hardly noted asymmetry in Heidegger's treatment of European languages and Japanese language. The relation between Heidegger's notion of the "Nothing" (*das Nichts*) and the Buddhist idea of "emptiness" or "Nothing" (*śūnyatā* in Sanskrit; *kong* 空 in Chinese and *kū* 空 in Japanese) is perhaps the trickiest issue. Sometimes Heidegger emphasizes their fundamental difference; sometimes, particularly in "A Dialogue," he suggests their close similarity.

IKI AND THE DANGER OF DIALOGUE

Iki refers to the aesthetic sensibility of a merchant class that was developed in the pleasure quarters in the Edo period of Japan (1603–1867).[2] According to Hisamatsu (1963, 64), the word *iki* comes from ideas concerning living, breath, going, and spirits or temperament.[3] He explains,

> [*Iki*] can be thought of as an aesthetic complex—connotatively, as combining outward coquetry with inner boredom; denotatively, as embracing such contrasting qualities as refinement and coarseness, or showiness and restraint. (Hisamatsu 1963, 64)

Among the three major rubrics of aesthetic tastes Hisamatsu lists, that is, humour (*kokkei*), sublimity (*sobi*), and elegance (*yubi*), *iki* falls into the last category, elegance.

Kuki's work on *iki* is in no way a simplistic application of traditional European aesthetics to Japanese art, as Heidegger suggests in the beginning of "A Dialogue."[4] He appropriates Heidegger's ideas with respect to the relation between a language and a people. He writes,

> [L]anguage is nothing but the self-manifestation of the past and present mode of being of a people, and the self-unfolding of a specific culture endowed with history . . . The relations between the two indicate organic compositional relations where the whole prescribes the part. (Kuki 1997, 28)

Evidently, a language and the "being of a people" are conceived in a holistic fashion, each incarnated into the other. The idea of coincidence between ethnic and linguistic boundary strikes one as similar to aspects of Heidegger's reflection on language, which can be traced back to von Humboldt's view of language.[5]

Kuki argues that *iki* is one of the Japanese words that are integrally embedded in the Japanese ways of being. There is no word in European languages that covers all the shades of meaning of *iki*. Its complete meaning is beyond that of such words as raffiné, elegant and coquettish. *Iki* is not an abstract concept, but a distinctive ethnic consciousness that penetrates the minutest areas of the life of the Japanese people. His study of *iki* purports to present "the hermeneutics of ethnic being" (Kuki, 118).[6]

Employing terminology and methodology from phenomenology, Kuki provides a complex representation of *iki*. Under the heading "intensional structure of *iki*," he considers *iki* to be a phenomenon of consciousness that involves spiritual qualities of Buddhist resignation or detachment from the world of evanescence, and the noble spirit derived from *bushidō* loyalty. He also investigates the extensional, objective expression of *iki* and examines the natural and artistic expression of *iki*.

The notion of *iki* appears in the very beginning of "A Dialogue" and recurs frequently. The Inquirer starts by describing his sense of impenetrability of *iki*. He states, "In my dialogues [*Gesprächen*] with Kuki, it was always the case that I could only have an inkling of what that word says from a distance [*aus der Ferne*]" (2/85).

In other words, he could not find his feet with Kuki when he tried to explain *iki*.[7] This stems from the incompatibility between European languages and conceptual systems and the Japanese world of art and poetry. Kuki attempted to "consider [*betrachten*] the nature of Japanese art with the help of European aesthetics" (2/86).[8] However, deeply rooted in European thinking, aesthetics is completely alien to Japanese ideas. As a result, "the proper nature of East Asian art is concealed [*verdeckt*] and shunted into a realm inappropriate to it" (14/102).

For Heidegger, Kuki's practice is not unrelated with the pervasive pro-European trends in Japan. Since the encounter with the European world, the majority of Japanese scholars consider that Western aesthetics can provide the necessary conceptual apparatus for comprehending and illustrating the basic concerns of their art and poetry (2/86).[9] Coupled with this consideration is the opinion that the Japanese language lacks classifying and conceptualizing capacity. As a result, there is a superficial East-West encounter in which East Asian people "chase after [*nachzujagen*] European conceptual systems" (3/87). In addition, the sweeping power of the modern technical world has encompassed every continent such that any encounter has been restricted to what is foregrounded (*Vordergründige*). Therefore, in spite of plenty of "assimilations" (*Angleichungen*) and "intermixtures" (*Vermischungen*), a "true encounter" (*wahrhafte Begegnung*) with European existence (*Dasein*) does not happen, and "perhaps cannot happen" (3/87).[10]

After revealing the danger (*Gefahr*) that the abundance of European categories mislead the Japanese people to depreciate what claims (*in den Anspruch nimmt*) their existence (*Dasein*), the Inquirer draws attention to a much more enormous danger. It threatens from a realm (*Gegend*) where no one discerns it. However, one needs to experience the danger exactly in this realm (3/88). What is this danger? The Inquirer spares no pains in playing the game of suspense.

I: . . . The danger arose from the dialogues themselves, in that they were dialogues.

J: I do not understand what you mean.

. . .

I: The danger of our dialogues concealed itself in language itself, not in *what* we discussed, nor in *the way in which* we tried to do so.

J: But Count Kuki had uncommonly good command of German, and of French and English, did he not?

I: Of course. *He* could say in European languages whatever was under discussion. But we were discussing [*erörterten*] *iki;* and here the spirit of the Japanese language [*japanische Sprachgeist*] remained closed to me— as it is to this day.

J: The languages of the dialogue shifted [*verlagerten*] everything into the *European.*

I: Yet the dialogue tried to *say* [*Sagen*] what is essential [*das Wesentliche*] of *East Asian* art and poetry.

J: Now I am beginning to understand better where you sense the danger. The language of the dialogue constantly destroyed the possibility of saying what the dialogue was about. (4–5/88–89; em. or.)

What Heidegger is concerned with is neither the content nor the way of proceeding of his discussion with Kuki, but the very language of their conversations. According to him, the word *iki* exemplifies "what is essential of *East Asian* art and poetry" (4/89; em. or.). This essence resides in and hence is enclosed in the Japanese language. When *iki* is conversed about in European languages, what it embodies is shifted into European conceptual systems and thus destroyed.[11] Therefore, the essence of *iki* was by no means communicated to Heidegger.

In section three of "A Dialogue," the theme of danger recurs. This time Heidegger is speaking of the danger not only in relation to his discussion with Kuki, but also in relation to his ongoing dialogue with the Japanese interlocutor:

I: . . . I now see *still* more clearly the danger that the language of our dialogue might persistently destroy the possibility of saying that of which we are speaking. (15/103; em. or.)

Then the Japanese interlocutor ascribes the danger to the constitution of European languages in terms of a fundamental distinction between sound and script on the one hand, and reference and sense on the other. This distinction implies a more fundamental metaphysical differentiation between the sensuous (*Sinnlichen*) and the non-sensuous (*Nichtsinnlichen*).

In the beginning of section four, with reference to the inevitability of addressing the danger of the on-going conversations between the Inquirer and the Japanese, in a subtle and almost unnoticeable way, the danger of their conversation is not explicitly attributed to European languages, but to "the concealed nature [*verborgenen Wesen*] of language" (21/111). From this place onward, the subterranean discourse about the nature of language ascends to the surface discourse. However, the danger of their discussion on the nature of language is far from being ignored. As a matter of fact, as the Inquirer states, in venturing this dialogue, they are exactly "walking toward the danger" (23/113).

Embedded in these dialogues is a hardly noticed asymmetry in Heidegger's treatment of European languages and East Asian languages. Readers of "A Dialogue" often take it for granted that his consideration of different families of languages rests on equal footing. Steven Heine describes Heidegger as "stress[ing] to the Japanese participant the 'danger' inherent in East-West dialogue which is based on limitations in language itself" (1990, 61). Denker makes the comment that "[t]he great danger of this dialogue is that the relation between the two cultures can only be discussed in either of the two languages" (80). This reading suggests relativism.

In my view, it is misleading to generalize the point of Heidegger's remark on the incomprehensibility of *iki* along the following lines: Since the essence of a word is embedded in its relative cultural and linguistic context, distortions will arise when this word is rendered into another language. A careful reading of "A Dialogue" shows that this assumption fails to capture the complexity of the relevant issue. Heidegger's observations do not proceed from a neutral position. What he is talking about is not the danger of any language when used to explain a notion embedded in another language, but specifically *the* danger inherent in European languages. Furthermore, the existence of this danger is independent of the actual use of European language(s), either in intercultural context or not.

In "A Dialogue," Heidegger's discussion of the danger of language only bears upon the transit of Japanese notions into European languages. He has never entertained the danger involved in the reverse direction, that is, European notions may be distorted when entering into the Japanese language. If there is anything being endangered in this intercultural exchange, it always belongs to the Japanese world, not to the European world. The European world unilaterally brings disorder, corruption, and threat, whereas European languages seem to be immune to the "danger" of corruption.

When occasionally the passage of European words into the Japanese language is mentioned, the word "danger" is never attached to these episodes. In one case, invoking the Japanese's role as translator of German poetry and philosophy, Heidegger has him stating that "I, coming from Japanese poetry, still have difficulty to experience European poetry in a way that does justice to its essential nature" (8/94). There is no hint that the essence of European poetry should be confronted with dangers of distortion or destruction when conveyed into the Japanese language. In contrast, the attitude toward translating from German into Japanese is overtly optimistic. On the basis of his experience of translating Heidegger's lecture on Hölderlin's poem "Homecoming" and Kleist's plays, the Japanese states,

> J: . . . while I was translating, I often felt as though I were wandering back and forth between two different language worlds, such that at moments a radiance shone on me which let me sense that the wellspring of Being [*Wesensquell*] from which those two fundamentally different languages arise was the same [*derselbe*]. (24/115; tr. m.)

On this occasion, the Japanese language does not form a barrier against the advent of European notions, nor does it incur danger of distortion. Rather, the translator experiences an ecstasy in which a common ground for the two languages of different nature is sensed.

That Heidegger applies the term "danger" only to European languages is consonant with the central presuppositions of his philosophical enterprise. As explicated in Chapter three, "danger" in Heidegger's usage is not an ordinary word with a negative sense, but a technical term with a positive sense. It is closely bound up with the destiny of Being. European languages are the embodiment of Western metaphysical thinking that derives from a correspondence to the originary disclosing of Being. The initial disclosing of Being is not thought through. Being finds distorted reflection in European languages that have a dualistic structure. However, this distortion itself belongs to the structure of the history of Being. In this sense, if the forgottenness of Being itself can be characterized as a "danger," then this danger is a mode of Being's disclosure; it is attached to the region of that "undefined defining something" (22/112). A renewal of metaphysical thinking and the overcoming of the danger can only be prepared where the danger originates.

The revitalization of the inception of Western historicity can only be brought about by a transformative thinking that traces the realm where the danger originates. Explorations of what remains unthought and unarticulated can only be done by way of questioning the nature of language, the enriched *logos* in its full configurations. It is from this perspective of re-initiating the original great beginning of metaphysics that Heidegger elaborates on the "danger" of European languages in "A Dialogue" with as many emphatic gestures as possible.

The duplicity of Heidegger's connection with traditional Western metaphysics is manifest in his connection with aesthetics as depicted in "A Dialogue." With reference to the saying that in leaving behind metaphysics, Heidegger also leaves behind aesthetics that is grounded in metaphysics, the Inquirer explains, "But leaves it behind in such a way that we can give thought to the nature of aesthetics, and can direct it back within its boundaries" (42/138). Heidegger's position regarding aesthetics cannot be captured in terms of total rejection. For one thing, he caustically accuses Western aesthetics of enshrining a dualistic scheme of appearance and essence. For another thing, his criticism does not entail a simplistic dismissal of aesthetics, but instead purports to open up an originary thinking on the nature of aesthetics.

While highlighting a sense of impenetrability, Heidegger provides a series of hints at an alternative vision of *iki*. These hints are given along the line of the question what had been Kuki's motivation to go to Germany to study with him. This question appears for the first time in section one, following Heidegger's remark on a dialogue from house to house. This remark is slightly qualified: Heidegger refrains from saying that this dialogue is *entirely* (*ganz*) impossible, but that it is *nearly* (*beinahe*) impossible (5/90). Following this, the Japanese interlocutor states,

> You are right to say 'nearly.' For still it was a dialogue—and, I should think, an exciting one, because Count Kuki, in the workshops he held with us at Kyoto University, came back again and again to those dialogues [*Gespräche*] with you. Most often it happened when we pressed him in our effort to understand more clearly the reason that had prompted him at that time to go to Germany to study with you. (5/90)

This statement presents the first example of a possible East-West dialogue. It is one in which Kuki was learning from Heidegger. The Inquirer concurs that Kuki must have had special reasons for coming to study with him at the University of Marburg (6/91). A bit later the Inquirer asks the

Japanese interlocutor what prompted Japanese scholars, in particular Kuki, to pay special attention to the alleged transcript of his lectures of 1921. In the beginning of section three, at the Inquirer's reiteration of his puzzlement about *iki*, the Japanese presumes that Heidegger's meditation upon hermeneutics must have inspired Kuki's reflection on *iki* (13/101). In section five, the Japanese interlocutor more explicitly suggests that it was probably the promise of leaving aesthetics behind in the sense of directing it back within its boundaries that had attracted Kuki to study with Heidegger (42/138). A few pages later, he claims that he comes to see more clearly "how well-directed [*gut geleitet*] Count Kuki was when he, under [Heidegger's] guidance [*Anleitung*], tried to reflect on hermeneutics" (47/145).

In the meantime, the Japanese is also learning from Heidegger. While on one occasion the Inquirer states that the Japanese is nearer to the nature of language than all European concepts are (27/118), the Japanese is let to say, "When I can follow you in the dialogue, I succeed. Left *alone*, I am helpless" (33/126; em. or.). That the dialogue successfully ends owes significantly to the Japanese letting himself be steeped in Heideggerese.

Heidegger's perspective on *iki* gradually transforms itself. In the role of the Inquirer, he states, "[Kuki] used the European rubric 'aesthetics,' but what he thought and searched for was an other [*anderes*] . . ." (42/139; omission signs original). He suggests that perhaps now he is in a better position to expose what the word *iki* hints to the interlocutors in a veiled manner (*verhüllterweise zuwinkt*). This transpires after the nature of aesthetics has been clarified (43/140).

Despite the fear that any explication of *iki* would fall into the trap of traditional aesthetic representation, the Inquirer encourages the Japanese interlocutor to translate *iki*. The first translation of *iki* is "the gracious" (*Anmutende*) (43/140). This term should be distinguished from aesthetic subject-object relation. With the caution that any indication (*Hinweis*) would necessarily be entangled with the realm of the aesthetic, the Japanese interlocutor ventures another characterization of *iki*: "*iki* is the breath of the stillness of luminous delight" (44/141). The Inquirer expounds, "The delight comes from the manner of the hint beckoning on, beckoning to and beckoning fro" (44/141; tr. m.).

This is the place where section five comes to an end according to my division of the text. The "other" interpretation of *iki* brought about with the aid of Heidegger's transformative thinking of Western aesthetics and metaphysics is what finally helps the Japanese interlocutor overcome any hesitation about revealing the Japanese word for language.[12] The suitable stage is made ready for the consummate apparition of this intriguing word. As the

Japanese interlocutor states, "it is easier now to attempt an answer [to the most difficult question about what *koto* means] because we have ventured to explain *iki*" (45/142).

On the other hand, the reverse question whether and what Heidegger has learned from Kuki is not raised, not to mention considered. The dialogical relation between Heidegger and Kuki is obviously asymmetrical. While placing emphasis upon the indigenous nature of *iki* and on the danger of the European languages in which *iki* was conceptualized, Heidegger does not show any motivation to learn some Japanese language so as to experience the nature of *iki* in its original embedment. The overall presence of *iki* in Heidegger's essay is not aimed at demonstrating what inspiration Heidegger has drawn from non-Western sources.

A number of scholars have pointed out the discrepancy between Kuki's work on *iki* and Heidegger's deployment of it in "A Dialogue." According to May, "Heidegger's interpretation of *iki* can hardly be squared with Kuki's understanding of the idea" (18). Through careful textual studies, he suggests that Heidegger's quasi-poetical formulation of *iki* draws on Oscar Benl's treatise on the *Nō* play (May 1996, 18–19; Benl 1952). Karatani (1988, 621) comments, "Notwithstanding Heidegger's desire to see in *iki* a possibility for going beyond Western thought, he is in total ignorance of what *iki* is." He claims that Heidegger sees in Kuki's *iki* a description of *Abgrund*, that is, an abyssal depth beyond the structured depth of metaphysical thought. Yoneda (1989, 94) contends that Heidegger's presentation of *iki* draws on the notion of *fūga* (windblown elegance), which is central to the aesthetics of the haiku poet Bashō.

Park (2005, 326) suggests that, when writing "A Dialogue" thirty-odd years after his talks with Kuki, Heidegger may have confused *iki* with an altogether different Japanese aesthetic category, such as *yūgen,* which means "dark and mysterious beauty." He seems to be drawing on Heine's argument that *yūgen,* a notion popular in the Kamakura-period, marks a "more appropriate starting point for the conversation, than an aesthetic concept denoting the edo-period 'stylishness' of the 'floating world' (bordello culture)" (Heine 1990, 65).

The observation that Heidegger's description of *iki* has more affinities with *yūgen* may be right. However, it does not seem to be particularly relevant to argue that what Heidegger depicts is actually another notion. What is more likely to be the case is that he has integrated various Japanese sources that happened to be available to him in order to make his point concerning aesthetics and metaphysics. What is at issue has less to do with which Japanese notion is actually involved than with how a thinking correspondence to the Saying of language can be initiated (from Heidegger's perspective), and with what role *iki* plays in Heidegger's essay (as illustrated in this section).

KOTOBA

In the middle of "A Dialogue," the Japanese word for language is said to give a hint (*Wink*) of what the nature of language is (24/115).[13] The question of what this word is stays in the background throughout all subsequent conversations on the nature of language. The reason why it is being held back is that, to name this word, the Japanese interlocutor would be obliged to afford a translation in a European language. Since European language and philosophy embody a dualistic conceptual system, delivering the Japanese word in a translation or an explanation would bring it into the realm of conceptual thinking and thus distort its nature.

The Japanese word *kotoba* is derived from the native Yamato vocabulary. Literally it means the foliage of speech. Like many ancient words, *kotoba* lends itself to etymological play. This should be kept in mind when the "meaning" of *kotoba* comes to be at issue. In the *Iwanami Dictionary of the Ancient Language*, the linguist Ono Susumu explains that in ancient Japanese society, *koto* meant both reality or events (*koto* 事) and its expression in words (*koto* 言). Differentiation between reality and its verbal articulation was unknown until the Nara and Heian periods, when the word *kotoba* became independent from *koto* (thing) and expresses the surface of reality ("the leaves of things").[14]

There has been a range of literature on *kotoba* either from a philological or from a philosophical standpoint. The first important philosophical paper on *kotoba* was contributed by Watsuji Tetsurō in 1929. His general aim is to develop a theoretical Japanese language that is not far removed from contemporary usage. This language uses ancient Japanese words, instead of Chinese or European loan words. He draws on the etymological-philosophical significance of *koto* and makes three points. First, *koto* is to be contrasted with *mono* (者). *Mono*, the specific being of the content, presupposes Being (*koto*). Second, *koto* is the basis of the taking place of an action. Third, *koto* is "saying." Words (*koto*) are subsumed under "things" (*koto*). Words bring out the original nature of "things." *Koto* is the being of the possibility of unfolding.

It can be seen that there is a general consensus that *koto* in the ancient period means both what is or is happening (*koto*) and its expression in words (*koto*).[15] When these two folds of meaning are distinguished, the latter meaning is borne by the word *kotoba*. According to Tezuka, Heidegger inquired with great interest about the Japanese word for language, about which Tezuka reports as follows.

> The word you are asking about is *kotoba*. . . . the *koto* is connected with *koto* [meaning "matter" { 事 }] of *kotogara* [meaning "event" or "affair" (*Sache* { 事, 事柄 })]. The *ba* is a sound-transformation of *ha* { 葉 } and has connotations of "many" or "dense," as with leaves (*ha*) on a tree. If this is right, then the *koto* of "language" and the *koto* of "matter" are two sides of the same coin: things happen and become language (*kotoba*). The word *kotoba* may have its roots in this kind of idea.
>
> This explanation seemed to fit well with Heidegger's ideas. Taking notes on a piece of paper that was to hand, he said: "Very interesting! In that case, Herr Tezuka, the Japanese word for 'language,' *kotoba*, can mean *Ding* [thing]."
>
> There was perhaps an element here of forcing the word into a pre-conceived idea, but I was not in a position to contradict this interpretation. (May 1996, 60).[16]

Heidegger's interpretation of *kotoba* in "A Dialogue" bears tenuous similarity to the account Japanese scholars give of the "deeper" etymological roots of *kotoba*. May considers Heidegger's transformation of *kotoba* to be "a substantive inaccuracy" or even "distortion" (19). Marra claims that Tezuka's choice of the word *kotoba* was "prompted by his desire to please Heidegger by playing the philosopher's own game," since there is a variety of words from which to choose, such as *gengo* literally meaning "the speech of words" (Marra 2004, 555).

Under Heidegger's pen, *ba* means leaves, including and especially the leaves of a blossom—petals, like cherry blossoms or plum blossoms. *Koto* names "that which in the event gives delight itself, that which uniquely in each unrepeatable moment comes to radiance in the fullness of its grace" (45/142). When it is said that the twin words *iro* and *kū* hint toward the realm where their interplay comes to pass, *koto*, which is this realm, is defined as "the happening [*Ereignis*] of the lightening message of the graciousness that brings forth," "that holds sway over that which needs the shelter of all that flourishes and flowers" (47/144). Obviously, Heidegger interprets *kotoba* in an idiosyncratic manner in accordance with his own intonations on the nature of language.

HEIDEGGER'S NOTHING AND THE BUDDHIST EMPTINESS

Philosophers such as Parmenides, Eckhardt and Hegel have devoted serious thought to the notion of the Nothing.[17] In "What Is Metaphysics?" (1929),

Heidegger notoriously makes the question of the Nothing a central issue of metaphysics.[18] This lecture is the major textual basis on which Heidegger was charged of nihilism.

Against the practice of opposing Being and nothing in the Western metaphysical tradition, Heidegger discerns the existence of a unitary bond between these two notions. He claims,

> [T]he nothing does not merely serve as the counter-concept of beings; rather, it originally belongs to their essential unfolding as such. In the Being of beings the nihilation of the nothing occurs. [1929, 91/115]

The Nothing is what makes possible the unconcealment of beings. It is at work within Being. Heidegger provides a different justification of Hegel's remark in the *Science of Logic,* "Pure being and pure nothing are, therefore, the same" (1990, 82). For Hegel, neither Being nor Nothing is the truth. What is true is the movement by means of which Being passes over into Nothing, and Nothing into Being. Hegel calls this movement "becoming." Being and Nothing are inseparate and inseparable. In the meantime, they are also distinguished from each other. To say they are the same means that their distinction immediately resolves itself.

According to Heidegger, that Being and Nothing are the same is not because they are as indeterminate and immediate as one another, but because "Being itself is essentially finite and manifests itself only in the transcendence of a Dasein that is held out into the Nothing" [1929, 95/120]. In addition, Heidegger attributes another fold of meaning to the Nothing: the Nothing entails the act of nullification; it annuls beings. This does not mean that beings are destroyed; rather, the act of nullification is a predecessor to the appropriative event (Ereignis) [1943e, 238/312, note a].

In the postscript added to "What Is Metaphysics?" in 1943, Heidegger starts his exposition from the side of Being. This makes more explicit the inherent connection between Being and Nothing. Heidegger argues that scientific research attempts at investigating and explaining beings, but can never encounter the Being of beings as such. This is because, as the ground that makes possible any manifestation of beings, Being does not lend itself to objective ways of representation and explanation. In this sense, Being is radically other to beings. It is "that which is not"; it "essentially prevails as Being" [1943e, 233/306]. Being and Nothing are entangled with each other insofar as Being is *not* a Being. Being cannot be made sense of apart from its *not* being a being (that is, not an entity among others). This *not* points to the Nothing that opens up the expanse in which Being as such is disclosed.

In the introduction appended to "What Is Metaphysics?" in 1949, Heidegger approaches the classical question "why are there beings at all, and not rather Nothing?" in a way radically different from traditional metaphysics. According to him, this question should begin with that which is not a being, that is, the Nothing in the capitalized form [1949c, 290/382]. The Nothing is an alias of Being. It is that which is not a being.

In the *Contributions to Philosophy,* Heidegger explicitly claims that his questioning of the Nothing arises from the question concerning the truth of Being. The Nothing with which he is concerned is "the essential enquivering of Beyng itself and therefore is more-being than any beings" [1936–38, 187–88/266].

It is clear that, throughout the variation in configuring the question of Nothing and of Being, Heidegger has all along conceived the notion of Nothing from the perspective of the central question of Western metaphysics in a manner he considers as the most radical and authentic. This is the background against which he places a special emphasis on the fundamental difference between his ideas and Buddhism. In a rarely noticed passage in the *Contributions,* Heidegger writes,

> But how is the metaphysical renunciation of beings, i.e., renunciation of metaphysics, possible without falling prey to the "nothing"?
> Da-sein is the grounding of the truth of Beyng.
> The less a being man is and the less he insists upon the being which he finds himself to be, so much nearer does he come to Being. (No Buddhism! The opposite.) (*CP* 120/170)

Heidegger's use of the "nothing" in this place is completely different from his own notion of the Nothing. The "nothing" in this passage is associated with what is regarded as nihilism, to which is attributed the belief that the nothing is simply null, that there is no ground for anything, that living and dying do not make a difference. These ideas have often been associated with a popular (and vulgar) understanding of Buddhism.[19]

On this occasion, Heidegger stresses that his discourse of overcoming metaphysics and his reflection on Being in its truth (in its unconcealment) cannot be identified with Buddhist nihilism. His concern is with the most fundamental grounding of the truth of Being in Da-sein. If one uses the early Heidegger's terminology that still smacks of traditional Western metaphysics, one could say that the grounding of the truth of Being is in the meantime the ecstasis of Da-sein by means of which beings *as a whole* are negated. This is precisely what Heidegger attempts to elaborate in "What Is Metaphysics?"

in terms of the "Nothing." In the last paragraph of the preceding citation, Heidegger suggests that his emphasis on the Nothing does not drift away from the perennial question of Being; to the contrary, his aim is to bring out the most crucial feature of Being. Heidegger underlines that his philosophical project is fundamentally contrary to Buddhism. It does not fall prey to the Buddhist nothing. Rather than that, it attempts to articulate the highest truth of Being.[20]

It could be said that when writing "What Is Metaphysics?" and the *Contributions to Philosophy,* Heidegger did not yet know so much Buddhist ideas from his Japanese friends. However, in his meeting with the Thai monk Mani as late as 1963, Heidegger articulates similar considerations with regard to the radical difference between his concern and Buddhist thought (Petzet, 174). He claims that the Western and Buddhist view of humans are contrary to each other. With Western tradition, there is marked an essential distinction between the human being and other living beings, such as plants and animals. The humans are distinguished by their knowing relation to Being. The purpose for raising the question of Being anew is to inquire into the question about the nature of the human being. With Buddhist doctrines, there is not such a radical distinction between humans and other living beings. Man is just one among the myriad of living beings.[21]

Hartig claims that Heidegger's discussion with the Thai monk is "one of the most important encounters between original Buddhism and the *Seinsdenken* of Heidegger" (189). He may have in mind exchanges such as Heidegger responding to Mani's saying "nothingness is not nothing" that this is what he has always been saying all his life [1963a, 592], Mani's remark "Come to us, to our land, we shall understand you" [590], and Heidegger's final remark,

> Heidegger (to the interpreter): Please tell him that all the fame in the world means nothing to me when I am not understood and find no understanding. Therefore, I do not only thank you but I have experienced in this dialogue a confirmation, which has rarely come my way before. [1963a, 593]

Given that on the same occasion Heidegger has just emphasized the important difference between the orientation of his thinking and Buddhist beliefs, it is unconvincing to attribute undue weight to Heidegger's agreement that he has been saying similar things as Mani says. With regard to the other two remarks, it is not implausible that Mani's welcome is nothing more than a ready phrase prepared before coming to Europe to meet "the philosopher." Heidegger's last statement sounds to be exaggerated in implying that Mani is one of the very few people who can understand his philosophy. This is probably a rhetorical device designed to suggest the extent to which European philosophers have misunderstood him. Soon after his meeting with Heidegger, Mani disappeared from his religious order and was later discovered working for an American television network—much to Heidegger's chagrin.[22]

SHIKI AND KŪ

Heidegger invokes the famous Buddhist formula "*shiki* is *kū, kū* is *shiki*" ("form is emptiness; emptiness is form") in " A Dialogue." In his text, the twin words *shiki* and *kū* appear as *iro* and *kū* (*DL* 14/102). In the context of the Buddhist ideas of *shiki* and *kū*, which cannot be clearly differentiated, the first character should read *shiki,* not *iro.* Heidegger might have misread *shiki* as *iro* from his notes, or he was later given another reading.[23] Further, Heidegger made an obvious mistake in explaining *iro* (form) as meaning "colour" (*DL* 14/102); in fact, "colour" can only be said to be one aspect of the meaning of "form."[24]

The original Sanskrit for *shiki* is *rūpam* (*se* 色 in Chinese), for *kū* it is *śūnyatā* (*kong* 空 in Chinese). The formula "*shiki* is *kū, kū* is *shiki*" comes from the *Heart Sutra,* one of the most famous, and also the shortest, Buddhist scriptures. As with other sutras, this text assumes a question-and-answer structure. In it, there is only one question raised by the venerable Sariputra as to how one should achieve the profound perfection of wisdom. The long answer contains references to almost all the major categories of Buddhist thought, including the so-called "five aggregates."

The statement "Form is emptiness; emptiness is form. Emptiness is not other than form; form is not other than emptiness" is usually called the fourfold profundity that characterizes the five major Buddhist categories (aggregates). Form is the most basic of the five aggregates. It encompasses both visual forms such as color and shape, as well as non-visual ones such as sound, odor, and taste. Emptiness is the fundamental nature of reality. It signifies the absence of a self-causing and invariant self-nature or self-hood in any thing or person. Whatever exists does so by virtue of a perpetually shifting web of causes and conditions that result from other causes and conditions. Emptiness is present from the very moment of the conception of form. It does not exist apart from the phenomena it qualifies, and is not to be sought as something separate. Although emptiness is the mode of being of form, it does not negate form. Therefore, emptiness is form. Emptiness is dependent upon the form it qualifies.[25]

It is clear that the Buddhist notion of emptiness proceeds from very different considerations compared with Heidegger's notion of the Nothing. With the former, emptiness indicates the fundamental nature of reality. With the latter, the Nothing points to the radical gap between Being and beings in that Being is *not* a being. In the twentieth century, the Kyoto school philosophers elaborate on emptiness (or nothing), and make it the central notion of Eastern thought, such that "philosophers of nothingness" is their common epithet. According to Nishida, the West has taken Being to be the ground of reality, and the East has taken nothing as the ground. Nishitani furthers the efforts of integrating Buddhist resources into philosophical discourse. He argues that Heidegger's Nothing is still relative nothing in that it remains bound up with human subjectivity, whereas Nishida, Tanabe and himself share what sets them apart from traditional Western philosophy: absolute nothingness.[26] As he explicates,

> True emptiness is nothing less than what reaches awareness in all of us as our own absolute *self-nature*. In addition, this emptiness is the point at which each and every entity that is said to exist becomes manifest as what it is in itself, in the form of its true suchness.[27]

It is clear that the nothing of the Kyoto school philosophers is concerned with an ultimate nature of existence, which is elaborated in a sophisticated way, whereas Heidegger's Nothing can be said to be a detour, or an alternative device designed to highlight the centrality of the question of Being as distinguished from beings. Admittedly, there are mutual influences. Heidegger may well have appropriated Buddhist expressions into his writings on the Nothing without acknowledgment.[28] This is fully illustrated in May (1996, 21–34). On the other hand, Heidegger's development of the metaphysics of the Nothing, often associated with Eastern thought and deprecated as nihilistic or vacuous (as reflected in the marginal note in Heidegger's *Contributions* quoted above), may have inspired Japanese philosophers such as Nishitani to provide Buddhist ideas with a renewed positive re-interpretation in accordance with contemporary academic standards.

The connections Heidegger makes between his idea of the Nothing and Eastern notions in "A Dialogue" are reflective of, or rather, derived from, the reception of his work in Japan. The Japanese translation of "What Is Metaphysics?" by Yuasa Seinosuke appeared as early as 1930.[29] This essay was much more welcome in Japan than in the West. Heidegger himself is aware of this situation. In his reply to Kojima Takehiko's letter in 1963, he states,

> That essay, which was translated into Japanese as early as 1930, was understood immediately in your country, in contrast with the nihilistic misunderstanding of what was said which is prevalent to this day in Europe. The nothing that is talked about there means that which in relation to what-is is never any kind of being, and "is" thus nothing, but which nevertheless determines what-is as such and is therefore called Being. [1963c, 225]

The first half of Heidegger's statement appears in "A Dialogue" as well,[30] and is repeated in a letter to Roger Munier dated 31 July 1969.[31] It is noteworthy that the second half of this remark accords well with what Heidegger urges in "What Is Metaphysics?": The Nothing is nothing because it is not any kind of being; the question of the Nothing is of a piece with the question of Being.

In "A Dialogue," the terms *shiki* (*iro*) and *kū* appear in the context of discussing *iki*. The Inquirer ascribes to Kuki a way of interpreting *iki* in terms of "sensuous radiance through whose lively delight there shines the radiance of something suprasensuous" (*DL* 14/101). The Japanese comments that this way of elucidation brings out what the Japanese experience in art. This is followed by the Inquirer's remark that their experience then moves within the difference between a sensuous and a suprasensuous world.[32] This distinction is the basis of Western metaphysics. At this point, the Japanese interlocutor invokes *iro* and *kū*:

> J: . . . Our thinking, if I am allowed to call it that, does know something similar to the metaphysical distinction [between the sensuous and suprasensuous]; but even so, the distinction itself and what it distinguishes cannot be comprehended with Western metaphysical concepts. We say *iro*, that is, colour, and say *kū*, that is, emptiness, the open, the sky. We say: without *iro*, no *kū*. (14/102)

The existence of a similar metaphysical distinction is said, strangely enough, to be the source of the danger of their dialogue. Below is the discussion that ensues:

> J: . . . while *iro* does indeed name colour, it yet means essentially more than whatever is observable by the senses. *Kū* does indeed name

emptiness and the open, and yet it means something other than that which is merely suprasensuous.

I: your suggestions, which I can follow only from afar [*aus der Ferne*], increase my uneasiness. Even greater than the fear I mentioned is the expectation within me that our conversation, which has grown out of our memory of Count Kuki, could turn out well.

J: You mean it could bring us nearer to the unsaid?

I: That would already offer us an abundance to think on. (14–15/102–103)

The Inquirer's "fear" is related to the alleged distortion of *iki* by the European metaphysical system. Greater than this fear is the expectation that their conversation could succeed, that is, could bring the interlocutors to the realm of the unsaid, to the single source. Normally speaking, fear and expectation are contrary psychological states. Their being juxtaposed in this place implies that they are two sides of the same coin. When the European language in which *iki* is explained has not yet been transported into the realm of its own source, the danger of distortion is persistently present. The Inquirer senses that, after many years of philosophical explorations, he is perhaps on the way to that unspeakable source (*DL* 8/93–94). This allows him to expect that his conversation with the Japanese, alleged to be Kuki's student, get onto a successful track.[33] That *iro* and *kū* mean more than what they name hints at the possibility of their transportation into the realm of the other thinking Heidegger is pursuing, the realm of the single source from out of which language speaks, the realm of the dialogue between Being's saying and man's listening.

In the last few pages of "A Dialogue," *kū* appears once again. In describing as "reach[ing] far [*weit*]" the Inquirer's question about the site in which the sense of a kinship between Japanese thinking and Heidegger's thinking and language comes into play, the Japanese interlocutor states, "The expanse [*die Weite*] is the boundlessness which is shown to us in *kū*, which means the sky's emptiness" (41/137; tr. m.). It remains unclear to what extent *kū*, as juxtaposed with the term "emptiness," can still be said to be a *Japanese* notion. These two words have been intermingled and fused into each other in Heidegger's own thinking. The import of the suggestion that *kū* and his Nothing are "the same" will be revealed in the next chapter.[34] My examination suggests that Heidegger's purpose of enlisting the Buddhist idea of nothing in "A Dialogue" is to elaborate and enrich his "single thought."

RASHŌMON AND THE *NŌ* PLAY

The film *Rashōmon,* directed by Akira Kurosawa, was based on two short stories by Akutagawa Ryunosuke (1892–1927), "Rashōmon" and "In a Grove."[35] Produced and initially opened in Tokyo in 1950, it was translated, subtitled, and transported to New York and opened one year later. Being awarded first prize at the Venice Film Festival in 1951, it won an Oscar prize in 1952. With the success of the film, Akutagawa's works were translated into English. The story of the film is of rape of the wife and murder of the husband, as narrated four times from the perspectives of four people. The audience is left to decide which account of the event approximates what actually happened.

According to the bandit, he saw the couple on their way a little past noon the previous day. As a gust of wind lifted the veil of the woman, he caught a glimpse of her face. That seemed to be the origin of the subsequent events. The bandit confesses to luring the couple into a grove and of killing the man in a duel at the woman's request after her violation. The woman told a very different story. According to her, after the bandit stained her honor and fled, she lost consciousness at the frightening expression of her husband that was full of distain. When she woke up, she found her husband stabbed dead. According to the ghost of the murdered husband who spoke through a medium, his wife requested the bandit to kill him before intending to leave with the bandit. Feeling shamed because of this, he killed himself. The woodcutter, who found the corpse, claimed that all these stories are lies. According to him, the husband refused to risk his life in a duel, and asked the bandit to kill his wife. Hearing this, the woman incited the two to engage in a duel; consequently the husband was killed.

In "A Dialogue," while the film *Rashōmon* is invoked as a prominent example of Europeanization, it is said that present in it are "subdued gestures [*Gebärde*]" (*DL* 16/104) and a sense of enchantment (*Bezaubernde*) that enacts the mysterious (*Geheimnisvolle*).[36] One of the "subdued gestures" is "a resting hand surrounding which is gathered [*sich versammelt*] a touch that remains infinitely remote from any touch" (16/104–105; tr. m.). This hand is "suffused and borne by a call [*Anruf*] calling from afar and calling still farther onward, because stillness has brought it" (16/105). Notably, such words as "gather," "gesture," "call" are all typically Heidegger's terminology.

Watching the film *Rashōmon* by oneself, one cannot find a scene in which a hand is given a focus of such kind, except for the two hands of the murdered man sticking out of the shrubs when the woodcutter found the corpse. Heidegger may not have considered ascribing a metaphysical significance or an aesthetic touch to this pair of stiff hands of a dead man. As a matter of fact, the film *Rashōmon* is set in a milieu in which the world is thrown out of joint: the decrepit *Rashōmon* gate, the suspense of a Hitchcockian style before the corpse is discovered, the violence, the betrayal, the robbery, and the inscrutability of everything. All these are evinced in the woodcutter's utterance in the beginning of the film: "I can't understand it. I just can't understand it at all." From this perspective, instead of treating it as an embodiment of the "enchantment" of traditional Japanese taste, it would be more apposite to describe this film as an allegory of the rootlessness of Japanese reality after the Second World War. This is the reality about which Tezuka expressed serious worry in his report on his conversation with Heidegger.

Following the reference to the hand, the Inquirer wonders why in view of such gestures, the Japanese uses the film as an example of Europeanization. In speaking of the realistic that belongs to the language of metaphysics, the discourse of the Japanese interlocutor necessarily entails the distinction between the real as sensuous and the ideal as non-sensuous. The Japanese explains that by the realistic he means the photographic objectivity derived from the technical-aesthetic framework of the film industry. This is, in the last analysis, a consequence of the outreach of the all-sweeping Europeanization. He admits that the difficulty of his speech is due to the fact that he has not yet found the proper language to express his thoughts. To acquire the adequate way of expression, he needs exactly the language of the Inquirer.

In the following exchanges, it is suggested that a transformation can only occur from within the heart of Europeanization. The Japanese needs Heidegger's language, which stems from traditional Western metaphysics, in order to bring out the contrast in the film between the foreground world that is European or American, and the background world that is Japanese. It is also through the self-transformation of this metaphysical language that the otherness, or the promise, of the Japanese world could be brought into adequate articulation.

After the discussion of *Rashōmon*, the theme of the *Nō* play enters "A Dialogue." *Nō* is a theatrical performance involving singing and dancing, accompanied by a chorus and musicians. The protagonist usually wears a mask. According to Grazia Marchianò (1997), *Nō* avoids imitation; this makes it absolutely different from Greek-based European mimetic drama. She writes,

> The link between mind and nature, and between nature and artifice is given in visual expression in the *Nō* in the geometrical patterns of

immobile gestures, the tones of utterances which seem to erupt from the depths of the actor's being, the register of breaths which rise to gasps, irrevocable gazes, rending of the soul. (Marchianò 1997, 99)

The most famous and influential *Nō* playwright, actor and troupe leader is Zeami (1363–1443), whose real name is Kanze Motokiyo.[37] Being a practitioner of the Soto branch of Zen Buddhism, Zeami stresses development of mental awareness as sought in Zen. The *Nō* actor is expected to attain enlightenment (*satori*) through assiduous practice and training, and to incorporate this enlightenment into his performance. He should also be able to see himself from behind by means of his mind. An accomplished actor should also take account of the critical eyes of the spectators. The actor and the audience together should form a single theatrical experience. The best plays or performances do not pursue surface beauty, but possess ethereal beauty that is comparable to "white plum blossoms" or "snow piled up in a silver container." This kind of beauty is beyond any conscious technical manipulation. It evokes deep emotional resonance in the minds of the audience.

In "A Dialogue," it is claimed that the background world of Japan, or "that world itself," that is concealed behind the objective frame of a film, is experienced in the Japanese *Nō* play (17/106). Heidegger employs his idiosyncratic expressions to characterize this type of drama. With a *Nō* play, the emptiness of the stage calls for an unusual concentration (*Sammlung*), and "only a slight additional gesture on the part of the actor is needed to cause mighty things to appear out of a rare calmness [*Ruhe*]" (18/107). As an example, the Japanese makes the gesture of putting up an open hand and holds it above his eyes, which hints at the coming forth of a mountain landscape. From this episode onward, Heidegger begins to explicitly characterize Japanese notions in accordance with his locutions.

What follows is a concentrated discussion of gesture in a typically Heideggerian language: Gesture is the gathering of a bearing (*Versammlung eines Tragen*). Human beings bear their share to its encounter, but "what properly [*eigentlich*] bears, only bears itself *toward* [*zu-trägt*] us" (18/107–8; em. or.). A gesture unites originarily within itself what bears toward it and what bears itself. With this formulation, the danger remains that one understands the gathering as a subsequent union. What is required is to realize that "all bearing, including what bears toward it and what bears itself, springs [*entquillt*] first and only from the gathering" (19/108).[38] The gesture made by the Japanese interlocutor functions as a didactic or heuristic device to make the suggestive connection between East Asian emptiness and Heidegger's Nothing. When the Inquirer asks where to "look for the essence of that gesture," the reply is:

J: In a showing that is itself invisible, and that, so gathered, bears itself to encounter emptiness [*die Leere*] in such a way that in and through it the mountains appear.

I: That emptiness then is the same [*dasselbe*] as Nothing [*das Nichts*], namely, the essential which we attempt to add in our thinking, as the other, to all that is present and absent. (19/108; tr. m.)

The Inquirer speaks of "Japanese" emptiness (exemplified by the essence of the gesture in the *Nō* play) as "the same" as Nothing. Here, as in other cases, Heidegger is playing with both the literal sense (that is, identical) and the philosophical sense (that is, gathering in distinctiveness) of the "same." In the next chapter I will consider Heidegger's understanding of the "Same" and its bearing on his comportment toward East-West dialogue.

Chapter Nine
Do We Have Our Eyes on the "Same"?

The examinations conducted in Chapter eight constitute the basis of my *first reading* of "A Dialogue," which demonstrates that Heidegger has adroitly turned the topic of East-West dialogue, as broached in the opening part of his essay, into an architectonic monologue. In this chapter, I expose the strains and tensions that arise when Heidegger applies dialogue and the Same, the two notions central to his thought, to East-West dialogue. I show that Heidegger's fundamental concerns and presuppositions have prevented him from exploring the question of East-West dialogue. The disclosure of the relevant problematic constitutes my *second reading* of "A Dialogue on Language."

DIALOGUE

In order to gain a firm grasp of Heidegger's deployment of the thematic of East-West dialogue in "A Dialogue," his notion of dialogue calls for special examination. By the term "dialogue," Heidegger does not mean an ordinary conversation in the mundane human world. For him, a true dialogue can never be a free (and this means arbitrary and unhistorical) commutation or consultation between speakers. In his words, "not every speaking with one another [*jedes Miteinanderreden*] could be called a dialogue" (*DL* 52/151). For Heidegger, a true dialogue is a happening that historically determines man; it is appropriated to the Saying of Being.

Parkes argues that it accords better with Heidegger's ideas to translate the title of "A Dialogue," *„Aus einem Gespräch von der Sprache,"* as "From a Conversation on Language." According to him, in the German language, the word *Gespräch* is most commonly used for a mundane communicative exchange among human beings. For this reason, it is better to translate it with the English word "conversation." "Conversation" gives a greater impression that this essay is "derived from an actual conversation" than does the word "dialogue," which suggests "a freer, more literary composition" (1996, xvii). Parkes assumes that Heidegger has intended to give his essay a greater impression of reality. On another occasion, Parkes stresses that "*Aus einem Gespräch von der Sprache*" is not *über der Sprache* but *von der Sprache*. The word *von* suggests that "the conversation is as much (or more) *from* or by language as it is about it" (1987, 213; em. or.).[1] In the light of this ideal, "[t]he interlocutors strive to avoid speaking about language, trying rather to let the conversation be led by and issue from out of the essential being of language itself (*vom Wesen der Sprache her*)" (213). Because of this linguistic and philosophical insight, Parkes prefers to use the word "from" in the translation of the title.

These observations are quite insightful; and surely in some particular contexts "conversation" indeed serves as a better rendition of *Gespräch*. However, Parkes' argument is concerned with the overall import of what dialogue means for Heidegger. A problem with rendering *Gespräch* as "conversation" is that, if the conversation in "A Dialogue" does not proceed in the manner of attending to and taking into consideration of what the other interlocutor has to say, but rather depends upon something supposedly higher in status and primal in order, then one could hardly assume that it is Heidegger's intention to present this conversation as actual and ordinary as possible. Although Parkes is right in observing that *Gespräch* refers to everyday conversations between human beings, Heidegger's idiosyncratic use of this word has led to a semantic ascent, so to speak. *Gespräch* has become a special technical term in Heidegger's writings.[2] The term *Gespräch* needs to be understood in light of the integral framework of Heidegger's later thought.

In *What is Called Thinking?* (1951/52) Heidegger strictly distinguishes the German word *Konversation* from *Gespräch*. He expresses a depreciative opinion of *Konversation*, "Conversation [*Konversation*] consists in slithering along the edges of the subject matter, precisely without getting involved in the unspoken." Inasmuch as *Konversation* "express[es] the fact that the speakers are turning to one another," it can be called a *Gespräch*; "but true dialogue [*Gespräch*] is never a conversation," Heidegger asserts. Dialogue "leads the speakers into the unspoken." The "soul of dialogue" consists in the involvement [*Sicheinlassen*] of speakers among each other in "*that* realm and abode [*Aufenthaltsort*] about which they are speaking" (*WCT* 178/182; em. or.).

The context in which Heidegger makes this distinction is a discussion of the interpretation of a philosophical work. He considers that most interpretations remain at the level of conversation. This is sufficient in most cases. But as far the question "What calls on us to think?" is concerned, this is not sufficient; because this question asks for the unspoken call that "directs [*weist*] to the beginning of Western thinking, the beginning whose way [*Bahn*] we, too, today still follow in our thinking, though Western is for the moment submerged in European thinking" (*WCT* 178/182; tr. m.).

It is clear that Heidegger's notion of dialogue is essentially connected with the beginning of Western thinking, and with the necessity of corresponding to what remains unspoken in that beginning. The dialogue between a Japanese and an Inquirer unfolds primordially "*as a historic one* precisely in its attempt to reflect on the nature of language" (*DL* 34/128; em. ad.; tr. m.). The primary concern is with the historic nature of every thinking dialogue. To enter into such a dialogue, a deconstruction of the history of Being is called for.[3] For Heidegger, a dialogue with past thinkers, notably with Greek philosophers, is not a simplistic return to Heraclitus or Anaximander. Although the Greeks have experienced the unconcealment, they have not thought it through and articulated it adequately. One needs to "think what Greeks have thought in an even more Greek manner" (39/134), to think it from out of the essential origin.

In the essay "The Way to Language" (1959), Heidegger characterizes the nature of language as "monologue." He remarks that "Monologue," the title of Novalis' poem, "points to the mystery of language: language speaks singularly and solely [*einzig und einsam*] with itself alone" (*OWL* 111/239).[4] He emphasizes, "The monological character of the nature of language has its joining [*Gefüge*] in the disclosing design [*Aufriß*] of Saying. . . . language *is* monologue" (*OWL* 134/265; em. or.). Language is monologue in the sense that it is originarily appropriated to Saying. On the other hand, an authentic dialogue is "determined by that which speaks to those who seemingly are the only speaker—men" (*DL* 52/151–52). It is a speaking "*from* [*von*] language," "*from out of* the nature of language [*vom* Wesen der Sprache *her*]" (51/150; em. or.).[5] Hence, dialogue in its true nature unfolds itself as a monologue, in that it lets language speak from out of itself.

THE TURN OF THE DIALOGUE

Heidegger's notion of dialogue provides the background against which one could understand better the overall composition of "A Dialogue." As can be seen from the outline delineated in the beginning of Chapter eight, two fundamental queries act as the organizing threads for Heidegger's composition of "A Dialogue." The first query concerns what is "an authentic explanation" of Heidegger's conception of hermeneutics. It is raised in the early half of the essay, when the Inquirer is immersed in the recollection of his intellectual maturation (11/98). The second query concerns what word in Japanese corresponds to the nature of language. It appears in the middle of the whole essay, following the recurrence of the phrase "language is the house of Being" (23/113). Heidegger prescribed a long reflection to the Japanese, with his eyes closed and his head lowered. When the Japanese resumes the conversation, he admits the existence of a Japanese word for the nature of language, which is nevertheless not a word for the speaking and using of language (23/114). The Inquirer supplements that that is how it should be because the nature of language cannot be a matter of linguistic concern.

In the first half of "A Dialogue," the two queries just mentioned run paralleling one another. The withheld Japanese word for the nature of language is constantly linked to Heidegger's familiar phrase for the nature of language and for hermeneutics: "language is the house of Being." In the middle of "A Dialogue," it is claimed that the two queries ask for the same (30/123). Henceforth, they appear more recognizably as twin threads in close interplay with each other.

The interplay and eventual integration of these two organizing questions correspond to the deliberate interchange of the roles of the Inquirer and the Japanese. In the early parts of the dialogue, the Japanese interlocutor seems to be rash in making self-assured assertions with respect to the application of European conceptual apparatus; whereas the Inquirer takes a cautious stance toward the assimilation of Japanese notions to European concepts, and keeps on warning the Japanese against making hasty claims. It is alleged that the Japanese notion *iki* is disfigured when rendered into European languages and therefore is resistant to the (European) understanding of the Inquirer. All these take place against the background in which the "complete Europeanization of the earth and of man" (15/103) seems to have desiccated the sources of the essential.

Analogous to the turn of Being itself, and to the turn of Heidegger's own thinking, a turn occurs to the Japanese's speech as well. Transformed by the Inquirer's instillation, he is led onto the right track of questioning and responding, and begins to speak Heideggerese. In sections five and six there is very little differentiation between the roles of the Japanese and the Inquirer. As I argue in Chapter two, Heidegger may well have conceived the path of his philosophical exploration as a lively exemplification of the turn (*Kehre*) of Being itself. Paralleling with an account of his intellectual maturation, there also occurs a turn to their discussion of Japanese notions. That their conversation comes to fruition is owing to the interlocutors' having their gaze on the Same, "the indefinable something" (13/99) which alone allows a dialogue to succeed.

In the final two sections, it is suggested that Japanese notions and ideas hint toward the source, and thus can be explicated, provided that the explanation is embedded in the special language of Heideggerese. The language of the dialogue seems to have succeeded in overcoming the danger of the metaphysical language. Hence, the space is opened for letting language/Being speak for itself. After the longest section (about sixteen pages) devoted to the question of hermeneutics, in which language (as Saying) plays a fundamental role in bringing about an authentic dialogue with past thinkers,[6] *it seems* that a dialogue from house to house has become possible, and is taking place. The ordinary intercultural dialogue, as exemplified in the Kuki-Heidegger dialogues that are inevitably threatened by the danger of European languages, is transformed into the authentic dialogue on the nature of language between the Japanese interlocutor and the (European) Inquirer.

Eventually, *iki* can be elucidated, and the Japanese, somehow the personification of the "probing intimations" (*vermutenden Andeutungen*), is finally emboldened to reveal the Japanese word in its Romanization: *kotoba* (45/142). This word hints at and beckons the essential being (*Wesende*) (that is, "that which is like a saga" (47/145)), which is named by the German word *die Sage*. *Die Sage* is the "more fitting word" (*ein gemäßeres Wort*) for the nature of hermeneutics. The question of the Japanese word for language completely coalesces into the reflection on the nature of Saying (*die Sage*) (49/148).

Analogous to the turn of the dialogue between the Inquirer and the Japanese, Heidegger must have expected that a turn occur to the readers of "A Dialogue," such that they engage into, or follow up his single thought on the essential turn (or rather, movement) of language and Being. Bernasconi's suggestion of a double reading of Heidegger has captured something like this. He claims that Heidegger's "saying not-saying" (*sagenden Nichtsagens*) amounts to

> an invitation to a certain kind of reading where we hear first the metaphysical at work throughout language and then in a second reading the silence, the concealment, that resounds in it. (1985, 93)

A scholar who adopts this way of reading by means of which his own thinking follows closely the complex structure of the turn in Heidegger's text and is hence transformed would be someone who stays close to what I call an internal approach to Heidegger. Admittedly, this approach may safeguard one in getting Heidegger right, since that is the way in which Heidegger expects one to read him. However, "the task of thinking," to use Heidegger's phrase, may have something that exceeds getting him right.

The essay "A Dialogue on Language" as a whole could be seen in this light: it is orchestrated in such a way that the text itself serves as an exemplification, or an Ereignis, of what according to Heidegger should happen in "an authentic dialogue *from* language" (53/152; em. or.). That the dialogue takes place between a Japanese and an Inquirer shows the distance between two interlocutors who come from two radically different worlds. The two major lines of inquiry, one concerning the "authentic explanation" (11/98) of hermeneutics and the other one concerning the Japanese word for language run paralleling each other in the early half of the text and then are revealed to be actually "ask[ing] for the Same" (30/123). When asked whether he finds such trails that direct thinking back to the region of its source, the Inquirer states, "I *find* them only because they are *not* of my own making, and are discernible only quite rarely, like the wind-borne echo of a distant call" (37/124; em. or.). The trails that direct their dialogue are not of an individual's making, but are revealed in the beginning of Western philosophy. The authentic dialogue is one which, as Heidegger's thinking does, tries "to fetch, to bring together, to gather in, what is concealed within the old" (36/131).

The topic of East-West dialogue could be seen as a site where Heidegger is experimenting with his configurations of the essential Saying of Being, in which resides his notion of dialogue. The discussion of the Japanese word for language and of hermeneutics proceeds in exactly the "same" mode as an authentic dialogue does. From this perspective, we could be completely in agreement with Nancy that the alterity of Japanese thinking is totally subsumed under the alterity of language.[7] The conclusion would then be that "A Dialogue" is an architectonic monologue. It has nothing to do with East-West dialogue.[8]

While this interpretation conforms to the general drift of "A Dialogue," a series of questions remain. If Heidegger does not have in mind Japanese notions or ideas he knows of, why does he, especially in the first half of "A Dialogue," invoke the topic of East-West dialogue and highlight Japanese themes (even if later on they either retreat without traces or become assimilated into Heidegger's pre-conceived scheme of composition)? Why does he broach the vexing question of East-West dialogue on various occasions in the 1950s (albeit without elucidating his thought on it)? I would claim that Heidegger *has* considered applying his key ideas of "dialogue" and the "Same" to East-West dialogue, but only to find this experiment intertwined with tensions and ambiguities. I will come back to this after an elucidation of his notion of the Same.

THE SAME

The Same and Belonging-Together

In "The Principle of Identity" (1957), Heidegger starts his elucidation of the Same by opposing it against the traditional concept of identity. The formula of the principle of identity A=A expresses equality (*Gleichheit*) of the two elements A and A. However, τὸ αὐτό, the Same (*das Selbe*), means something essentially different from "identical," which is ὅμοιον in Greek (*WCT* 240/147). These two Greek words are different; but it is precisely in their being distinct that they belong to each other. Heidegger explains, "For something to be the same, one is always enough" (*ID* 23–24/86). Therefore, the formula A=A fails to define A as the Same.

Translating Plato's phrase ἕκαστον ἑαυτῷ ταὐτόν as "jedes selber ihm selbst dasselbe" (each itself the same with itself), Heidegger happily announces, "Our German language, like the Greek, offers the advantage of clarifying what is identical with the same [*demselben*] word, with its joining [*Fuge*] of different configurations" (24/87; tr. m.). By "the same word," he refers to the dative *ihm*. Accordingly, Sameness (*Selbigkeit*) implies "the relation of 'with,' that is, a mediation, a connection, a synthesis: the unification into a unity" (25/87).

In the history of Western thought, the unity of identity is regarded as an essential trait of the Being of beings. Being identical with itself is considered as part and parcel of the Being of beings. Were the claim of identity not made, Heidegger emphasizes, "beings could never appear in their Being" (26/88). This is the dominant mode in which sameness figures in the history of metaphysics. However, the Same itself has not been adequately considered.

Parmenides experiences identity in a fundamentally different way. He does not represent identity as a metaphysical feature of Being of beings, but presents it as that to which Being and thinking belongs. He has the intimation that "thinking and Being belong together in the Same [*das Selbe*] and by virtue of this Same" (*ID* 27/90). Heidegger cites Parmenides' fragment 3: τὸ γὰρ αὐτὸ νοεῖν ἐστίν τε καὶ εἶναι; the common translation of this passage is, "For it is the same thing, to think and to be" (*WCT* 240/146; *M* 97/235). He modifies this translation as, "The Same namely is experiencing (thinking) as well as Being" (*ID* 27/90). In this way the sentence starts with "Das Selbe."[9] Heidegger obviously treats τὸ αὐτό as the grammatical subject of Parmenides' fragment and coins a philosophical term out of it. As he writes in "Moira,"

> The enigma-word [*Rätselwort*], τὸ αὐτό, the Same, with which the saying begins, is no longer a predicate repositioned to stand first, but rather

the subject—what lies at the ground, what bears and holds [*das Tragende und Haltende*]. (*M* 95/45; tr. m.)

According to Heidegger, metaphysicians after Parmenides represent identity as a characteristic of Being. With Parmenides, however, Being is determined as a characteristic of identity that determines Being. In *What is Called Thinking?*, Heidegger explains that the Same does not mean "of a kind" (*einerlei*), since if Being and thinking are of a kind, then one can replace one for the other indifferently (*WCT* 240/147). This is the least of what Parmenides would have meant.

On the basis of this philological/philosophical twist, Heidegger elaborates his reflection on the Same acquired thereof.[10] The Same means belonging-together (*Zusammengehören*). The standard way of understanding "belonging-together" takes "together," that is, unity, as what is decisive, and interprets "to belong" as, "to be assigned and placed into the order of a 'together,' established in the unity of a manifold, combined into the unity of a system, mediated by the unifying center of an authoritative synthesis" (*ID* 29/92). Heidegger adds, "Philosophy represents this belonging-together as *nexus* and *connexio,* the necessary connection of the one with the other" (29/92). The together, *nexus* and *connexio,* for him, speaks of a necessary mediation that prevails in the identity. Such a conception is approximated in German speculative Idealism, which was prepared by Leibniz and Kant and consummated with Fichte, Schelling and Hegel. From thence onward, the unity of identity is no longer characterized as mere abstract oneness (*Einerlei*) with no regard to internal mediation.

For Heidegger, the emphasis needs to be moved to the side of "belonging" (*Gehören*) in the phrase "belonging-together." It is the sense of "belonging" that holds sway in the gathering of "belonging-together." What is at issue is not to think of "belonging-together" in terms of the unity by means of togetherness, but to *experience* this togetherness in terms of belonging (*ID* 29/92). Taking over the hint provided by Parmenides, one can say that the belonging-together involves both thinking and Being in their belonging-together in the Same. Since thinking is the most distinctive characteristic of man, Heidegger argues, the belonging-together concerns man and Being. To think of the belonging together is not to assimilate components into a unity. It purports to be a matter of experiencing the belonging-together in a more originary manner. This means I paraphrase: Man needs to uphold the difference between Being and thinking in their common rootedness in the source, that is, the Same, that which lets Being and apprehending relate and concern one another mutually.

In its original sense, Being means presence; yet Being does not present itself arbitrarily and incidentally. "Being is present and abides only as it concerns man through the claim it makes on him" (31/95). Man is the only being who allows Being to arrive as presence. In other words, man is the only being who can let himself open to Being and answer to Being's call. Heidegger writes, "Man *is* essentially this relationship of responding to Being, and he is only [*nur*] this. This 'only' does not mean a confinement, but rather a super-measure [*Übermaß*]" (31/94; em. or.; tr. m.). Belonging to Being holds sway in man. The belonging to each other of man and Being grants them essential determinations, which have so far been interpreted in terms of metaphysical categories and mediations. Proceeding from a classical conception of man and of Being, traditional metaphysics represents the togetherness of man and being as coordination (*Zuordnung*) and conceives and interprets this coordinating relation in terms of either man or Being. However, Heidegger claims, the belonging-together itself remains unthought. In his own words, "We do not as yet enter the domain of the belonging-together" (32/96). The first and foremost question is "whether and how a belonging to one another first of all is at stake in the 'together'" (30–31/94).

In order to enter the domain of belonging-together, one needs to take departure from traditional representational thinking in accordance with which man is regarded as rational agent, and Being as the ultimate ground that sustains all beings. This moving away from traditional conceptions is a leap (*Sprung*). This leap is "the abruptness of the unbridged entry [*Einkehr*] into that belonging which alone can grant a toward-each-other [*Zueinander*] of man and Being" (33/97).[11] The leap assumes the same mode as Ereignis. It is the movement by means of which one enters into the realm of the belonging. Heidegger writes,

> The *belonging*-together of man and Being in the manner of mutual challenging drives home to us with startling force that and how man is delivered [*vereignet*] to Being and Being is dedicated [*zugeeignet*] to the essence of man. Within the framework [*Ge-stell*] there prevails a strange delivering and dedicating. One must simply experience this owning [*Eignen*] in which man and Being are delivered [*ge-eignet*] to each other, that is, we must enter into what we call *the event of appropriation* [*Ereignis*]. (*ID* 36/100; em. or.; tr. m.)

While the Same, the belonging, is first and foremost "that in which and from out of which" man and Being originate as delivered to each other, "leap" shares the same configuration and dynamism as the "Same." The Same is essentially bound up with Ereignis in which Being and thinking are gathered together.

Historic Significance of the Same

For Heidegger, the Same is the matter of thinking, the task of thinking, and the way of thinking. As he writes in "Moira," "What is silently concealed in the enigma-word τὸ αὐτό is the revealing bestowal [*entbergende Gewähren*] of the belonging-together of the duality and the thinking that comes forward into view within it" (*M* 95/46). More crucially, the Same is in its nature historic. In drawing "The Principle of Identity" to an end, Heidegger reiterates that one can only think within the space of play (*Spielraum*) of tradition (*Überlieferung*) (*ID* 41/106). The *Gelassenheit* (releasement) of thinking is not arbitrary, unscrupulous letting-be. It is subject to the law of thinking in the most originary way. Heidegger explicates in "*What is Called Thinking?*,"

> The thinker needs only a single [*einzigen*] thought. And for the thinker the difficulty is to hold fast to this single and one thought as the single "to be thought of" for him [*das einzig für ihn zu-Denkende*]; to think this One as the Same, and from [*von*] the Same to say the Same in the corresponding way, . . . in such a way that we ourselves are claimed by the Same. The limitlessness [*Grenzenlose*] of the Same is the sharpest limit set to thinking. (*WCT* 50/20; tr. m.)

The limitlessness of the Same, the space of play (*Spielraum*) of tradition is the limit that makes thinking possible, and within which thinking has to conduct its course. Man has to hold fast to the "single and one thought" that is bequeathed to him from the ancient and "torrential" times when time opens itself up into the triple fold of past, present and future. In thinking back on the first beginning, man enters into the realm in which alone the other beginning can unfold. Thinking at the source of the historicity of the first beginning is the one and only way in which what is granted at the *Anfang* of history can become meaningful. In *Contributions to Philosophy*, Heidegger describes this historic structure as dialogue:

> Thinking in the crossing brings into dialogue [*Zwiesprache*] what has first been of Beyng's truth and that which in the truth of Beyng is futural in the extreme—and in that dialogue brings to word the essential sway of Beyng, which has remained unquestioned until now. (*CP* 5/5f)

Man (thinking) and Being share the same dialogical structure in their dialogue with each other. This dialogical structure has the same joining as the structure of temporality. In "Hölderlin and the Essence of Poetry" (1936), Heidegger relates his discussion on dialogue with the Same. In a draft of an unfinished poem, Hölderlin sings,

> Much has man experienced.
> Named many of the heavenly one,
> Since we have been a dialogue [*Gespräch*]
> And able to hear from one another. (*EHP* 56/38)

On the basis of the last two verses, Heidegger says that humans are a dialogue: "Man's being is grounded in language; but this actually occurs only in *dialogue* . . . language is essential only as dialogue" (*EHP* 56/38; em. or.). He asserts that being able to hear is "based upon the possibility of the word" (57/39). Humans are a dialogue. This, Heidegger claims, "always also signifies we are *one* dialogue" (57/39; em. or.). What does the "one" indicate? Heidegger continues,

> The unity [*Einheit*] of a dialogue consists in the fact that in the essential word [*wesentlichen Wort*] there is always manifest [*offenbar*] that one and the same [*das Eine und Selbe*], on which we are unanimous [*einigen*], on the basis of which we are united [*einig*] and so are authentically [*eigentlich*] ourselves. Dialogue and its unity bears our Dasein. (*EHP* 57/39; tr. m.)

Why does Heidegger place emphasis on the idea of "one and the same"? Should it be taken in the literal sense? If not, what does it imply? A few lines later, Heidegger repeats,

> Since when have we been a dialogue? If there is to be *one* dialogue, the essential [*wesentliche*] word must remain related to what is one and the same. . . . But the one and the same can be manifest only within the light of something that remains. . . . But this occurs in the moment in which time opens itself up in its dimensions. . . . Only since "torrential time" has been broken up into present, past, and future, has it become possible to agree upon something that remains over time. We have been *one* dialogue since the time when there "is time." Ever since time arose and was brought to stand, since then we *are* historic. Both—to be *one* dialogue and to be historic—are equally ancient, they belong together, and they are the same [*dasselbe*]. (*EHP* 57/39–40; em. or.; tr. m.)

Man as the one dialogue is essentially related with "the essential word" (*wesentliche Wort*), which names the "same" as the grounding word (*Grundwort*) and as the enigma-word (*Rätselwort*).[12] The "one and the same" can be manifest only as one experiences it as the belonging of Being and thinking. It is named as the Same in the first beginning of philosophy. The emphasis in the above quotation on time and historicity, coupled with an ontological account of the structure of temporality, is a sustaining core of Heidegger's philosophy. It means something like this: The initial utterance of the grounding words such as the Same brings about the dawning of human mind and makes humans (Western man) historic. A true hearing is possible and necessary only because the epochal event of unconcealment *has* happened in the first beginning, which needs to be reheard in the other beginning. That humans are one dialogue implies that a true dialogue is characterized by oneness and singularity, in the sense of being grounded upon and directed toward the inceptive event in which Being is shown for the first time in the beginning of history, that is, toward the "one and the same."

Appealing to both literal and ontological senses of the "same," Heidegger states that being one dialogue and being historic are the "same." This means that the gathering of Being and thinking (the one dialogue) is possible only *as history* and makes sense only when understood in relation to the ontological structure of temporality. It is historic since it embodies in itself a call for correspondence to what was said and to be said in the first beginning, and for the initiation of the other beginning that is to say what is unsaid in what is said.

Occasionally, Heidegger uses the word Same to explicate the intricate relations concerning the history of Being. In the *Contributions to Philosophy,* Heidegger states within brackets, "Being and Beyng is the same [*dasselbe*] and yet fundamentally different [*grundverschieden*]" (*CP* 120/171).[13] By "Being," Heidegger refers to the Being of beings in the traditional metaphysical sense; by "Beyng," he means Being as thought in its originariness. By the "Same," he attempts to convey the sense in which there is an inner bond between Being and Beyng. Yet the new way of thinking Beyng radically distinguishes itself from the precedent metaphysical approach to Being. Insofar as the supposedly "radical distinction" between thinking of the other beginning and past metaphysical thinking makes sense only because they are the "Same," only because they share the same matter of thinking, their distinction falls within the purview of the "Same."

In "Anaximander's Saying," Heidegger makes the connection between dialogue and the Same more explicit.

> We seek a clearer dialogue not for its own sake but solely for the sake
> of that which wishes to come to language in such a dialogue, provided
> it comes of its own accord. This is *that same* which, in different ways, is
> destined to concern both the Greeks and us. It is that which brings the
> dawn of thinking into the destiny of the West. It is as a consequence
> of this destiny that the Greeks first became, in the historical sense, the
> Greeks. ([1946a, 253/336]; em. ad.)

It is clear that the Same is that which brings the dawn of thinking, that which
comes to language in an authentic dialogue, and that which forms the bond
between the Greeks and contemporary Western people.

On another occasion, Heidegger uses the idea of the Same to describe
intellectual relations between philosophers. In his lecture course held in
1936 on Schelling's treatise on the essence of human freedom, Heidegger
remarks, "the greatest thinkers at bottom never understand each other, precisely because, in the form of their own singular greatness, they each will or
want the Same" ([1936c, 13/11]; tr. m.).

This assertion is made in reference to Hegel's relation to Schelling.
According to Heidegger, both philosophers adhere to a distinctive approach
to fundamental questions of metaphysics, and hence there is a breach
between them. Since philosophizing is quite an individual matter, and a
philosopher's thinking is unavoidably bound up with his own ways of being
in the world, the greater his thinking is, the greater is its singularity. Nevertheless, their philosophizing in each of their ways inevitably arises as a correspondence to the claim of Being, as a reflection on the question of Being.
As Heidegger states in his lecture course on Parmenides, "Essential thinking
must always say only the same, the old, the oldest, the beginning, and must
say it primordially" [1942/43, 77/114]. Being determines that every genuine thinker thinks the question of Being. The Same in this context means
that there is a fundamental structure at work that unites these two "greatest thinkers" [1936c, 13/11]. This structure is none other than the history
of Being. Being has different grantings to different thinkers without their
knowing this. It is in this sense that the greatest thinkers at bottom never
understand one another.

The Same and the "Single Source"

The essay "A Dialogue on Language" is one of the few writings where the
idea of the Same is pervasive throughout the text. For example, the Japanese
expresses uncertainty whether the Inquirer has his eyes on "the Same" (*das
Selbe*); the response to this is that this will be revealed in their dialogue itself

(*DL* 12–13/99–100). In relation to the "undefined defining something," the Japanese says that he has in mind "the Same" as what the Inquirer intends, that is, the nature of language (22/112). Another place where the word Same occurs is,

> J: . . . while I was translating, I often felt as though I were wandering back and forth between two different language worlds, such that at moments a radiance shone on me which let me sense that the wellspring of Being [*Wesensquell*] from which those two fundamentally different [*grundverschiedenen*] languages arise was the same [*derselbe*].
>
> I: You did not, then, seek for a general concept [*allgemeinen Begriff*] under which both European and East Asian languages could be subsumed.
>
> J: Absolutely not. (*DL* 24/115; tr. m.)

The Same that seems to ground the "fundamentally different" language worlds cannot be regarded as a general concept by means of which European and East Asian languages can be united. This is because a general concept is neutral, and thus does not have a historic nature. It is clear from the previous section that the Same in its essential nature belongs essentially to the axis of european-occidental-grecian history. If one should consider applying the Same to other languages of a completely different nature, how could this story remain untroubled? This is probably what Heidegger has in mind in making fleeting remarks on East-West dialogue in the 1950s and 1960s. He is speculating on the possibility whether or not the space of play (*Spielraum*) of the Same (or the Ereignis) could have the elasticity to gather together both Eastern and Western notions without losing the singularity of the history of Being.

In "A Dialogue," Heidegger hints at the idea of the Same when reminiscing on his exploration of the nature of language,

> The prospect of the thinking that labours to answer to the nature of language is still veiled, in all its vastness. I do not yet see whether what I am trying to think of as the nature of language is also adequate for the nature of the East Asian language; whether in the end—which would also be the beginning [*Anfang*]—a nature of language can reach the thinking experience, a nature which would offer the assurance that European-Western saying and East Asian saying will enter into dialogue such that in it there sings something that wells up from a single source [*einzigen Quelle*]. (*DL* 8/93–94; em. or.)

The word "also" indicates, to whatever extent, that Heidegger is considering, or has considered, the application of his insight to such issues as: whether his thinking on the nature of language can bring about a beginning in which the nature (Being) of language and thinking are gathered together, whether European-Western saying and East Asian saying can enter into dialogue in the mode as he delineates, that is, to correspond to the saying of Being, to let themselves be appropriated by the inceptive event (Ereignis), such that the initial belonging-together of Being and thinking (that is, the Same) is manifested and articulated. That the end would also be the beginning hints at the structure of temporality in which the future (what is to be said) and the past (what has been said) are gathered together. The tonality of "that one and the same on which we are unanimous" in "Hölderlin and the Essence of Poetry" cited in the previous section finds its counterpart in the phrase "single source" in this passage.

The suggestion that the dialogue between the Japanese and the Inquirer is guided by the single source finds expression throughout the essay in various formulations. Sometimes it is said that they stay on the path of the dialogue only because they, without knowing it, "were obedient to what alone allows a dialogue to succeed" (22/112). In some cases the single source is referred to as the "undefined defining something."[14] To initiate a true dialogue, one needs "[t]o give heed to the trails that direct [*weisen*] thinking back into the region of its source [*Quellbereich*]" (37/124). In the middle of the essay, it is said that when the Japanese asks the Inquirer about hermeneutics, and when the Inquirer asks about the Japanese word for language, they ask each other "the same,"

> J: Thus when I ask you about hermeneutics, and when you ask me what our word is for what you call language, we ask each other the Same [*das Selbe*].
>
> I: Clearly, and that is why we may confidently entrust ourselves to the hidden drift of our dialogue. . . .
>
> J: . . . as long as we remain inquirers. (*DL* 30/123; omission signs original)

Here, the word dialogue appears as well. In seemingly identifying the thrust of the question about the Japanese word for language with that of his explorations of the nature of language in terms of hermeneutics, Heidegger is presumably experimenting with extending the idea of the Same and of dialogue to things from supposedly very different worlds, keeping a close eye on where it would lead.

To make the inquiry about the Japanese word for language is characterized as "walking toward the danger" (23/113). The term "danger," as shown earlier, is closely associated with Heidegger's enterprise of commencing the other beginning that is embedded in the first beginning of (Western) philosophy. In designing this episode, Heidegger may bear in mind a motif from Plato's "Sophist" on which he lectured in 1924–25.[15] In the "Sophist," there is the presence of a visitor from Elea, home of Parmenides and Zeno. In order to complete his account, the visitor has to show that it is possible to speak of things that appear to be true but in fact are false. However, insofar as speaking falsely is saying "what is not," this would contradict his teacher Parmenides' idea. Thus, he is obliged to engage in "parricide" in order to show why Parmenides was wrong.[16] In speaking of the danger of conversing about the nature of language, Heidegger probably feels an acute sense of parricide. He has to go against traditional Western metaphysicians in order to retrace the originary source of the nature of language.

Can the Same Transfigure Itself?

In "The Principle of Identity," the Same means belonging-together, the gathering of Being and thinking. That the question about the Japanese word for language and the question about hermeneutics ask the Same could have the following implications. One should not regard Eastern and Western thinking as static entities; their nature can be brought into a co-correspondence to the Saying of the nature of language. Although each of them may have different grantings from Being that unfold into different histories, East and West can be gathered together by the movement of the Same, of Ereignis. In the meantime, the distinctiveness of East and West will remain.

This may be what Vetsch has in mind in attributing to Heidegger an account for intercultural dialogue according to which diversity shines in the Same. According to Vetsch's Heideggerian interpretation, the Same is the unifying unity that embodies different cultures. It lights up in similar structures of different cultures, but does not show itself. The Same is a value-unquestioned, dynamic, a-categorical unity. It allows a cultural manifoldness to unfold historically (84).

This is a wonderful picture in which East-West encounter could be described as the "intermingling scent [*Ineinanderduften*] of cherry blossom and plum blossom on the same [*selben*] branch" (*DL* 53/153).[17] This picture is similar to Heidegger's suggestion, as recorded in Tezuka's "An Hour with Heidegger," that East and West "must engage in dialogue at such a kind of depth" (May 1996, 62).[18] Granted that Heidegger has wondered about the feasibility of this kind of picture, it proves extremely difficult to spell out what this East-West dialogue could entail. It could be a dialogue in which, in and through an Ereignis whose spectrum is considerably broadened, both East and West re-enact their respective historic beginnings. This is articulated by the Japanese interlocutor in "A Dialogue":

> Professor Tanabe often came back to a question you once put to him: why it was that we Japanese did not call back to mind the time-honoured beginnings [*ehrwürdigen Anfänge*] of our own thinking, instead of chasing ever more greedily after the latest news in European philosophy (*DL* 37/131; tr. m.).

In this remark, Heidegger is considering the plausibility of an East-West dialogue according to which, in analogy with his advocacy for the West to go back to the great beginning of Western philosophy, the East attempts to renew their own beginnings as well. For Kolb, this vision involves relativistic implications. According to him, in Heidegger's account, "there is not . . . any obvious way for two different grantings of presence to come into conflict within an individual or within the spirit of a nation. There seems no way for either salvation or perversion to come from outside" (1986, 231). For Mehta, the differences between East and West do not hamper their mutual communication. This is because, as a scholar of Asian origin, he strongly believes that his ancient thinkers have also reflected upon the (same) question of Being and of language, albeit in quite different ways.[19] To place it in his own words, "May it not be that man as man (irrespective of whether he is Greek, or Chinese, or Indian) has some comprehension of Being insofar as, as man, he has dealings with essents?" (1976, 468)

The question is, how to make sense of the Same in and through which different traditions enter into dialogue? In accordance with the relativistic reading such as Kolb's, the same would at most be similarity of structures of *Ereignisse* that make it possible for the corresponding tradition to retrieve its own beginnings. Proceeding from the universalistic reading such as Mehta's, the same is structuralistic, or functionalistic insofar as, as Heidegger insists, the Same cannot be a "general concept" (*DL* 24/115) under which East and West could be subsumed. One could see that, for the relativist, there is a plurality of *Ereignisse;* for the universalist, there is solely one authentic Ereignis. However, both agree that if *Ereignis* cannot be anything substantial, then it must have a formalistic feature. On the other hand, a universalist who is inclined to ascribe a concrete content to the Same would acknowledge that there are at least common concerns or questions shared by East and West, if not common histories and answers.

For Heidegger, Western-European philosophy is the sole thinking that is determined by the duality of beings and Being and marks the dawning of the human mind; that philosophy is Western is a tautology (*WIP* 30/31); there is not such a thing as Chinese or Indian philosophy (*WCT* 224/228). Serious thinking can only arise from within the same lineage that is born of the first beginning. A reversal can only be achieved by the self-transformation of Western-European thinking, because this is the *topos* where Being has shown itself in the beginning of history, and has determined the destiny that unfolds as the *Ge-stell.*

Given his stress on a "thick" description of the evolvement of Western historicality, Heidegger cannot possibly accept the formalism as suggested by either relativistic or universalistic readings. Then, what would he think about the last proposal that there are at least common concerns or questions shared by the East and West, if not common histories and answers? To be more specific, one may have to admit that Being has also shown itself to the East. In conformity with Heidegger' thinking, Ereignis (or the enactment of the other beginning) is possible, is *not-yet,* only because Being's original Saying *has already been* heard by the early Greeks. Heidegger will have great difficulties in deciding whether or not the East *also* has heard Being's original Saying. What could be a possible solution for this dilemma? One needs to notice that Heidegger does not attribute to Japanese history a "great beginning" (*große Anfang*), but "time-honoured beginnings" (*ehrwürdigen Anfänge*) (*DL* 37/131). Could this differentiation protect Heidegger's story of the unique history of Being from endangerment? Before trying to find a reply to this question, I take a look at the two senses of otherness at play in "A Dialogue," which are suggestive of the difficulties involved when the Same enters into the context of intercultural dialogue.

Two Senses of Otherness

Apart from the suggestion that "a dialogue from house to house remains nearly impossible" made in the opening part of "A Dialogue" (*DL* 5/90), on a few occasions when the dialogue is getting onto the right track, Heidegger emphasizes fundamental differences between East Asian and Western thinking. For example, Heidegger makes his Japanese interlocutor remark that "As far as I am able to follow what you are saying, I sense a deeply hidden kinship with our thinking, precisely because your path of thinking and its language are *so totally other* [*so ganz anders*]" (*DL* 40–41/136; em. ad.). May interprets this passage as Heidegger's confession that "there is a 'deeply hidden kinship' between East Asian thought and his own attempts at thinking" (46).[20] Although he notices that Heidegger "is not further prepared . . .

to explicate the content or extent of this kinship," May does not give much attention to the latter half of this quotation wherein Heidegger's path of thinking and its language are defined as "totally other" to Asian thought. In another place, Heidegger makes the Japanese visitor remark something similar: "*Totally from afar* [*ganz aus der Ferne*] I sense a kinship between our word that is now before my mind [that is, *kotoba*], and your phrase [the phrase "language is the house of Being"]" (*DL* 24/114; em. ad.). In endorsing "a kinship" between the Japanese word *kotoba* and his own phrase, Heidegger does not forget to stress that these two are related in a certain kinship "*totally from afar.*"[21]

In my view, the otherness that Heidegger invokes could be seen from two different perspectives, which suggest similar conclusions. One is that this otherness is an internal otherness, which accords with the differentiating-unifying nature of the Same. While grounding an intimate bond between the East and the West, the Same at the same time bespeaks a fundamental distinctiveness. The otherness is not an inscrutable, impenetrable external otherness; but rather refers to an East interpreted in the light of Heidegger's vocabulary and framework of thinking. The internal otherness of the East represents the necessary tension that contributes to the structure of the belonging-together of the Same.

The other way of interpreting the otherness is to regard it as an indication of Heidegger's awareness that, despite abundant input of his hermeneutic endeavors and maneuvers with regard to Japanese notions such as *kotoba*, he can in no way rest assured that East Asian notions have yielded to his appropriation. He is aware that his experiment with extending the ideas of dialogue and the Same to East-West dialogue turns out to be completely embedded in his own thought, and that East Asian ideas have hardly been considered in their own right.

With the hindsight on Heidegger's concrete occasions of engagements with *kotoba, dao,* and other East-Asian notions, it is clear that the role of the East in the scheme of the "Same" of East and West is significantly marginalized. The general drift of Heidegger's thinking tends toward a picture of East-West dialogue in which the East is invited to join in, or to be of aid to, the central task of leaping into the other beginning of the Western metaphysical tradition.

In view of his presupposition about the singularity of the history of Being, one can see that it proves difficult, almost impossible, for Heidegger to truly engage with Eastern ideas. This would involve either a revision of his presuppositions, or an acceptance of different philosophical concerns and questions. Heidegger finds it demanding to accept either of these alternatives, both of which imply that his story about the history of Being cannot be absolute or ultimate.

If dialogue for Heidegger can only be initiated from within the house of Being, if an authentic dialogue only concerns "that one and the same" that is historic, then one can only speak of a dialogue from house to house insofar as the East engages (or immerses) itself in the project of retrieving Being from within the One House of Being, whose history finds correspondence in Heidegger's thinking. Insofar as Asian ideas and languages are presumably uncontaminated by the *Ge-stell*, they may be able to render help to the project of entering into the other beginning. However, the time is not yet ripe to take them as the starting point or the frame of reference of inquiries.

Heidegger would not worry whether his view involves features of Eurocentrism. This is because, for him, the singular story of the history of Being is more than an ontic narrative of Western historicality. It is a unique story about the origin of man and of the world in the ontological sense. In the meantime, the Other is invited to join, through the medium of a dialogue with early Greek thinkers, in the project of retrieving the first beginning and embarking onto the other beginning.[22]

From his experience of imaginative experimentation of employing his key idea of the "Same" in "A Dialogue," Heidegger may have realized that this attempt leads either to formalistic implications, which he would no doubt denounce, or to something like an authentic dialogue in (co-)correspondence to Being's own Saying. He attempts to qualify this authentic dialogue by making the subtle hierarchical differentiation between the Western "great beginning" and the Japanese "time-honoured beginnings" (*DL* 37/131). However, this qualification is hardly noticeable to most readers. Heidegger's proposal for an "authentic dialogue" (53/152) sounds profound and ineffable, but hardly convincing to be an East-West dialogue.

Conclusion

An answer to the question, "What defines Heidegger's comportment to East-West dialogue?" is to be multi-facetted. There cannot be an answer without equivocation. This is not only because Heidegger's path of thinking is unceasingly underway, but also because this question itself seems to be a *Holzweg* that criss-crosses with a number of other *Holzwege* and *Wegmarken* on Heidegger's route of philosophical reflection.

Heidegger's denouncement of metaphysics has misled some scholars to believe that his philosophical enterprise is set radically against the Western metaphysical tradition. This belief opens avenues for the claim that Heidegger considers that Asian traditions, which are uncontaminated by the dualistic conceptual system of Western metaphysics, have resources in store for the proper thinking of the question of Being and of the nature of language. This may well be an idea Heidegger sometimes entertains. However, before leaping to such a conclusion, one needs to notice that, in the whole of his philosophical undertaking, Heidegger has never changed his belief that Western-European philosophy is the sole thinking that is determined by the duality of beings and Being, the sole thinking that marks the dawning of the human mind. That philosophy is Western is a tautology (*WIP* 31/30). There is no such thing as Chinese or Indian philosophy (*WCT* 224/228). Serious thinking can only arise from within the same lineage that is born of the first beginning. Instead of disposing Western tradition, Heidegger's ultimate expectation is for Western-European metaphysics in the true sense of the word to occur in the other beginning, and for Western-European Dasein to correspond to the call of Being and to reflect on the question of Being from out of its ground.

Heidegger has never provided more clues concerning his reflection upon East-West dialogue than in "A Dialogue." In the latter half of this text, it *looks* as if East and West have entered into a "deep-level" dialogue in the

same mode as what he delineates as authentic *Gespräch*, which is a monologue of Being that is to be heard by man, a dialogue in which "there sings a
single source" (*DL* 8/94), with the interlocutors having their gaze upon "the
Same" that gathers Being and thinking, and an Ereignis, an appropriating
event, in and through which the superficial conceptions of East and West as
immobile entities are let go. However, the question remains, "Do the East
and the West have their gaze on the 'Same' in this deep-level dialogue?"

Given that, for Heidegger, the "Same" cannot be anything general
in the sense of having metaphysical essence, two slightly different replies
to this question suggest themselves. One takes the "Same" to be a similarity in terms of structures of respective Ereignis (according to a relativistic
reading); the other considers that the "Same," as the single event, can only
be functional in the sense of not possessing a content (according to a universalistic reading). It is not possible for Heidegger to accept the formalistic
implications entailed by these two suggestions.

Discussing Heidegger's phrase of a "dialogue from house to house" in
terms of relativism and universalism *seems* to be at odds with Heidegger's
thinking, since this terminological pair is derived from the tradition of
essentialistic thinking (either there are many "incommensurable" unique
essences or there is one unique essence). In this study I have used these
terms with sensitivity to their specific meaning when applied to Heidegger.
They mainly serve as conceptual tools for delineating what is at issue and
what is *not* at issue in Heidegger's thought. In Chapters two and six I have
demonstrated the ways in which Heidegger's writings lend themselves to
relativistic and universalistic interpretations, neither of which, however,
captures the general orientation of his thinking. On Heidegger's own
terms, a "dialogue from house to house" can make sense only insofar as
the East engages itself in the project of retrieving Being from within the
One House of Being that is, out of necessity, built on the great beginning
of (Western) history.

Heidegger's imaginative experimentation of applying his key idea of
the "Same" to East-West dialogue in "A Dialogue" has shown him that this
experiment is intertwined with tensions and ambiguities. Occasionally, he
plays with the idea of projecting East-West dialogue into an undeterminable future (in "three hundred years"). This postponement in a way provides him with justification to evade addressing East-West dialogue in any
detail. However, as long as he keeps the guiding assumptions of his thought
intact, even when an authentic East-West dialogue as he foresees should
happen in the future, it would inevitably be visited by similar irreconcilable
tensions and ambiguities.

On the basis of the investigation carried out in this work, I suggest that one can obtain a perspicuous representation of Heidegger's ambivalence and evasion with respect to the issue of East-West dialogue from the following perspectives. First, Heidegger's primary concern, in the context of his central tenet that Being has been forgotten and that the *Ge-stell* has been dominating the whole globe, is to prepare for the inception of the other beginning, which is possible because of the occurrence of the first beginning with early Greek thinkers. For him, what is embedded in the *Anfang* of Western philosophical tradition is not ontic triviality, but is endowed with unique ontological significance. Therefore, the more urgent and primary undertaking than that of engaging into a dialogue with the East is for the West to achieve self-transformation by way of a dialogue with early Greek thinkers and their language.

From this perspective, one can better understand why Heidegger resolutely refuses to conceive of East-West dialogue as one in which both parties are engaged in genuine interactive communication with mutual attunement and contestation (which is not a Gadamerian dialogue) simply under the pretext that this conception is superficial and lacks historical dimension. The prospect of such a dialogue requires him to expose the fundamental ideas and guiding themes of his philosophy to challenge and revision. He would have to acknowledge the existence of crucial elements of contingency that persist both in East-West dialogue and in the historical development of Western philosophy. This represents too much of a concession for Heidegger to grant.

Second, because of his exacerbating worry about the *Ge-stell*, as well as his limited and yet sustained exposure to intellectual sources from Asia, Heidegger has, now and again, entertained the "preliminary" thought that ancient Asian traditions, insofar as they have not been affected by the *Ge-stell*, might be of help for the enactment of the other beginning, that what he has been striving for may have been articulated by ancient Asian thinkers, that with respect to the essence of art "the Japanese actually [already] have it" (*KD* 214). He appropriates expressions and ideas from Eastern sources and fits them into his own writings, and plays with the idea of a "fruitful confrontation with East-Asian 'thinking'" [1968, 230].

The problem is, how could it be possible for the East to render "help" from *outside* the history of Being? On the one hand, contemporary East Asian thinkers can help in the rather trivial sense that insofar as East Asia is now part of the *Ge-stell*, they can participate in the "planetary" European project of going back to the first beginning and preparing for the other beginning of Western philosophy. On the other hand, leaving it unclear whether "East-Asian 'thinking'" refers to contemporary or ancient Asian thought, Heidegger occasionally hints at the cosmological necessity that the early confrontation of the Greeks with the Asiatic be repeated as a confrontation between European philosophy and East Asian thinking.

Heidegger has been intrigued and struck, especially since the 1940s, by the experience that traditional East Asian languages seem to nicely convey what he intends to say, although it may well be the case that these languages strike him inasmuch as they have already been rendered into Heideggerese. In the meantime, Heidegger is well aware that notwithstanding similarities, there are fundamental differences between his tenets and the general orientation of Asian thinking, in which, for example, is absent the centrality of the role of human beings. Furthermore, he is only willing to appropriate sources from East Asian traditions with the provision that they fit well into and serve as support for his single path of thinking.

Nevertheless, it seems that Heidegger cannot simply disregard the *ontic,* if not ontological, significance of his encounter with East Asian thought— though he cannot resolve the question of how and why of this significance for his *Denkweg*. On numerous occasions of such encounters, he may have been faced with the irresolvable dilemma, "How to include and how *not* to include East Asia in the history of Being?"

Entangled with these conflicting considerations, despite occasional oblique references to East-West dialogue and his thought experiment in "A Dialogue," Heidegger has not been able to provide any substantial account of it. The event of East-West dialogue as he hints at cannot enjoy the same status as the "only one and first beginning" (*CP* 4/5), nor can there be room for it to be part and parcel of the other beginning. It is an event whose occurrence can at most be anticipated, both in the sense that is consistent with the modality of Ereignis, and in the sense that Heidegger fails to provide any condition of possibility for its actuality.

Notes

NOTES TO THE INTRODUCTION

1. The first volume of *Der Untergang des Abendlandes* was published in 1918; the second, subtitled "Perspectives of World History," in 1923. On Heidegger's intellectual relation with Spengler, see Zimmerman (2001).
2. See for example Franklin Perkins, *Leibniz and China. A Commerce of Light* (Cambridge: Cambridge University Press, 2004).
3. In 1966 Heidegger had an interview with the German weekly magazine *Der Spiegel,* on the condition that the content of their interview was not going to be revealed until his death. The relevant document appeared in *Der Spiegel* on 31 May 1976 under the title "Only a God Can Save Us." The text published there differs slightly from the one published in Neske and Kettering (1988) and reprinted in the *Gesamtausgabe* in 2000. The latter version was edited by Hermann Heidegger, Heidegger's son and executor, on the basis of Heidegger's own copy. Soon after the interview in 1966, *Der Spiegel* journalists made editorial revisions twice of the text. Although formally speaking Heidegger approved these revisions, *Der Spiegel* did not provide Heidegger with either the original tape recording or a clear indication of the revisions they had made, which included adding subtitles, squeezing in questions and deleting sentences. See Herman Heidegger, "Comments on *Der Spiegel* Interview," in Neske and Kettering (1990, 233–236). The citation in the main text [1966a, 113/679] will be discussed in Chapter three.
4. Pöggeler (1987a, 50; 1998, 269). In a later publication, Pöggeler cites "had learned more from Chinese" again without giving the source (1999, 107–108).
5. The scholars who misquote this reference that is crucial for the central argument of some of them include Parkes (1992, 406n68), Cho (1992, 307; 1993, 149), May (1996, 8), Zhang (1998, 311). In citing this remark, Bilimoria notes his surprise at it since according to him Heidegger's conversations and dialogues were to a larger extent with the Japanese (1991, 7).

6. The original sentence runs, „wiewohl er von früh an . . . mit Japanern zusammengearbeitet habe. Vom Chinesen habe er indessen mehr gelernt" (Fischer-Barnicol 1977, 102).

7. Gadamer's influence on the understanding of Heidegger by such scholars is already visible in an article of 1970 by Mehta, in which the central task of comparative philosophy is understood as understanding and interpretation (1970, 306).

8. I use the terms "Asian philosophy (thought, traditions)" and "Eastern thinking (thought, ideas)" interchangeably. A slight difference in usage, I presume, is that the word East refers to the broad range of non-Western traditions and is often used in contrast with the word West; whereas the term Asian is more closely associated with specific schools of thought.

9. *Ereignis* has been translated as "appropriation," "propriation," "appropriating event," "e-vent," or "the event of occurrence." I often leave Ereignis untranslated.

NOTES TO CHAPTER ONE

1. In Chapter seven I discuss Heidegger's contact with Indian thought. Compared with the flourish of Heidegger-related studies in Japan, scholarship in China is evidently impoverished. This is undoubtedly related with the tumultuous social and political history in China in the twentieth century, and in particular with the rule of authoritarianism in the academic circle from the 1950s to 1980s, whose negative aftermath remains visible to this date. Xiong Wei (1911–1994), who studied with Heidegger in the 1930s, played a role in introducing Heidegger to China. Xiong wrote, "[Heidegger] has never attempted to convey knowledge, but rather to induce one to think, to think and to say poetically. This makes his lectures very enjoyable. I was really led into a fresh world" (1997, 383). On another occasion, he recalls a moment during Heidegger's seminar on Kant's transcendental dialectic in 1935, when Heidegger remarked, "This is not difficult; it isn't Chinese!" (*Das ist nicht schwer, das ist doch kein Chinesisch!*) (1992, 293).

2. This article originally appeared in *Shisō* (Tokyo), October 1924, and was reprinted in *Tanabe Hajime zenshū* (*The Complete Works of Tanabe Hajime*), 4:17–34. For its German translation see "Die neue Wende in der Phänomenologie—Heideggers Phänomenologie des Lebens" (trans. Johannes Laube), in Buchner (1989, 89–108).

3. About these translations, see Kōzuma Tadashi, "Bibliografie der Heidegger-Übersetzungen und der deutschsprachigen Heidegger-Texte in Japan," in Buchner (1989, 245–262).

4. Cf. Hamada (1994), who comments, "Without [Köbel] the history of Japanese philosophy would have developed otherwise" (8).

5. Cf. Yuasa (1987, 156).

6. In his speech on the occasion of Heidegger's eightieth birthday, Tsujimura Kōichi, one of Yamanouchi's students, claimed that his teacher was the first Japanese who studied with Heidegger (1969, 159).

7. "Sei no sonzaigaku ka shi no benshōhō ka," *Tanabe Hajime zenshū,* 13:525–80.

8. Okakura Kakuzō, *The Ideals of the East* (London: John Murray, 1903); *The Book of Tea* (Rutland VT: Tuttle, 1979 [1906]). On his relation to Kuki, see Pincus (1996, 25–54).

9. On Kuki's relation with French philosophy, see Light (1987).

10. These lectures were soon published in French with the title *Propos sur le Temps,* a copy of which belongs to Husserl's personal library (library code K.U. Leuven, FHUS BA 985).

11. Kuki, *Le problème de la contingence,* trans. Omodaka Hisayuki (Tokyo: University of Tokyo Press, 1966). Originally published as *Gūzensei no mondai* (Tokyo: Iwanami Shoten, 1935). Reprinted in *Kuki Shūzō zenshū* (*The Complete Works of Kuki Shūzō*), vol. 2 (Tokyo: Iwanami Shoten, 1981).

12. There are two English translation of this book: Kuki Shūzō, *Reflections on Japanese Taste. The Structure of Iki,* trans. John Clark (Sydney: Power Publications, 1997); Hiroshi Nara, *The Structure of Detachment: The aesthetic vision of Kuki: With a translation of Iki no kōzō* (Honolulu: University of Hawai'i Press, 2005). Originally published as *Iki no kōzō* in *Shisō* (Tokyo: Iwanami Shoten, 1930). Reprinted in *Kuki Shūzō zenshū* (*The Complete Works of Kuki Shūzō*), vol. 1 (Tokyo: Iwanami Shoten, 1981).

13. According to Tada Michitaro and Yasuda Takeshi. See Dilworth (1998, 194).

14. For an exposition of the relation between Watsuji's philosophy and Heidegger's, see Liederbach (2000).

15. Cf. Yuasa (1987, 167); Blocker and Starling (2001, 129).

16. A copy of the Japanese original and a German translation of this haiku is in Neske (1977) 232–233 (trans. Tsujimura and Buchner).

17. Zen is the Japanese reading of the Chinese word *chan* 禅, which is derived from the Sanskrit *dhyāna* (meditation). *Chan* Buddhism was developed in China in the sixth and seventh century and later spread to Japan. It was made the national religion of Japan in the thirteenth century. In opposing the "adherence to scriptures" advocated by other schools, *chan* Buddhism emphasizes daily practice such as meditation and manual work, and attainment of sudden enlightenment (satori). Because of its introduction to the West through the writings of such figures as D. T. Suzuki and Masao Abe, this branch of Buddhism is more known in the Western world as Zen Buddhism, rather than *chan* Buddhism.

18. A number of publications on this matter have appeared in the international journal *The Eastern Buddhist* as well. Willfred Hartig (1997) provides a comprehensive overview of the literature concerning Heidegger and Zen-Buddhism; he

also appends a long list of scholars from East Asian countries who have visited Heidegger and/or published on Heidegger and Buddhism.

19. It is a matter of debate whether or not the trend of thought as represented by the Kyoto School was complicit with Japanese fascism and militarism. The articles in Heisig and Maraldo (1994) examine the awakenings of consciousness with a nationalistic tendency as represented in the new trend of Zen thought and the Kyoto school. For a severe critique of this representation, see Parkes (1997) and Michima (1992). In a more recent article, Sandford (2003) explicitly relates Heidegger's influence with Japanese fascism.

20. Cf. Liederbach (2000, 11); Ōhashi (1989b, 26).

21. The three *Festschriften* are: Gadamer (1969), Klostermann (1970), Klostermann (1977). The last edition was published on the occasion of Heidegger's death. It consists of transcripts of recorded speeches delivered to Heidegger in honour of his eightieth year. Tsujimura's address occurs on page 60.

22. Tsujimura (1969), in Buchner (1989, 159–165).

23. But he also remarks in the same text that embedded in the kinship between Heidegger's thought and Zen Buddhism is a deep chasm (*tiefe Kluft*).

24. In his early years, Hisamatsu's faith in Buddhism was destroyed while studying natural sciences. It was through following a course by Nishida that he retrieved his faith and began to study philosophy. After 1935, he taught philosophy and Buddhist theology at the Imperial University of Kyoto, while living a secluded life in a Zen monastery.

25. Suzuki Daisetz Teitaro (1870–1966) was educated at Tokyo University and in the United States and later on taught at leading universities in Japan, Europe, and the United States. His English publications on Zen Buddhism are well known in the West.

26. After noting the rumor that Heidegger was quite impressed by Suzuki's writings on Zen (referring to Chang 1977a) and suggesting that Heidegger finds in the Japanese writer something similar to "the step back," David Kolb draws attention to the relativistic implications of these gestures in saying "this is not strictly an influence opening the West to new possibilities but an encouragement to live our tradition in the way in which all grantings of unconcealment should be lived" (1986, 233).

27. Chang (1974, 1975, 1977a, 1977b, 1977c), among other publications. Chang obtained a PhD at Columbia University in 1962 before working at the University of Hawai'i.

28. These are the first two verses of chapter 48 from the *Daodejing*: 為學者日益，為道者日損.

29. May gives as reference for the first line *Zhuangzi* 22 and for the second line *WCT* 9/7. Heidegger was familiar with Wilhelm's translation of the *Zhuangzi* (cf. [1962b, 29n2]; Petzet 1983, 24).

30. Again in a translation of Wilhelm (1911). See further Chapter six.

31. For example Elberfeld (2000, 153), Strolz (1984, 92), Wohlfahrt (2003, 49), and Cho (1993, 148).

32. Fu also argues that although Heidegger's notion of Ereignis bears affinity to Daoist naturalism, it is influenced by Christian eschatology.

33. This review is posted on http://faculty.vassar.edu/brannor/heidegger.html.

34. A slightly revised version appears as a chapter in Pöggeler (1998). John Maraldo perceives quite a number of strained and questionable comparisons in some of the articles, and wonders "what causes so many commentators to seek a non-Western, often Daoist or Zen, counterpart to so many seminal Heideggerian themes" ("Review of *Heidegger and Asian Thought*—Graham Parkes," *Philosophy East & West* 40 (1990): 100–105; 102).

35. For a comprehensive overview of German-language literature on Heidegger's Asian connection see Elberfeld (2003), a chapter in the *Heidegger Handbuch* of 2003.

36. Weinmayr's article from this collection, which is a comparison of Heidegger and Nishida, has been translated into English in 2005 (Weinmayr 2005).

37. These pieces are [1958a], [1958b], [1963c], [1966b], [1968], [1969a], [1974a].

38. According to Ram Adhar Mall, one of the pioneers, intercultural philosophy stands for a "new orientation in and of philosophy, and it accompanies all of the different concrete philosophical traditions and forbids them to put themselves in an absolute, monolithic position" (2000, xii).

39. Others include Willfred Hartig (1997), Klaus Seeland (1998) and A.W. Prins (1996).

40. In translating Reinhard May's work, Parkes disposes the archaic phrase "*ex oriente lux* (light from the East)," and uses "hidden sources" culled from Heidegger's essay "Hints" (*Winke*). Parkes (1996, 65) cites, "If the language of human beings is in the word, only then is she in order. If she is in order, then the assurance of hidden sources [*verborgenen Quellen*] hints at her" [1941b, 33].

41. *The Analects*, Book two, section four.

42. According to Petzet, it is a significant work in Heidegger's own eyes and it opens up a pathway that "connects Heidegger's thinking with the world of the Far East" (1993 [1983], 166). For Parkes, this is "the only extended engagement with Asian philosophy in Heidegger's published works" (1987, 213). A more recent article (Park 2005) attempts to make a few critical remarks in a Gadamerian spirit, which, however, are ambiguous and inconsistent with its positive interpretation of Heidegger's text.

43. John Macquarrie (1994, 120) suggests that in this essay Heidegger is conversing with Nishitani Keiji. Miles Groth (2004, 146) presumes that the Japanese may be modeled on Hisamatsu Shinichi.

44. Tezuka's main publications include *In Search of the Spirit of Western Europe, Modern German Poets, Studies on [Stefan] George and Rilke* (all in Japanese).

Among his translations are Heidegger's *Elucidations of Hölderlin's Poetry,* "What are Poets for?," and "A Dialogue on Language," as well as Nietzsche's *Thus Spoke Zarathustra,* Goethe's *Collected Poems,* Carossa's *The Year of Beautiful Deceptions,* and Hesse's *Siddhartha.*

45. When Tezuka translated "A Dialogue on Language" ("Kotoba ni tsuite no taiwa") into Japanese he added three texts of his own, published in *Haidegga zenshū (The Complete Works of Heidegger),* 21:137–166 (Tokyo: Risō 1968). I will refer to the Japanese texts as Tezuka (1968). Most of my references will be to "An Hour with Heidegger" ("Haidegga to no ichi jikan") and to its English translation (by Parkes) in May (1996, 59–64). (There is a Japanese and German bilingual version in May 1989, 82–99; pagination of the Japanese original is 21:159–166.) Then there is "Three Answers," one answer of which (the one by Heidegger) was translated into German together with "An Hour with Heidegger" (Buchner 1989, 137–181, Vetsch 1992, 189–197; pagination of the Japanese original of all three answers is 21:151–158). Finally, there is an "Afterword" ("Kaisetzu," 21:137–50), which has not been translated into any Western language.

46. Tezuka (1968, 139–40); Cited partly in English translation in Parkes (1996, 66, translator's notes, No. o) and in German in Yoneda (1984, 91n1).

47. In a conversation with Panikkar, Heidegger admitted that in "A Dialogue," he had "occasionally put his own thoughts in the mouth of the Japanese partner" (1977, 175).

48. After this exchange, Tezuka asked a question about the meaning of "nature" for Hölderlin, to which Heidegger answered that nature had a metaphysical meaning as well as a sense of fatherland for him.

49. Cho studied in Germany in the 1950s and held visiting positions there several times. The presence of Heidegger's "Japanese connection," as distinct from the Chinese connection, seems to be stronger in the German literature. This might have formed the background against which Cho attempts to explain away the significance of Japanese themes in "A Dialogue," and argues that it is in essence a dialogue with Laozi.

50. Heidegger's collaboration with Hsiao and reference to the word *dao* will be discussed in Chapters six and seven.

NOTES TO CHAPTER TWO

1. Heidegger has never offered an intellectual autobiography. Once he explains that if he would do so, his sayings would be treated as fixed "opinion" (*Meinung*), rather than "direction" (*Weisung*) of the path of independent reflection, such that, what is still to be thought would fall into oblivion [1962c, xiii].

2. See Chapter four.

3. My statement in made with the awareness that Heidegger's corpus contains multiple possibilities of exegeses, and his philosophy has been interpreted and applied to a variety of disciplines with special attention to the role of the ontic being-in-the-world. For my purpose of elucidating his position with regard to East-West dialogue, his stress on the centrality of the question of Being is most relevant.

4. Among these materials are, "A Dialogue on Language" [1953/54]; "A Recollection" [1957b], which was originally the inaugural speech to the Heidelberg Academy of Sciences in 1957; his letter to William J. Richardson in April 1962 in response to the latter's questions about his philosophy [1962c], and "My Way to Phenomenology" [1963b].

5. See van Buren (2005, 19). He regards this transition as a turn in Heidegger's thinking that is as profound as the turn in the years following the publication of *Being and Time*.

6. According to Kisiel, "The underscoring of '-logian' in fact shifts the focus to the philosophical foundations of theology in the fundamental experiences which phenomenology aims to explore" (2002, 13).

7. Cf. Taminiaux (1994, 70).

8. A similar disclaimer is, "this change is not a consequence of altering the standpoint, much less of abandoning the fundamental issue of *Being and Time*" [1962c, xvi].

9. Emad and Maly, translators of the *Contributions,* render *Seyn* as be-ing. However, *Beyng* seems to be a more suitable translation. Heidegger may have been inspired by Hölderlin, who uses *Seyn* in a short philosophical writing in 1795: "*Seyn*—expresses the joining of Subject and Object" (Hölderlin, 515).

10. Sheehan also invokes the phrase *auf einen Stern zugehen,* only that he insists on identifying Ereignis as the "one and only star" that guided Heidegger's journey (2001b, 4).

11. This lecture course deals with the hymns "Germania" and "The Rhine." The lecture notes were published as *GA* 39 in 1980 [1934/35]. There are two other lecture courses on Hölderlin: one on "Remembrance" [1941/42], which is related to, and yet to be distinguished from the lecture on "Remembrance" [1943c]; the other one was devoted to the hymn "The Ister" [1942]. In addition, several lectures on Hölderlin were published in 1996 as *GA* 4 under the title *Erläuterungen zu Hölderlins Dichtung*. A few other relevant writings and notes appear in *GA* 75 under the title *Zu Hölderlin—Griechenlandreisen* [2000c].

12. See *DL* 7/92.

13. The notes for this lecture course were published as late as 1998 as *GA* 38, under the title *Logik als die Frage nach dem Wesen der Sprache* [1934].

14. Cf. *ID* 33n1; Stambaugh (1973, x).

15. This is Heidegger's own retrospective comment on *Being and Time* made in the "Letter on Humanism" (*LH* 243/318).

16. On other occasions, Heidegger states that what is meant by the *Wesen* of language "cannot be anything linguistic," that is, it cannot be a subject of philology (*DL* 23f/114); nor has it to do with "metalinguistics," scientific, or philosophical investigation of languages in the ordinary sense (*OWL* 58/160).

17. Cf. [1946b, 239/313, 243/318, 274/361], [1946c, 232/310], [1953/54, 5/89, 22/111, 24/115], [1955–56, 96/143], [1955–57, 39/104], [1959c, 135/267], [2001, 181/226].

18. Heidegger often uses the word "man" without explication of its connotation. From the context it presumably refers to Western man who has the potential to hear the call of Being, and to stand into the open and thus to achieve his essence.

19. In "Letter on Humanism" Heidegger speaks more about this dimension. Only in *ek-sisting* is man claimed by Being, and has language as his abode. Heidegger explains that *ek-sistence* does not coincide with *existentia*. *Ek-sistence* means "standing out into the truth of Being," while "*existentia* (existence) means in contrast *actualitas*, actuality as opposed to mere possibility as Idea" (*LH* 249/236).

20. For the above quotations, see *OWL* 94–5/200–1.

21. Elisabeth Hirsch translates *die Sage* as "the primal utterance" (1970, 263).

22. These agitated exclamations bear kinship with Karl Barth's dialectical theology that is developed in his commentary on *The Epistle to the Romans* published in 1922. Barth's thought represents a defense on behalf of God, to whom no culture has access, against the God of culture. Heidegger once remarked that "the only spiritual life of the age was in Karl Barth" (cited in Safranski 1998, 111–112).

23. For Heidegger, Ereignis is "not simply an occurrence, but that which makes any occurrence possible" (*TB* 19/20).

24. Cf. Ihde (1973); Taylor (2002).

25. Rorty and Lafont assume that such expressions as "language speaks," the "single star," "single word(s)," and the reflection in terms of the essence of language are clear indications of reification of language. Charles Taylor (2005) nevertheless discerns in these characterizations a constitutive theory of language.

26. Martin Kusch (1989) defines "language as the universal medium," and "language as calculus" as two opposite views of language. Characterizing Heidegger's reflection on language as embodying a version of "universal medium," Kusch also claims that there is a "linguistic relativism" in Heidegger (6–7). He provides a scheme of eight main ingredients of the conception of language as the universal medium. "Linguistic relativism" is one among them. However, as Jitendrana Mohanty points out, "Language as the universal medium" is already a reduction of the world to a language. "Language as calculus" is a further reduction of language to grammar and/or logic. Both views are abstract reductions derived from

"the difficulty of empirically grounding the claim to radical difference between two cultures" (2000, 97–8).

27. By the term "neutralized" and "neutralization," I mean the orientation of interpretation that does not take into account the fact that Heidegger's remarks are intended as at once ontological and ontic.

NOTES TO CHAPTER THREE

1. Emad and Maly's translation "the one and only first beginning [*dem einzig einen und ersten Anfang*]" obscures the implication that there is only one first beginning.
2. Joseph P. Fell argues that the first beginning is the other beginning "in disguise" (1971, 237). He considers that the other beginning represents "a future and merely 'possible' terminus toward whose realization his thinking is 'underway'" (213).
3. For example, May, Mehta, Thurnher, and others, whose views are referred to in subsequent chapters.
4. In the concluding paragraph of the "Letter on Humanism" [1946b], Heidegger speaks of philosophy and metaphysics as identical: "The thinking that is to come is no longer philosophy, because it thinks more originarily than metaphysics—a name identical to philosophy" (*LH* 276/364). In this place, he is using the word "philosophy" in the narrow sense.
5. These two occasions are, "And who of us can decide whether or not one day in Russia and China the ancient traditions [*uralte Überlieferungen*] of a 'thought' will awaken which will help make possible for man a free relationship to the technical world?" [1966a, 111/677]; "By thinking the clearing and characterizing it adequately, we reach a realm that can perhaps make it possible to bring a transformed European thinking into a fruitful confrontation with East-Asian 'thinking'" [1968, 230]. See for further discussion of these citations the last section of this chapter.
6. In "Overcoming Metaphysics," Heidegger connects world wars with the abandonment of Being, "The 'world wars' and their character of 'totality' are already a consequence of the abandonment of Being. . . . Contending with a long war is only the already outdated form in which what is new about the age of consumption is acknowledged" (*OM* 84–5/91).
7. This was originally delivered on 9 June 1938 as a lecture entitled "The Founding of the Modern World Picture." It was the last of a series of lectures on this theme.
8. Heidegger deploys remarkably similar formulations in thematizing on language and on technology. For example, "the essence of technology is by no means something technological" [1953a, 311/7]; "the essential *being* of language cannot be anything linguistic" [1953/4, 23–24/114]. He uses the term "danger" in both cases (see *QT* and *DL*).

9. In his lecture course on Plato's *Sophist* in 1924/25, Heidegger discusses the relation between τέχνε and ἀλήθεια in these terms. Much later Heidegger characterizes τέχνε as a kind of knowledge in the sense of making manifest and bringing to presence [1962b, 135/15]. Zimmerman summarizes Heidegger's notion of τέχνε as "the disclosive occasioning that makes presencing and bringing-forth possible" (1990, 233).

10. Similar remarks are made in [1949a, 60] and [1962b, 134/13]. Feenberg rightly observes that Heidegger's notion of the essence of technology is disconnected from actual devices (2000, 449).

11. Cf. *QT* 320/15.

12. Hölderlin, *Sämtliche Werke*, vol. IV, p. 190. Cited in [1946c, 222/295] and *QT* 333/29.

13. A similar remark is, "Assuming we could look forward to the possibility that the *Ge-stell*—the mutual challenge of man and Being to enter the calculation of what is calculable—were to address itself to us as the event of appropriation [*Ereignis*] which first surrenders man and Being to their own being; then a path would be open for man to experience in a more originary way—the totality of the modern technological world, nature and history, and above all their Being" (*ID* 40/105).

14. The same idea is repeated in [1969c, 61/367].

15. Apart from ancient Chinese, Indian, and Greek traditions, Jaspers also refers to the Middle Eastern traditions such as the Iranian and Palestinian ones.

16. In the same letter, Heidegger states that the only possibility of finding the essential ownness of man is to search from inside the governing domain of the *Ge-stell* [1963c, 224–25].

17. The same passage appears in his letter of greetings to a Symposium in Beirut in November 1974 [1974b].

18. These authors include, for example, Loscerbo (1981); Rojcewicz (2006); Zimmerman (1990).

19. Heidegger has deliberately used the same title as Jünger's. The English translations are different because of the different meaning they ascribe to the word *über*.

20. The use of the word *Zwiesprache* instead of *Gespräch* (which is what Heidegger normally uses in the phrase East-West dialogue) may be connected with his pessimistic tone in this particular essay. A *Gespräch* speaks from out of the nature of Being and its language, whereas a *Zwiesprache* has to proceed under the guidance or sheltering of a thinking on originary Being. It seems to be more closely related with the Greek world. See the following passage:

> At the outset of the destining of the West, in Greece, the arts soared to the supreme height of the revealing granted them. They brought to light the presence of the gods and the dialogue [*Zwiesprache*] of divine and human destinings. (*QT* 339/34)

The *Zwiesprache* of divine and human destinings is made possible by the unconcealment of Being in ancient Greece. Heidegger's use of *Zwiesprache* in "On the Question of Being" [1955a] denotes his uncertainty whether a *Zwiesprache* between East and West could be possible, given that the gods have fled, Being withdrawn, the earth and heaven as depicted in Hölderlin's poetry vanished, and the powerful planetarization is reigning supreme.

21. In this connection, Halbfass rightly remarks that the enigmatic future "dialogue" with the East, to which Heidegger refers, cannot be planned and organized. What we may have to learn above all is *Gelassenheit*, a serene willingness to wait, and *not* to plan for this future (1988, 170).

22. Buchner was the editor of *Japan und Heidegger*. In a letter to Max Müller on 5 October 1966, Heidegger endorsed Müller's decision to appoint Hartmut Buchner, for the reason that he was well qualified and in addition had at his disposal East Asian experience that was not easy to obtain [2003b, 55f].

23. This concern about the depth of East-West dialogue echoes what Heidegger states during his meeting with Tezuka: "East and West should enter into dialogue at this kind of depth" (May 1996, 62; tr. m.). Cf. Chapter nine.

NOTES TO CHAPTER FOUR

1. Essentially related to *Heimat* is the word *Geheimnis* (secret, mystery), to which Heidegger ascribes a unique sense in light of Being-historic thinking. The true mystery is not "a particular mystery about this and that," but is rather the "one" (*Eine*), "the concealing of what is concealed as a whole, of beings as such" (*ET* 148/194), with concealment meaning "the authentic un-truth that is most ownnest [*Eigenste*] to the essence of truth" (148/193).

2. The italicized part of the citation is what Heidegger cites from the preface of Hebel's Alemannic Poetry (1802). He gives as the reference "*J. P. Hebels Werke*, Bd. 1, S. 197, ed. Wilh. Altwegg."

3. Cited from an earlier preface to "Homecoming / To Kindred Ones" [1949d, 234].

4. In the "Letter on Humanism," Heidegger speaks of the West (*Abendland*) in terms of the "nearness to the source" as well [*LH* 257/338].

5. Heidegger's view on the "inner relationship of the German language with the language of the Greeks and with their thought" [1966a, 113/679] has been often referred to. Cf. [1941a, 14] and *DL* 24/87.

6. Already in 1939 Heidegger wrote a note on the philosophical misinterpretation of "homeland [*Vaterland*]" in Hölderlin's writings [1939b, 277]; cf. also "Das abendländische Gespräch" [1946–48, 167].

7. "Istros" and "Ister" are the Greek and the Roman names for the lower course of the river whose upper course is called the Danube.

8. The German for these two lines is,
   nemlich zu Hauß ist der Geist
   Nicht im Anfang, nicht an der Quell. Ihn zehret die Heimath.

9. In the lecture course on Hölderlin's "Remembrance," Heidegger makes similar remarks,

   If things remain at the stage of rejecting the foreign, or to eliminate it completely, then the necessary opportunity for passing through the foreign and with it, the possibility of the homecoming in the own and thereby this itself will be lost. [1941/42, 190]

10. According to Gosetti-Ferencei, Hölderlin's relation to Greece is situated in the context of his subscription to the Kantian ideal of freedom; whereas Heidegger seeks in his references to Greece the possibility of a reversal of thinking and Being, whose authenticity has been lost in the advent of metaphysics and humanism (2004, 281).

11. Heidegger's argument may be supported by the following passage from a letter of Hölderlin in 1801:

    Yet what is familiar must be learned as well as what is alien. This is why the Greeks are so indispensable for us. It is only that we will not follow them in our own, national [spirit] since, as I said, the *free* use of *what is one's own* is the most difficult. (Pau 1988, 150; square brackets original)

    It seems that Hölderlin's advice that the Germans should not simplistically follow the Greeks derives from the emphasis that the familiar has to be learned as well, and this is the most difficult.

12. Pöggeler also points out that it is by means of a "difference which joins together [i.e. conjoining in distinction]" that Hölderlin seeks to come from the foreign to what is one's own (1987b, 180).

13. For example, when translating one of Heidegger's lecture courses on Nietzsche, David Krell renders *morgenländische Geschichte* as "the history of antiquity" [1937a, 132/395].

14. Quoted in Brusotti (2004, 47).

15. The German original reads: "Wird dieses Abend-Land über Occident und Orient hinweg und durch das Europäische hindurch erst die Ortschaft der kommenden anfänglicher geschickten Geschichte?"

16. Compared with the occidental, Europe seems to better represent the spiritual unity and the contemporary state of the West. Cf. "Does the occidental still exist? It has become Europe. Europe's technological-industrial domination has already covered the entire earth" (*EHP* 201/177); cf. also, "Today we know that the Anglo-Saxon world of Americanism is determined to destroy Europe, and thus our homeland, and thus the origin of the Occidental" (*HHI* 54/68).

NOTES TO CHAPTER FIVE

1. What is in square brackets is added in the 1953 edition.

2. Cf. Bernasconi (1995b, 252, n1).
3. Nietzsche, *Human, All too Human,* as cited by Scheiffele (39–40).
4. *Briefwechsel zwischen Wilhelm Dilthey und dem Grafen Paul Yorck v. Warten-burg, 1877–1897* (Halle-an-der-Saale: Max Niemeyer, 1923), 61. Quoted from *Being and Time* [1927, 452/400].
5. Cf. Inwood (1999, 67–69).
6. Heidegger's distinction between *Geschick* and *Fatum* bears resemblance to Leibniz's differentiation between three types of *Fatum:* 1. *Fatum Mahometa-num,* which is inscrutable and inescapable; 2. *Fatum Stoicum,* which human beings can understand and thereby achieve inner tranquility; 3. *Fatum Christianum,* which is sent by a benign deity (Gottfried Wilhelm Leibniz, *Theodicy* (1710), § 58). It is clear that the first type suggests something like an inscrutable Asiatic *Fatum* as characterized by Heidegger; whereas the third type is similar to Heidegger's notion of *Geschick.*
7. See *DL* 3/87.
8. Cf. the last paragraph of "Ways toward Discussion":

   If we move the historic *Dasein* of both these neighbouring nations [*Nachbarvölker*] into the field of vision of those reflections, which go beyond the renewal of the basic structure of occidental Being, only then a real space for neighbourhood reveals itself in its broadest width [*weitesten Weite*]. If peoples want to enter this space, and that means to say, wish to give it form creatively, then the basic conditions of true understanding should stand clearly before the inner eye. There are two conditions: the enduring will to listen to one another and the measured pace of courage for self-determination. The one does not let itself be deceived and weakened by fleeting results of disingenuous understand-ing [*Verständigung*]. The other makes the participants sure of them-selves and only then able to be open with the other. [1937b, 21]

9. Bernasconi observes that Heidegger acknowledges the importance of the Asiatic for the Greeks "only so long as that was not the issue at hand" (1995a, 348). In his view, Heidegger's exclusion of the Asiatic from the ori-gin of occidental metaphysics and his denial of the possibility of Christian philosophy are the preconditions for another beginning of thinking.
10. The word *Bewahrung* has the connotation of guarding, shielding, protect-ing, preserving, and saving from.
11. With reference to Heidegger's saying that only by confronting the Asiatic, which was the most foreign, could the Greeks have built the fundament of Western history [1937b, 21], Ōhashi (1989a, 130) claims that, from Hei-degger's point of view, this experience with the Asiatic is not only contained in the "first beginning," but also present in or paralleled with the "other begin-ning." If one were to talk about an "other beginning," not only the "other" in connection with the first beginning, but also the "other" with respect to the Western world (that is, the East Asian world that stays immune from the rule

of modern technology), should be included in thinking. I would suggest that one should understand Heidegger's relevant remarks in the context of his times. Furthermore, Ōhashi has ignored the fact that the militant tone in which Heidegger speaks of the early Greeks' confrontation with the Asiatic is certainly distinct from a supposedly positive dialogue with the East in the present age.

12. Cf. *HHI* 4/5; *EHP* 105/81, 108/83, 160–163/139–41.
13. Bernasconi claims that Heidegger has tried to diminish, or to efface Hölderlin's evocation of the role of Asia, which conforms to the same practice in his mention of confrontation with the Asiatic (1995a, 345). To the contrary, Pöggeler thinks that "contrary to Hölderlin, Heidegger distinguished the Greek from the Oriental" (1987a, 54). Neither of them provides sufficient arguments for their views.
14. Cited from Petzet (1993, 164).

NOTES TO CHAPTER SIX

1. *Daodejing, dao,* and *Laozi* are contemporary standard *pinyin* transliterations of the Chinese characters (道德经 , 道 , and 老子). Transliterations on the basis of the Wade system, which was commonly used in the past, are *Tao Te Ching, Tao,* and *Laotse* (or *Lao Tzu*). I write *dao* in lower case in agreement with a pluralistic understanding of *dao*. Such scholars as Chan Wing-tsit (1963) and A. C. Graham (1989) have questioned the legitimacy of attributing the authorship of the *Daodejing* to a single legendary figure called Laozi. In this book I use the name "Laozi" as the implied author(s) of the *Daodejing.*
2. Cited in Legge (1961, xiii).
3. For an overview of *Daodejing*'s translations as of 1998, see Hardy (1998).
4. In an earlier essay Hansen (1983b) had already hinted at a pluralistic interpretation of *dao.*
5. *dao ke dao ye, fei heng dao ye* 道可道也 , 非恆道也 [Mawang Dui A] ; *dao ke dao, fei chang dao* 道可道 , 非常道 [Wang Bi].
6. Ames and Hall render the first verse of the *Daodejing* as, "Way-making that can be put into words is not really way-making." Underlying the translation of *dao* as "way-making" is a sophisticated interpretation of the *Daodejing* as embracing a world view which they describe as "acosmotic" (2003, 13–15). I prefer Ivanhoe's translation, "A Way that can be followed is not a constant Way" (2002, 1). This rendering is consistent with ancient Chinese grammar in that it treats the meaning of the two words of *dao* as belonging to the same field of meaning with different functions.
7. All these three versions are available in Gao Ming (1996).
8. *Zhuangzi* is the *pinyin* transliteration of the name of the philosopher and his work, 庄子. The Wade transliteration is *Chuang Tzu*. An older German transliteration is *Dschuang-Dsï*. Similar to the case of the *Daodejing,* there

are also doubts whether the collection called the *Zhuangzi* can be attributed to a single author.

9. For an account of this incident, see Petzet (1993, 17–19). The story of the happiness of the fish is originally from chapter 17 of the *Zhuangzi.*

10. See Pöggeler (1999, 111).

11. „Dschuang-Dsï, Das wahre Buch vom südlichen Blütenland. Aus dem Chinesischen verdeutscht und erläutert von Richard Wilhelm. Eugen Diederichs, Jena 1923, S. 7. Vgl. S. 33 ff" [1962, /29].

12. See Graham (1981, 63–65, 88–89) and Watson (1968, 72–3, 123) for translations of the stories of the tree and of the fish.

13. The etymological details that Heidegger provides pertain so closely to the German language that the English translator has simply omitted the relevant paragraph.

14. The first quotation is from Hegel (1971, vol. 18, 146); the second from Hegel (1982, vol. II, 556); the third again from Hegel (1971, vol. 12, 71).

15. As early as 1842, Stanislaw Julien translates *dao* as *voie: Le livre de la voie et de la vertu.*

16. Reinhard May claims that Heidegger's use of *dao* in these two paragraphs self-evidently shows that he is pursuing transcultural thinking (1996, 35–44).

17. This exchange with Jaspers is discussed more fully in the next chapter.

18. Zhang (1998, 302–303) is obviously following Cho in stating that *dao* has the same significance for Heidegger as "logos" and "Ereignis" have, though without referring to Cho's work. On the factual basis of Heidegger's reference to *dao* in these two essays, his citation from chapter 28 of the *Daodejing* [1957a, 56/93] and of Zhuangzi's idea of the useless tree [1962b] (Zhang 1998, 315–328), and in particular on the ground of his change of the word *Wesen* (*yong*) into *Sein* when citing from a German version of chapter 11 [1943b] (Zhang 2005), Zhang seems to have found the incontrovertible evidence for Heidegger's special bond with *dao.*

19. Pöggeler considers that Heidegger's connection of *Weg* and *bewegen* is etymologically plausible in German, but this etymological play of words is not possible in Chinese (1999, 113).

20. In the original publication of the lecture "Basic Principles of Thinking" in *Jahrbuch für Psychologie und Psychotherapie,* vol. 6 (1959), it is incorrectly printed, "Laotse sagt (Kap. XVII; übersetzt von V. v. Strauss)." In the English translation by Hart and Maraldo (1976), this mistake is retained: "Lao Tzu says (Ch. 17)," and the reference to von Strauss is deleted. Although this is corrected in the *Gesamtausgabe* (vol. /9, 1994) with more detailed bibliographic information provided in a note (p. 93), the mistaken reference to chapter 17 (instead of 28) has been repeated throughout the secondary literature (e.g. Elberfeld 2000, 154; Zimmermann 1981, 256).

21. Ular's translation is, "to feel oneself as clear, to show oneself as dark" (*Klar sich fühlen, dunkel sich zeigen*) (20); Wilhelm's translation is, "Who recognizes

light, and nevertheless dwells in darkness" (*Wer Licht erkennt, und dennoch im Dunkel weilt*) (30). Almost all English translators render the character 白 *bai* as "white," or "whiteness," and take this verse to be an illustration of the relation between polarities.

22. Other pairs of contraries mentioned in chapter 28 of the *Daodejing* are male versus female, and clean versus soiled.

23. Pöggeler's interpretation of Heidegger's use of Laozi's verse is quite different from mine. He puts emphasis on the phrase "dark light" in Hölderlin's verses which Heidegger quotes before citing from the *Daodejing*. Pöggeler connects the "dark light" with the red Bordeaux of southern France. In the wine pressed from the grapes Hölderlin sees the fruit of earth and sky. Pöggeler explains, "Humans, who live in a world which features a finite historical openness from the midst of a concealing mystery, are themselves a light that must conceal itself in the darkness of that mystery" (Pöggeler 1998, 281). According to Pöggeler, the theme of Laozi's chapter 28 concerns the unity within which male and female, light and dark, honour and disgrace are combined. Compared with this, the light which science and technology bring into the world is destructive in its measureless glare. Pöggeler considers that the contraries used in Laozi's chapter can be interconnected with Heidegger's characterization of the world as a "limited openness of a livable world" (1998, 281). However, he does not address Heidegger's twist in using Laozi's verse.

24. Cf. "On the Essence of Truth" [1930b].

25. Cf. D. C. Lau (1958, 350).

26. See Heidegger *Nachlass* catalogue number 85.3/17 (Deutsches Literaturarchiv, Marbach); also cited in Petzet (1993, 181). In the 1983 German edition of this book, Petzet mistakenly ascribes the translation to Richard Wilhelm. This is corrected in the English translation. Ernst Jünger (1895–1998) is a well-known novelist and essayist. In the early period of his career, he was allegedly an ardent militarist and nihilist. This was changed in the 1940s. He became one committed to a strong belief in peace, European federation, and individual dignity.

27. Heidegger has kept to the translation of Ulenbrook (1962) except for one place in the fourth line. It was originally "und des Himmels Weg sehen." Ular translates this sentence as "Ohne hinauszusehen, kann man durchschauen" (34); Wilhelm's translation is "Ohne aus dem Fenster zu blicken, kann man des Himmels SINN erschauen" (52); von Strauss' version is, "nicht ausblickend durchs Fenster, sieht man des Himmels Weg" (214).

28. A defense of Heidegger is that he is only disparaging the superficial and insignificant foreign, while concerned with the authentic foreign. I have already explicated that the authentic foreign Heidegger has in mind is the Greek.

29. Ames and Hall think that phrases in D. C. Lau's translation of chapter 47 such as "By not setting foot outside the door . . ." and "By not looking out

of the window . . ." are suggestive of this idea (151). However, interpreting the "by" structure as pointing to a necessary condition seems to be strained.

30. Heidegger writes, "To be someone with a famous name is a gruesome thing. Even the Foreign Institute in Stuttgart has sought me out *here* and has sent a Japanese person, who invited me to Japan for several months during next year" (*ZS* 251/315; em. or.).

31. The word *vor* that Heidegger emphasizes may indicate a sense of future. We are before the unseemingly simplicity, since it is always coming.

32. Von Strauss translates *yong* as *Gebrauch;* Wilhelm translates it as *Werk.* Zhang (2005) attaches great importance to Heidegger's change of Ular's word *Wesenheit* into *Sein.* Zhang comments that this linguistic modification indicates the great extent to which Heidegger has engaged in a dialogue with Laozi, since Heidegger has read his notions of "ontological difference" and "Being" into Laozi's thinking. On this textual basis, Zhang makes the claim that Heidegger has written *Sein und Zeit* in dialogue with Laozi. It seems that Zhang is not aware of current established interpretation of *you* and *wu* and therefore the question whether Heidegger's consideration of the question of "Being" and "ontological difference" can be ascribed to Laozi unquestionably has not occurred to him.

33. Von Strauss' translation of *wu* is *Nichtseyn;* Wilhelm's is *Nichts* except for *Nichtsein* on the last occasion.

34. A Chinese author claims for the same way of periodization as mine. But the point he makes out of this is different. He argues that *wu* is as important as *you,* both being abstract notions (He Shibin 2005, 41). Zhu Qianzhi's version ([1996] 1984) of this chapter also reads *you* as going with *wu.*

35. See Graham (1990, 412, 343–351). Cf. also Ames and Hall (2003, 91).

36. Wohlfart (2003) speculates that Heidegger may have been inspired by the original meaning of the Chinese character *wu* 無.

37. Hsiao (1987, 102–103). Quotation marks original; there is only one square bracket in the original manuscript in the Heidegger Archive.

38. Ular's rendering of these two lines is,

> Wer von den Jetzigen dürfte, durch seiner Klarheit Grösse,
> die innere Finsternis klären?
> Wer von den Jetzigen dürfte, durch seines Lebens Grösse,
> den inneren Tod beleben? (12)

39. In Hsiao's "literal" Italian translation the two lines read "non trabocca mai/ e poichè non trabocca" (Siao 1941).

40. Heidegger indicated the source as, „IX. Spruch (übers. v. J. Ulenbrook Schünemann 1962)" [1965b, 617].

41. This refers to a kind of vessel that stands in position but overturns when full.

42. Heidegger *Nachlass,* catalogue number 94.143.2/7 (Deutsches Literaturarchiv, Marbach). In another letter to von Harbou (catalogue number

94.143.2/10), Heidegger quotes from several poems of Bashō from the translation of Helwig (Werner Helwig, *Wortblätter im Winde* [Hamburg: Goverts, 1945]). Heidegger may have obtained the latter book from his friend Emil Pretorius, who was responsible for the cover design of it.

NOTES TO CHAPTER SEVEN

1. Cited in IJsseling (1992, 318–9). According to IJsseling, this letter comes from an unknown private collection. He noted down this remark from an extract published in an auction catalogue.
2. I postpone the discussion of some relevant passages from "A Dialogue" to Chapter nine.
3. Medard Boss' contact with Heidegger is covered in the last section of this chapter.
4. Presumably, the lecture referred to is "Language" [1950a].
5. Another reason could be that, although Heidegger's interest in East Asian classics traces back to before the 1930s, it is only much later, in the 1950s or so, that he came to realize the relevance of Asian *languages*. At that time he is of too senior age to learn any new language. However, this reason seems to be trivial compared with Heidegger's ontological account as will be shown in this chapter. The point of the rhetorical question why Heidegger did not learn a bit more Asian languages should not be taken as a demand made by the author of this book. It is derived from immanent consideration of Heidegger's own standpoint.
6. Heidegger, *Sonzai to jikan,* trans. Keikichi Matsuo (Tokyo: Keisōshobō-Verlag, 1960); second edition 1966; third edition, with a letter from Heidegger, 1969; fourth edition 1973, fifth edition 1977.
7. For example, in "A Dialogue," Japanese intellectuals are described as "chas[ing] after European conceptual systems" (*DL* 3/87).
8. It is unclear whether it is by mistake that in his quotation Parkes leaves out the word "precarious [*mißlichen*]."
9. In contrast, in that period of time, Heidegger does comply with a number of similar requests from other sides. He wrote letters of greetings to the participants of two conferences in 1966 in the U.S.A. (*GA* 16, 650, 684). As late as 1974, he wrote "a word of greetings" for the 500th issue of the Japanese journal *Risō* (*GA* 16, 744–45) and another one to the participants of a symposium held in Beirut in November 1974 in celebration of his eighty-fifth birthday (*GA* 16, 742–43). Finally, as late as 1976, he sent greetings to the participants of the tenth Heidegger colloquium in Chicago (*GA* 16, 747–48).
10. Published as an appendix in Hartig (1997, 268–270).
11. Cf. *ID* 73/142, already cited in Chapter two.
12. Cited in Hecker (1990, 91; 1986, 62).

13. The reference to "the Buddhist monk" is to Bhikku Mahā Mani ([1963a], Petzet 1993, 170–181).

14. Hsiao for the first time reported this event in "Wir trafen uns am Holz-marktplatz" (Hsiao 1977). It was later on translated (with a few deletions) by Parkes and published under the title "Heidegger and Our Translation of the *Tao Te Ching*" (Hsiao 1987).

15. Oral communication to Cho cited in Cho, "Heidegger and Laozi," lecture delivered at Beijing University, 2001.

16. This passage (Hsiao 1978, 122) was omitted from the English translation (Hsiao 1987).

17. At the end of Chapter one I have discussed Cho's over-interpretation of Heidegger's connection with Laozi, which appeals to Heidegger's attempt at translating the *Daodejing* as part of his evidential support.

18. For the passage from the *Mencius* see Hisao (1987, 96).

19. Hsiao also worked on Herder's *Encyclopaedia,* and was a Chinese language teacher at Freiburg University. From 1974 until his death in 1986, he was professor at Fu-Jen University in Taipei. Among the topics of the doctoral dissertations he supervised are the notions of *you* and *wu* in Daoist thinking and comparative studies of Heidegger and Laozi.

20. In Hsiao's own Italian version of the *Daodejing, dao* remained untrans-lated (Siao 1941). The Chinese version on the basis of which they worked together was the edition by Chiang Hsi Chang (*Lao Tse Chiao Ku,* Shang-hai, 1937).

21. For example, during his meeting with Bhikku Māha Mani on 5 December 1963, Heidegger said that he knew Laozi "only through the German media-tors—for example, Richard Wilhelm" (Petzet, 174). He did not mention his attempt of translation at all. Petzet admitted that only after Heidegger passed away did he know of the translation attempt (181).

22. As reported by Zhang (1998, 309).

23. See Buchheim (1989, 206–207; "Diskussionsbericht").

24. During the same meeting, Heidegger presented a German translation of the *Zhuangzi* and posed questions to Chang (1977a, 419).

25. It remains unclear to which document Hartig refers. At the time of carry-ing out my research, by order of the Heidegger family, unpublished parts of Heidegger's *Nachlass* were closed to consultation until further notice. Thus it was impossible for me to check the relevant material.

26. In 1957 and 1958, Hisamatsu traveled around the world and delivered lectures in the United States, including one together with Suzuki at Harvard Univer-sity. During his stay in Europe, he visited such prominent thinkers as Paul Til-lich, Martin Buber, Gabriel Marcel, Paul Bultmann, and C. G. Jung.

27. L. Alcopley is the penname of Alfred L. Copley, a biologist and artist in New York. Hannah Arendt, of whom L. Alcopley was a friend, contributed

the English translation. Since her translation is quite free, I render my own translation.

28. During his meeting with Tezuka, one of Heidegger's questions is framed in exactly the same way: "Which words in Japanese are the customary terms for appearance [*Erscheinung*] and essence [*Wesen*]? I don't want technical terms. Can't one express these ideas in words that are used in everyday speech?" (May 1996, 60–61)

29. *EHP* 162/140, 105/81, 108/83, respectively.

30. Heidegger had planned the *Zollikon Seminars* to come out at a much later time as part of his *Gesamtausgabe;* it was published as *GA* 89 in 2001. With the support of F. W. von Herrmann, Boss was able to see it published as a separate volume ahead of schedule in 1987.

31. Boss' experience in India as a psychiatrist is recorded in his book *Indien-fahrt eines Psychiaters* (Pfullingen: Neske), 1959; 4th edition 1987 (Bern-Stuttgart-Toronto: Verlag Hans Huber). English version: Boss (1965).

32. Erna M. Hoch worked as a psychiatrist, psychotherapist, and doctor in various positions and places in India from 1956 to 1988. In her work she seeks to integrate Western conceptions of psychiatry under the influence of Heidegger's Dasein-analysis with sources from Indian tradition.

33. Pandey was a representative of Kashmiri Shaivism. His major work includes a monumental book on Abhīnavagupta (10–11th century), the main exponent of this school, commentaries on Abhīnavagupta's main treatises, and a book on Western aesthetics.

34. *Daseinsanalyse* (Basel: Karger), 2 (1985): 1–36. The English version of Hoch's report entitled "Messenger between East and West" is included in her book entitled *Sources and Resources. A Western psychiatrist's search for meaning in the ancient Indian scriptures* published in 1991.

35. Cited in Hoch (1991, 251). Small capitals in the original have been suppressed.

36. Because of limit of space, I cannot engage in a detailed presentation and examination of Hoch's report. For an illuminating discussion of Sanskrit words for being, see Mohanty (1992, 150–183).

37. "Für die Inder ist der Schlaf das höchste Leben." In the English version, "die Inder" was translated as "the Hindu" [1966/67, 132/212].

38. In the opinion of Mehta, this remark is the only positive (and casual) reference to Indian thought in Heidegger's writings (1987, 24).

NOTES TO CHAPTER EIGHT

1. For each section I give in brackets the page numbers of the English edition with the line number following the semicolon.

2. The Edo period, also called the Tokugawa period, is a time of internal peace, prosperity and cultural flourishing. Economic growth led to the rise of a

lively urban culture whose peak phase is called the *Genroku* epoch. *Genroku* arts centered on the "floating world"—pleasure quarters, theatres, restaurants and courtesans. Apart from the haiku of Matsuo Bashō, the well-known wood print art *Ukiyo-e* appeared during this time.

3. Hisamatsu, *The Vocabulary of Japanese Literary Aesthetics* (1963). This is an abridged English version of his six-volume *Nihon Bungakushi* (*History of Japanese Literature,* 1955–1960). Hisamatsu is the same Japanese scholar who held discussions with Heidegger on art and thinking.

4. Steven Heine rightly argues that Kuki's work on *iki* clearly shows his "strong reaction to his studies in France and Germany during the 1920s in two ways: it reflects the influences he absorbs from European philosophers, including Bergson, Sartre, Husserl, and Heidegger, and it fulfills his desire to identify and explicate the essence of Japanese culture and thought to the West" (1990, 70).

5. Wilhelm von Humboldt relates languages to the spirit of a people, "Language is, as it were, the outer appearance of the spirit of a people; the language is their spirit and the spirit their language; we can never think of them sufficiently as identical" (1988, 35).

6. Marchianò summarizes Kuki's account for *iki* as follows, "*Iki* and its various artistic, poetic, decorative and cultural manifestations, is a phenomenon of consciousness which is either absent or present in a person, an environment, a society, a historical period, or an artistic climate, precisely to the degree that one wishes to distinguish and cultivate it, making it the model for one's aesthetic life. Wherever the premises for this wish do not exist, *iki* means next to nothing: the trivial aspect of the loving encounter which gave rise to it is its dismal residue" (103).

7. I am using the phrase "find his feet" with Wittgenstein's remark in mind, that is, even if we have a mastery of a foreign language, we may not be able to understand the people who speak this language—"We cannot find our feet with them [*uns nicht in sie finden*]" (1953, 190). Both Wittgenstein and Heidegger would agree that a mechanistic "mastery" of a foreign language cannot induce a "feel" with the people who speak this language. Nevertheless, this insight leads to different routes: while Wittgenstein resorts to forms of life through which the world of togetherness is disclosed, Heidegger relies on the Greek-German lineage in which any sense of authenticity has to be grounded.

8. Ōhashi (1989c, 99) rightly remarks that Kuki himself would not have approved Heidegger's observation that he attempted to seize *iki* with the help of European aesthetics.

9. Aesthetics occupied a special place in the development of modern Japanese thought. Nishi Amane (1829–1897), who studied at the University of Leyden for a few years, translated the term "aesthetics" as *zenbigaku* (the science of good and beauty) in his book *New Theory of the One Hundred and the One* (Hyakuichi Shinron, 1874); later on he modified this translation

as *bimyōgaku* (the science of the beautiful and mysterious) in a series of lectures delivered in 1877, published as *Bimyōgaku Setsu* (*The Theory of Aesthetics*). Because of his efforts of persuasion, the Japanese Ministry of Education invited several foreign scholars, such as Ernest F. Fenollosa and George W. Knox, to lecture on aesthetics at Tokyo Imperial University in the late nineteenth century. Cf. Marra (1999, 2–3, 18–22).

10. This claim is qualified, in that the Japanese interlocutor states that he would be the last to risk affirming this; otherwise he would not have made the journey to Germany (to visit Heidegger).

11. This idea is echoed in Kuki's statement that *iki* is one of the words embedded in the Japanese ways of being, and cannot find a counterpart in European languages (Kuki, 118). Gadamer observes something similar, "What can be considered established is only the negative insight that our own basic concepts, which were coined by the Greeks, alter the essence of what is foreign." Preface to W. Dilthey's *Grundriss der allgemeinen Geschichte der Philosophie* (Frankfurt 1949), 18n, cited in Halbfass (1988, 164).

12. It is alleged that this hesitation has to do with the fear that as long as that word is uttered, it would inevitably be accompanied by an act of translating it into the European languages, and thus would be conveyed into the domain of Western metaphysical thinking.

13. Heidegger uses the word *Wink* or *Winke* very often in the context of his discussions of Hölderlin's poetry. Hölderlin writes that *Winke* are the language of the gods. According to Heidegger, the poet's free creativity has two constraints: the *Winke* of the gods and the voice of the people. The poet receives these hints and passes them on in his own hinting words to his people.

14. Sonoda (1989, 154) expresses a similar view: *koto* is the general name for everything that happens at all. In ancient times there was no difference between *koto-ba* and *koto*. When the Japanese came to distinguish between events and their linguistic expressions, *kotono-ha* or *koto-ba* became the label for language. According to Ogawa Tadashi (1992, 193), *ba* as in *kotoba* means periphery in the sense of the environment far away from the centre. Language consists of signs that merely show the "border" of events and the world; its nature is not to bring the world into appearance.

15. In the view of Kimura Bin, *koto* corresponds to the moment prior to the split of subject and object. This is what Nishida calls "pure experience" (*junsui keiken*). Cf. Marra (1994).

16. Explanations in round and square brackets of this paragraph are original. Additions between braces are mine.

17. The German word for "nothing" is *nichts*. Its nominalized form, *(das) Nichts,* is employed especially in the phrase *creatio ex nihilo*. God created the world out of *das Nichts*. When used to refer to a particular non-being or non-entity, *das Nichts* functions as a count noun and can take singular or plural forms (cf. Inwood, 144).

18. "What is Metaphysics?" is the inaugural lecture Heidegger delivered to the Freiburg University faculties on July 24, 1929. In 1943 and 1949, Heidegger appended an afterword and an introduction to it respectively. It is commonly agreed that this lecture marks the turning point of Heidegger's thought toward the later period.

19. By "popular (and vulgar) understanding of Buddhism" I mean those simplistic presentations of Buddhism that cannot be uncritically accepted or assumed in the scholarly arena.

20. Compared with Heidegger's differentiation of his thought from Buddhist ideas, it seems that Hegel exhibits a more balanced attitude. According to Hegel, nothing, understood as "the void," is the absolute principle in oriental systems, especially in Buddhism. In reference to what he thinks as an oriental proverb, "all that exists has the germ of death in its very birth, that death, on the other hand, is the entrance into new life," Hegel considers that this articulates the essential unity between being and nothing. However, this articulation presupposes that being and nothing are set apart in empirical time, and that their transition also takes place in concrete time. Being and nothing, as well as their mutual alternation, are not conceived in their pure abstraction. As a consequence, being and nothing in oriental thinking are not absolutely the same (Hegel 1990, 81–83).

21. To quote from the record of his conversation with the Buddhist monk Mani, Heidegger remarks, "I believe that in contrast to Buddhist teaching Western thinking makes a distinctive division between humans and other living organisms such as flora and fauna. Man is distinguished by having language, that is, he stands in a 'knowing' relationship to Being. And this question of Being has never been asked in the history of Western thinking so far—or to express this more clearly: Being itself has held itself hidden so far—in this respect. Therefore this question needs to be posed in order to obtain an immediate answer, What and how man is" [1963a, 590–1].

22. See Petzet (1993, 181). Pöggeler (1998, 276) wonders whether the whole conversation between Heidegger and Mani was not perverted from the start by the monk's wish to talk to "the" German philosopher, since philosophy itself is never embodied in an idol. He also notes the fact that Mani left his order soon afterward. Whether Mani started working for an American television network has not been confirmed, but it is certain that he left his order soon after his visit to Germany (Hartig 1997, 200).

23. This is suggested by Parkes (1996, 66, note q).

24. In a lecture on philosophy of religion delivered at the Institute of Philosophy, K. U. Leuven on May 4, 2000, John Maraldo also pointed out that Heidegger mistakenly took *shiki* as meaning "colour" in "A Dialogue." During his meeting with Heidegger, Tezuka adduces the words *shiki* and *kū* when Heidegger inquires about the Japanese terms for appearance (*Erscheinung*) and essence (*Wesen*). He explains, "*shiki* would be colour and colouring, and, by extension,

appearance; and though *kū* originally means emptiness, or sky (*sora*), it also means 'the open' (the opened-up world)" (May 1996, 62). On the basis of this reply, Heidegger may have mistaken *shiki* as meaning "colour."

25. Cf. Lopez (1988, 57–94); also cf. Dan Lusthaus, "Buddhist philosophy," in *Routledge Encyclopedia of Philosophy* (London and New York: Routledge, 1998).

26. According to Hans Waldenfels, hidden in Nishitani's *What is Religion?*, is a sustained argument that Heidegger's notion of the Nothing belongs to the Western tradition and is characteristically distinct from the nothing of the Asian tradition; however, due to Nishitani's personal relation with Heidegger, he does not put forward explicit criticisms (Waldenfels 1976, 104f). For a comparative study of Heidegger and Nishitani's thinking on the nothing, see Dallmayr (1992). He finds some of Nishitani's criticisms of Heidegger's notion of the Nothing dubious or puzzling.

27. Cited in Heisig (2001, 222).

28. Nishitani once remarked that Heidegger himself did not stress the connection of his philosophy with Buddhism. It is Buddhist philosophers who highlight the existence of this connection (1966, 150).

29. Yuasa Seinosuke came to Germany in 1926, and began to study with Heidegger in 1929. He stayed in Germany until the late 1930s (see Parkes 1992, 388).

30. In "A Dialogue," Heidegger writes, "J: . . . we in Japan understood at once your lecture 'What is Metaphysics?' when it became available to us in 1930 through a translation which a Japanese student, then attending your lectures, had ventured.—We marvel to this day how the Europeans could lapse into interpreting as nihilistic the Nothing of which you speak in that lecture. To us, emptiness is the loftiest name for what you mean to say with the word 'Being'" (*DL* 19/108f).

31. Heidegger writes, "The reaction to the piece [i.e. "What is Metaphysics?"] in Europe was: nihilism and enmity to 'logic.' In the far East, with the 'nothing' properly understood, one found in it the word for being" (letter to Roger Munier on July 31, 1969; [2003: 88]).

32. In "A Dialogue," *Erscheinung* and *Wesen* are replaced with a pair of Greek words, αἰσφητόν and νοητόν (*DL* 14/102).

33. Tezuka remarks that he "has neither attended [Kuki's] lectures nor known him in person" (1968, 140).

34. Probably in the "same" sense Heidegger makes the following remark in his discussion with Hisamatsu in 1958.

> Hisamatsu: The point you are making here can also be found in Zen-languages. Zen-language is regarded as free expression. It is so free, that, only when it has been pronounced, can grammar form itself.
>
> Heidegger: My thinking follows the same direction. [1958d, 191]

35. For an informative and "postmodern" account of *Rashōmon* in the context of its invocation in "A Dialogue," see Naas (1997, 63–90).

36. In his memoir, Petzet mentions his trip together with Heidegger to see the Japanese film *Rashōmon,* "which in those days was causing a great sensation" (189). When they watched the film is not mentioned. It must have been late 1952 or early 1953.
37. The families who have been the depositaries of instructions in Zeami's *Book of the Secret Nō* have remained the same for five centuries.
38. The word "bearing" later on unites the supposedly Japanese gestures and Heidegger's hints. "[Hints] are enigmatic. They beckon to us. They beckon *away.* They beckon us *toward* that from which they unexpectedly bear themselves toward us" (*DL* 26/117; em. or.). Hints and gestures both "belong to an entirely different realm of nature [*anderen Wesensraum*]" ((26/117). They make possible a transformed thinking about the nature of Being and of language.

NOTES TO CHAPTER NINE

1. Heidegger himself has attached importance to the word *von* in the title. In his actual meeting with Tezuka, he said that what he wanted to hear from him was "something *of* [*von*] the Japanese language—not just something *about* [*über*] language, but the language itself" (May 1996, 60). In his memoir on Heidegger, Petzet misquotes the title as "Aus einem Gespräch *über* die Sprache" (Petzet, 166; em. ad.). The English translator of Petzet's book draws attention to this mistake as well. This indicates that Heidegger's use of the word *von* is nothing ordinary.
2. In the German language there are a number of words that cover the same range of meaning: *Gespräch, Zwiegespräch, Zwiesprache, Konversation, Dialog.* Heidegger has used all these words (and other related ones). In "A Dialogue," he only uses *Gespräch.* When the German original is not indicated in my citations, it is always *Gespräch* that is used.
3. It is probably in view of the historic nature of Heidegger's notion of dialogue that Fóti translates *Gespräch* as "destinal interlocution" (1992, xv).
4. The phrase "language speaks" is repeated often in the 1950s: [1950a, 194/19], [1955–56, 96/143]. Cf. [1959c]: "We not only speak *the* language, we speak *from out of it.* . . . We hear the speaking of language . . . Language speaks by saying, i.e. by showing" (124/254–55; tr. m.); "language itself has woven us into its speaking" (112/242); "language speaks singularly and solely with itself alone" (111/239).
5. In making this remark, Heidegger knows that he is necessarily confronted with a hermeneutical circle. Because "[a] dialogue from language must be called for from out of language's nature. How can it do so, without first entering into a hearing that at once reaches that nature?" (*DL* 51/150). Nevertheless, he dismisses this problematic immediately in saying that to talk about a hermeneutical circle "always remains superficial" and that he

would "avoid a presentation" of it "as resolutely as [he] would avoid speaking about language" (51/150).

6. This section is preceded by a noticeable shift of the roles of the Inquirer and the Japanese interlocutor: "I: . . . in order that your reflection may swing freely, almost without your prompting, let us exchange roles, and let me be the one who gives the answers, specifically the answer to your question about hermeneutics" (28/120).

7. Nancy suggests that "A Dialogue" is essentially a performance of hermeneutics, "that which is staged is hermeneutics itself" (227). It is dialogue itself that "A Dialogue" proposes as the nature of language.

8. Closely following the surface discourse and clues Heidegger provides in "A Dialogue," and ignoring Heidegger's stress on the otherness of Japanese thinking, Wang (1995) argues that a thoughtful dialogue between the different languages of East and West is possible if it occurred in an event of appropriation of original Saying/co-responding between men and being itself. In this perspective an authentic East-West dialogue is the same as an authentic dialogue. However, it remains doubtful whether Heidegger would really think so. If they are totally identical, then what would East-West dialogue add to Heidegger's "Western" dialogue?

9. The German reads "Das Selbe nämlich ist Vernehmen (Denken) sowohl als auch Sein" (*ID*/90). It is not clear why Stambaugh translates this as "For the same perceiving (thinking) as well as being" (*ID* 27/).

10. Jaspers once describes Heidegger's making "the Same" the subject of the sentence as "an act of grammatical violence" (*HJC* 174/184).

11. The phrase "toward-each-other" reminds one of the "being-toward-each-other [*Zueinanderwesen*] of vastness and stillness in the same [*selben*] Ereignis of the message of unconcealment of the two-fold" (*DL* 53/153).

12. In "Hegel and the Greeks." Heidegger lists the following grounding words (*Grundworte*) in relation to Hegel's reflection on them: Hegel's the all, reason, concept, and actuality, to which Heidegger adds truth (unconcealment) [1958b, 328–32/434–39]. In my view, one could say that the Same is a grounding word as well.

13. In "Moira," Heidegger remarks that τὸ αὐτό "prevails as the unfolding of the twofold [of Being and beings]—an unfolding in the sense of disclosure" (*M* 95/46).

14. Ibid.; cf. *DL* 12/99, 13/99, 28/120.

15. *Platon: Sophistes, GA* 19 (1992).

16. Plato, *Sophist*, see in particular sections 241–242.

17. According to May (1996, 18) Heidegger borrows this image, *without acknowledgement*, from a Japanese poem Oscar Benl cites in his "treatise," mentioned in "A Dialogue" while discussing the *Nō* play (17f/106). The relevant lines read: "To smell a plum blossom / In a cherry blossom / And let both bloom / On a willow branch—thus would I wish it" (Benl 1952,

202). (In a footnote Benl mentions that the author of the poem is Nakahara Tokinore.) May draws attention to the striking similarities between the two passages. To him, the fact that Heidegger appropriates Asian sources testifies that he is thinking transculturally. May fails to consider the question whether or not Heidegger's use of these sources has a Euro-centric, or Heideggo-centric tendency.

18. According to Tezuka Heidegger said this when Tezuka mentioned "the open" as a possible translation of *kū*. May comments, "This sentence of Heidegger . . . was recounted word for word by Tezuka" (May 1996, 14). As the actual conversation took place in German, Tezuka recorded it from memory in Japanese, and May translated it back into German, it sounds overhasty to say that it was "recounted word for word." Tezuka's account in Japanese of this remark by Heidegger is, "東と西とは、こういう深処 に おいて話し会わなければならない" (Tezuka 1968, 165). There exist three German translations of this passage. May's own version is: „Ost und West müssen in einer derartigen Tiefe zu einem Gespräch finden" (May 1989, 93). Hartmut Buchner translates as, „In einer solchen Tiefe müssen sich der Osten und der Westen im Gespräch treffen" (Buchner 1989, 177). The translation by Oshima Yoshiko (in Vetsch 1992, 193) does not mention the word *Gespräch,* „Osten und Westen müssen in dieser Tiefe besprochen werden."

19. From a Heideggerian perspective, it can be said that this kind of belief arises under the sway of the *Ge-stell.* Even Asian scholars themselves cannot have access to their own traditions; instead, they interpret them in terms of Western concerns with the question of Being.

20. Some Heidegger scholars express similar views as May's. For example, Pattison states: "Heidegger's own essay 'Conversation with a Japanese' acknowledges that there was a possible rapport between his own thought and Japanese philosophy" (2000, 201).

21. This explains Heidegger's duplicitous attitude toward East Asia on many occasions. As Ogawa observes, Heidegger has on the one hand friendly interest but on the other doubting strangeness towards Japan (1992, 183).

22. This gesture is well conveyed in the following remark by Klaus Held, who is speaking for Heidegger,

> Other cultures, too, will thereby have a chance—their first real chance—to preserve their individuality, not in raising barriers against European thought, but in participating in the process of European self-criticism. (1995, 16; cf. 1993)

Bibliography

WORKS BY HEIDEGGER

1921. Drei Briefe Martin Heidegger an Karl Löwith. In Papenfuss and Pöggeler 2 (1990) 27–39.

1923. *Ontology: The Hermeneutics of Facticity.* Translated by J. van Buren.
Indiana: Indiana University Press. *GA 63: Ontologie (Hermeneutik
der Faltizität).*

1924. *Concept of Time.* Translated by W. McNeill. Oxford: Blackwell (1992).
Der Begriff der Zeit. In [2004b] 105–125.

1927. *Being and Time.* Translated by J. Macquarrie and E. Robinson. San Francisco: Harper (1962). *Sein und Zeit.* Tübingen: Niemeyer (2001).

1929. *What Is Metaphysics?* In [1998] 82–97. Was ist Metaphysik? In [1976]
103–122.

1930a. *The Essence of Human Freedom.* Translated by T. Sadler. London: Continuum (2002). *GA 31: Vom Wesen der menschlichen Freiheit. Ein-
leitung in die Philosophie* (1982).

1930b. On the essence of truth. In [1998] 136–154; also in [1949d] 292–324 and
[1993] 115–138. Vom Wesen der Wahrheit. In [1976b] 177–202.

1934. *Logik als die Frage nach dem Wesen der Sprache.* Vol. 38, *Gesamtausgabe.*
Frankfurt am Main: Vittorio Klostermann (1988).

1934/35. *Hölderlins Hymnen "Germanien" und "der Rhein."* Vol. 39, *Gesamtausgabe.* Frankfurt am Main: Vittorio Klostermann (1980).

1935. *Introduction to Metaphysics.* New Haven (Connecticut): Yale University
Press (2000). GA 40: *Einführung in der Metaphysik* (1983).

1935–36. The origin of the work of art. In [2002] 1–56; also in [1994a] 15–86 and
[1993] 139–212. Der Ursprung des Kunstwerkes. In [1977b] 1–74.

1936–38. *Contributions to Philosophy (From Enowning).* Translated by P. Emad
and K. Maly. Bloomington: Indiana University Press (1999). *GA
65: Beiträge zur Philosophie (Vom Ereignis)* (1989).

1936–46. Overcoming metaphysics. In Wolin (1993) 67–90; also in [1973] 84–
107. Überwindung der Metaphysik. In [2000d] 67–98.

1936/37.   *The Will to Power as Art. Nietzsche I.* Translated by D. F. Krell. New
            York: Harper & Row. *GA 43: Der Wille zur Macht als Kunst.*

1936a.   Hölderlin and the essence of poetry. In [2000a] 51–65. Hölderlin und
            das Wesen der Dichtung. In [1996] 33–48.

1936b.   Europa und die Deutsche Philosophie. In Gander (1993) 31–41.

1936c.   *Schelling's Treatise on the Essence of Human Freedom.* Translated by J.
            Stambaugh. Athens (Ohio): Ohio University Press (1985). *GA
            42: Schelling: Vom Wesen der menschlichen Freiheit* (1988).

1937/38a.   *Basic Questions of Philosophy.* Translated by R. Rojcewicz. Bloomington:
            Indiana University Press (1994). *GA 45: Grundfragen der Philoso-
            phie* (1984).

1937/38b.   A retrospective look at the pathway. In [1938/39] 363–378. Rückblick
            auf den Weg. In *GA 66* [1938/39] 409–428.

1937a.   *The Eternal Recurrence of the Same.* Translated by D. F. Krell. Vol. II,
            Nietzsche. San Francisco: Harper & Row. Die ewige Wiederkehr
            des Gleichen. In [1961] I, 255–472.

1937b.   Wege zur Aussprache. In [1983] 15–21.

1938.   The age of the world picture. In [2002] 57–85; also in [1975] 115–
            154. Die Zeit des Weltbildes. In [1977b] 75–114.

1938/39.   *Mindfulness.* Translated by P. Emad and T. Kalary. London—New York:
            Continuum (2006). *GA 66: Besinnung* (1996).

1939a.   *On the Essence of Language: The Metaphysics of Language and the Essenc-
            ing of the Word, concerning Herder's Treatise On the Origin of Lan-
            guage.* Translated by W. T. Gregory and Y. Umma. Albany NY:
            State University of New York Press (2004). GA 85: *Vom Wesen der
            Sprache* (1999).

1939b.   Zur politischen Missdeutung des "Vaterlands" bei Hölderlin. In [2000c]
            277–278.

1941/42.   *Hölderlins Hymne "Andenken."* Vol. 52, *Gesamtausgabe.* Frankfurt am
            Main: Vittorio Klostermann.

1941a.   *Basic Concepts.* Bloomington: Indiana University Press (1993). *GA 51:
            Grundbegriffe* (1981).

1941b.   Winke. In [1983] 23–33.

1942.   *Hölderlin's Hymn "The Ister."* Translated by W. McNeill and J. Davis.
            Bloomington: Indiana University Press (1996). *GA 53: Hölderlin's
            Hymne "Der Ister"* (1983).

1942/43.   *Parmenides.* Translated by A. Schuwer and R. Rojcewicz. Bloomington:
            Indiana University Press (1992). *GA 54: Parmenides* (1982).

1943a.   *Heraklit.* Vol. 55, *Gesamtausgabe.* Frankfurt am Main: Vittorio Klos-
            termann (1979).

1943b.   Die Einzigkeit des Dichters. In [2000c] 35–44.

1943c.   Remembrance. In [2000a] 101–173. Andenken. In [1996] 79–151.

1943d.   "Homecoming / To kindred ones." In [2000a] 23–65. Heimkunft / An
          die Verwandten. In [1996] 9–32.
1943e.   Postscript to "What is Metaphysics?" In [1998] 231–238. Nachwort zu
          "Was ist Metaphysik?." In [1976b] 303–312.
1944/45. *Feldweg Gespräche.* Vol. 77, *Gesamtausgabe.* Frankfurt a/M: Vittorio
          Klostermann.
1945.   Letter to the Rector of Freiburg University, November 4, 1945. In Wolin
          (1993) 61–66. Antrag auf die Wiedereinstellung in die Lehrtätigkeit
          (Reintegrierung). Brief an das Akademische Rektorat der Albert-
          Ludwigs-Universität vom 4. November 1945. In [2000b] 397–404.
1945–46. Hölderlins Dichtung ein Geschick. In [2000c] 349–365.
1946–48. Das abendländische Gespräch. In [2000c] 57–196.
1946a.   Anaximander's Saying. In [2002] 242–281. Der Spruch des Anaxi-
          mander. In [1977b] 321–374.
1946b.   Letter on humanism. In [1998] 239–276; also in [1993] 213–266.
          Brief über den "Humanismus." In [1976b] 313–364.
1946c.   Why poets? In [2002] 200–241. Also with the title 'What are poets
          for?' in [1975a] 87–140. Wozu Dichter? In [1977b] 269–320.
1947.   The thinker as poet. In [1975a] 1–14. Aus der Erfahrung des Denkens.
          In [1983] 75–86.
1949a.   Einblick in das was ist. *Bremer Vorträge 1949.* In [1994] 3–78.
1949b.   The turning. In [1977] 36–49. "Die Kehre." In [1994] 68–77.
1949c.   Introduction to "What is Metaphysics?" In [1998] 277–290. Einlei-
          tung zu "Was ist Metaphysik?." In [1976b] 385–384.
1949d.   *Existence and Being.* Chicago: Henry Regnery Company.
1950a.   Language. In [1975a] 189–210. Die Sprache. In [1959b] 9–34.
1950b.   The thing. In [1975a: 163–186]. Das Ding. In [2000d] 165–188.
1951.   Logos (Heraclitus, Fragment B 50). In [1975b] 59–78. Logos (Heracli-
          tus, Fragment 50). In [2000d] 211–234.
1951/52. *What Is Called Thinking?* Translated by J. G. Gray. New York: Harper
          & Row (1968). *Was heisst Denken?* Tübingen: Niemeyer (1997).
          GA 8: Was heisst Denken? (2002).
1952.   Moira (Parmenides, VIII, 34–41). In [1975b] 79–101. Moira (Par-
          menides, Fragment VIII, 34–41). In [2000d] 235–262.
1953/54. A dialogue on language: between a Japanese and an Inquirer. In [1971]
          1–56. Aus einem Gespräch von der Sprache: Zwischen einem
          Japaner und einem Fragenden. In [1959b] 85–156; also in *GA 12*
          (1985) 79–146.
1953a.   The question concerning technology. In [1993] 311–341; also in
          [1977a] 3–35. Die Frage nach der Technik. In [2000d] 5–36.
1953b.   Science and reflection. In [1977a] 155–182. Wissenschaft und Besin-
          nung. In [2000d] 37–66.

1955–56. *The Principle of Reason.* Translated by R. Lilly. Bloomington and India-
          napolis: Indiana University Press (1991). *GA* 10: *Der Satz vom
          Grund* (1997).
1955–57. *Identity and Difference.* Translated by J. Stambaugh. New York: Harper
          & Row (1969). Bilingual edition: *Identität und Differenz.*
1955a.   On the question of being. In [1998] 291–322. Zur Seinsfrage. In
          [1976b] 385–426.
1955b.   Memorial address. In [1966c] 43–57. Gelassenheit. In [2000b] 517–529.
1956.   *What Is Philosophy?* Translated by W. Kluback and J. T. Wilde. Sche-
          nectady, NY: The New College and University Press. Bilingual
          edition: *Was ist das, die Philosophie?*
1957/58. The nature of language. In [1971] 57–110. Das Wesen der Sprache. In
          [1959b] 157–216; also in *GA* 12 (1985) 147–204.
1957a.   Grundsätze des Denkens. Freiburger Vorträge 1957. In [1994] 79–176.
          Originally published in Jahrbuch für Psychologie und Psycho-
          therapie, vol. 6 (1959). Pp. 79–96 (the first lecture, "Principles of
          thinking") has been translated into English in Hart and Maraldo
          (1976) 46–58.
1957b.   A Recollection. In *Heidegger. The Man and the Thinker,* edited by T.
          Sheehan, 21–22. Chicago: Precedent Publishing. This translation
          first appeared in *Man and World* 3 (1970) 3–4. German origi-
          nal in *Jahreshefte 1957/58 der Heidelberger Akademie der Wissen-
          schaften.* Reprinted in "Vorwort" in [1972].
1958a.   Words. In [1971] 139–156. Das Wort. In [1959b] 217–238.
1958b.   Hegel and the Greeks. In [1998] 323–336. Hegel und die Griechen. In
          [1976b] 427–444.
1958c.   Die Kunst und das Denken. Protokoll eines Colloquiums am 18. Mai
          1958 (Martin Heidegger and Shinichi Hisamatsu). In Buchner
          (1989) 211–215; also in [2000b] 552–557. English, German,
          and Japanese text in Alcopley (1963).
1958d.   Wechselseitige Spiegelung. Aus einem Gespräch mit Martin Heidegger
          (Hisamatsu Shinichi and Martin Heidegger). In Buchner (1989)
          189–192.
1959a.   Hölderlin's earth and heaven. In [2000a] 175–207. Hölderlin's Erde
          und Himmel. In [1996] 152–181.
1959b.   *Unterwegs zur Sprache.* Stuttgart: Günther Neske.
1959c.   The way to language. In [1971] 110–138; also in [1993] 393–426.
          Der Weg zur Sprache. In [1959b] 239–268; also in *GA* 12 (1985)
          227–258.
1960.   Sprache und Heimat. In [1983] 155–180.
1961.   *Nietzsche.* 2 vols. Pfullingen: Neske.
1962–64. On time and being. In *On Time and Being,* New York: Harper and Row
          (1972). *Zur Sache des Denken.* Tübingen: Niemeyer (1969).

1962a.   *Sojourns: The journey to Greece.* Translated by J. P. Manoussakis. Albany: State University of New York Press. Aufenthalte. In [2000c] 213–246.

1962b.   Traditional language and technological language. *Journal of Philosophical Research* 23 (1998):129–145. *Überlieferte Sprache und Technische Sprache,* St. Gallen: Erker (1989).

1962c.   Preface. In Richardson (1962) ix-xxiii.

1963a.   Aus Gesprächen mit einem Buddhistischen Mönch. In [2000b] 589–593.

1963b.   My way into phenomenology. In *TB* [1962–64] 74–82. Mein Weg in die Phänomenologie. In Zur Sache des Denken (1969) 81–90.

1963c.   [Letter to Kojima Takehiko]. Part of "Ein Briefwechsel (1963–1965)." In Buchner (1989) 216–227.

1965a.   Zur Frage nach der Bestimmung der Sache des Denkens. In [2000b] 620–633.

1965b.   Zum siebzigsten Geburtstag von Siegfried Bröse am 8. August 1965. In [2000b] 617–619.

1966/67. *Heraclitus Seminar 1966/67 (Martin Heidegger and Eugen Fink).* Translated by C. H. Seibert. Alabama: University of Alabama Press (1979). *Heraklit.* In [1986] 9–266.

1966a.   Spiegel Interview with Martin Heidegger. In Wolin (1993) 91–115; also in *Philosophy Today* 20 (1976) 268–284; also in Neske and Kettering (1990) 41–66. Spiegel Gespräch mit Martin Heidegger. In [2000b] 652–683; also in Neske and Kettering (1988) 81–114.

1966b.   Ein Brief von Martin Heidegger an Keikichi Matsuo. In Buchner (1989) 228.

1966c.   *Discourse on Thinking.* Translated by J. M. Anderson and E. H. Freund. New York: Harper & Row.

1968.   Zur Frage nach der Bestimmung der Sache des Denkens. Vorwort für die japanische Übersetzung. In [2000b] 695; also in Buchner (1989) 230–231. Original edition, Kōza-Zen, 8 (Tokyo 1968) 321f.

1969a.   Aus der Dankansprache Martin Heideggers. In Buchner (1989) 166. Original edition, *Martin Heidegger-Ansprachen zum 80. Geburtstag am 26. September 1969 in Meßkirch,* Meßkirch (1970) 33–36.

1969b.   Gruss und Dank an die Teilnehmer der Heidegger-Konferenz in Honolulu auf Hawai. 17.-21. November 1969 (Briefe an Prof. A. Borgmann). In [2000b] 721–722.

1969c.   Seminar in Le Thor. In [2003] 35–63. *GA* 15: Seminare in Le Thor (1986).

1971.   *On the Way to Language.* Translated by P. D. Hertz. San Francisco: Harper and Row. *Unterwegs zur Sprache.* Stuttgart: Neske (1959).

1972.   *Frühe Schriften.* Frankfurt am Main: Vittorio Klostermann; also *GA* 1.

1973.   *The End of Philosophy.* Translated by J. Stambaugh. New York: Harper & Row.

1974a.   Grußwort anläßlich des Erscheinens von Nr. 500 der Zeitschrift *Risō*.
          In [2000b] 744–745; also in Buchner (1989) 232.

1974b.   A greeting to the symposium in Beirut. In Neske and Kettering (1990)
          253–254. Ein Grusswort für das Symposion in Beirut November
          1974. In Heidegger [2000b] 742–743.

1975a.   *Poetry, Language, Thought*. Translated by A. Hofstadter. New York:
          Harper.

1975b.   *Early Greek Thinking*. Translated by D. Farrell and F. A. Capuzzi. New
          York: Harper & Row.

1976a.   Modern natural science and technology. *Research in Phenomenology* 7
          (1977):1–4. Neuzeitliche Naturwissenschaft und moderne Tech-
          nik. In [2000b] 747–748.

1976b.   *Wegmarken*. Vol. 9, *Gesamtausgabe*. Frankfurt am Main: Vittorio Klos-
          termann.

1977a.   *The Question Concerning Technology and Other Essays*. Translated by W.
          Vernon. New York: Harper & Row.

1977b.   *Holzwege*. Vol. 5, *Gesamtausgabe*. Frankfurt am Main: Vittorio Klos-
          termann.

1983.   *Aus der Erfahrung des Denken 1910–1976*. Vol. 13, *Gesamtausgabe*.
          Frankfurt am Main: Vittorio Kostermann.

1986a.   *Seminare*. Vol. 15, *Gesamtausgabe*. Frankfurt am Main: Vittorio Klos-
          termann.

1986b.   *Briefwechsel 1953–1974. Martin Heidegger and Erhart Kästner*. Edited
          by H. W. Petzet. Frankfurt am Main: Insel.

1993.   *Basic Writings*. London: Routledge. Editor D.F. Krell.

1994.   *Bremer und Freiburger Vorträge*. Vol. 79, *Gesamtausgabe*. Frankfurt am
          Main: Vittorio Klostermann.

1996.   *Erläuterungen zu Hölderlins Dichtung*. Vol. 4, *Gesamtausgabe*. Frankfurt
          am Main: Vittorio Klostermann.

1998.   *Pathmarks*. Translated by W. McNeill. Cambridge: Cambridge Univer-
          sity Press. *GA* 9: *Wegmarken* (1976).

2000a.   *Elucidations of Hölderlin's Poetry*. Translated by K. Hoeller. Amherst NY:
          Humanity Books. *GA* 4: *Erläuterungen zu Hölderlins Dichtung*
          (1996).

2000b.   *Reden und andere Zeugnisse eines Lebensweges 1910–1976*. Vol. 16, *Gesa-
          mtausgabe*. Frankfurt am Main: Vittorio Klostermann.

2000c.   *Zu Hölderlin-Griechenlandreisen*. Vol. 75, *Gesamtausgabe*. Frankfurt am
          Main: Vittorio Klostermann.

2000d.   *Vorträge und Aufsätze*. Vol. 7, *Gesamtausgabe*. Frankfurt a/M: Vittorio
          Klostermann.

2001.   *Zollikon Seminars. Protocolls-Conversations-Letters*. Translated by F. Mayr
          and R. Askay. Evanston: Northwestern University Press. *GA* 89:
          Zollikoner Seminare, Protokolle-Gespräche-Briefe (2000).

2002.   *Off the Beaten Track.* Translated by J. Young. Cambridge: Cambridge University Press. *GA 5: Holzwege* (1977).

2003a.   *Four Seminars. Le Thor 1966, 1968, 1969, Zähringen 1973.* Translated by A. Mitchel and F. Raffoul. Bloomington & Indianapolis: Indiana University Press. *Vier Seminare.* In [1986] 271–421.

2003b.   *Martin Heidegger. Briefe an Max Müller und andere Dokumente.* Edited by H. Zaborowski and A. Bösl. Freiberg/München: Verlag Karl Alber.

2003c.   *The Heidegger-Jaspers Correspondence (1920–1963).* Edited by W. Biemel. Amherst NY: Humanity Books. *Martin Heidegger/Karl Jaspers: Briefwechsel 1920–1963.* Walter Biemel and Hans Saner, eds. Frankfurt am Main: Vittorio Klostermann (1990).

SECONDARY LITERATURE

Alcopley, L [Alfred L. Copley], ed. 1963. *Listening to Heidegger and Hisamatsu.* Kyoto: Bokubi Press.

Ames, Roger T., and David L. Hall. 2003. *Daodejing "Making This Life Significant." A philosophical translation.* New York: Ballantine Books.

Bambach, Charles. 2003. *Heidegger's Roots: Nietzsche, National Socialism, and the Greeks.* Ithaca and London: Cornell University Press.

Barrett, William, ed. 1956. *Zen-Buddism: Selected Writings of D. T. Suzuki.* New York: Doubleday.

Beaufret, Jean. 1977. [no title]. In Klostermann (1977) 10–23.

Benl, Oscar. 1952 (publ. 1953). Seami Motokiyo und der Geist des No-Schauspiels: Geheime kunstkritische Schriften aus dem 15. Jahrhundert. *Akademie der Wissenschaften und Literatur (Wiesbaden/Mainz), Abhandlungen der Klasse der Literatur* (5):107–253.

Bernasconi, Robert. 1985. *The Question of Language in Heidegger's History of Being.* New Jersey: Humanities Press.

———. 1992. *Heidegger in Question: The Art of Existing.* New Jersey: Humanities Press.

———. 1995a. On Heidegger's other sins of omission—His exclusion of Asian thought from the origins of occidental metaphysics and his denial of the possibility of Christian philosophy. *American Catholic Philosophical Quarterly* 69 (2):333–350.

———. 1995b. Heidegger and the invention of the Western philosophical tradition. *Journal of the British Society for Phenomenology* 26:240–254.

———. 1997. Philosophy's paradoxical parochialism. In *Cultural Readings of Imperialism: Edward Said and the Gravity of History,* edited by K. A. Pearson, 212–226, London: Lawrence & Wishart.

Bilimoria, Purusottama. 1991. Heidegger and the Japanese connection. *Journal of the British Society for Phenomenology* 22:3–20.

Blocker, H. Gene, and Christopher L. Starling. 2001. *Japanese Philosophy.* Albany: State University of New York Press.

Boss, Medard. 1965. *A Psychiatrist Discovers India.* Translated by H. A. Arey. London: Oswald Wolff. Original edition, Indienfahrt eines Psychiaters, Bern-Stuttgart-Toronto: Verlag Hans Huber (1959 etc.); 4th edition (1987) including 'Nach dreißig Jahren.'

Brusotti, Marco. 2004. "Europäisch und über-Europäisch." Nietzsches Blick aus der Ferne. *Tijdschrift voor Filosofie* 66:31–48.

Buchheim, Thomas, ed. 1989. *Destruktion und Übersetzung: Zu den Aufgaben von Philosophiegeschichte nach Martin Heidegger.* Weinheim: VCH Verlagsgesellschaft.

Buchner, Hartmut, ed. 1989. *Japan und Heidegger. Gedenkschrift der Stadt Messkirch zum hundertsten Geburtstag Martin Heideggers.* Sigmaringen: Jan Thorbecke.

Carus, Paul, and D.T. Suzuki. 1898. *Lao-Tze's Tao-Teh-King.* Chicago: Open Court.

Chan, Wing-tsit. 1963. *The Way of Lao Tzu (Tao te ching).* Chicago: Chicago University Press.

Chang, Chung-yuan. 1974. Tao: A new way of thinking. *Journal of Chinese Philosophy* 1:137–152.

———. 1975. *Tao: A New Way of Thinking. A translation of the Tao Tĕ Ching with an introduction and commentaries.* Taipei: Dun Huang.

———. 1977a. The philosophy of Taoism according to Chuang Tzu. *Philosophy East & West* 27:409–422.

———. 1977b. Tao and Heidegger. *Lier en Boog* 2:66–74, 87.

———. 1977c. Reflections. In Neske (1977, 65–70).

Cheng, Chung-ying. 1978. Remarks on ontological and transontological foundations of language. *Journal of Chinese Philosophy* 5:335–340.

Cheung, Chan-Fai. 1998. One world or many worlds? On intercultural understanding. In *Phenomenology of Interculturality and Life-world,* edited by E. W. Orth and C.-F. Cheung, 150–171. Freiburg/München: Verlag Karl Alber.

Cho, Kah Kyung. 1992. Heidegger und die Rückkehr in den Ursprung. Nachforschungen über seine Begegnungsmotive mit Laotse. In Papenfuß and Pöggeler 3 (1992) 299–324.

———. 1993. Der Abstieg über den Humanismus: West-Östliche Wege im Denken Heideggers. In Gander (1993) 143–174.

Cooper, D. E. 1997. Heidegger's hidden sources: East-Asian influences on his work. *Asian Philosophy* 7 (3):242–244.

Dallmayr, Fred. 1992. Nothingness and *sunyata:* A comparison of Heidegger and Nishitani. *Philosophy East and West* 42:37–48.

de Boer, Karin. 2000. *Thinking in the Light of Time. Heidegger's Encounter with Hegel.* Albany: State University of New York Press.

Denker, Alfred. 2000. *Historical Dictionary of Heidegger's Philosophy.* Lanham/London: The Scarecrow Press.

Dilworth, D.A., V.H. Viglielmo, and A.J. Zavala, eds. 1998. *Sourcebook for Modern Japanese Philosophy: Selected Documents.* Westport (Connecticut): Greenwood.

Dreyfus, Hubert L., and Mark A. Wrathall, eds. 2005. *A Companion to Heidegger.* Oxford: Blackwell.

Elberfeld, Rolf. 2000. Laozi-Rezeption in der deutschen Philosophie. In *Philosophieren im Dialog mit China,* edited by H. Schneider, 141–165. Köln: Chora.

———. 2003. Heidegger und das ostasiatischen Denken. Annäherungen zwischen fremden Welten. In Thöma (2003) 468–473.

Emad, Parvis, and Kenneth Maly. 1999. Translator's Foreword [to *Contributions to Philosophy*]. In [1936–38] xv–xliv.

Feenberg, Andrew. 2000. The ontic and the ontological in Heidegger's philosophy of technology. *Inquiry* 43:445–450.

Fell, Joseph P. 1971. Heidegger's notion of two beginnings. *Review of Metaphysics* 25:213–237.

Fischer-Barnicol, Hans A. 1977. Spiegelungen—Vermittlungen. In Neske (1977) 87–104.

Fóti, Véronique M. 1992. *Heidegger and the Poets.* New Jersey/London: Humanities Press.

Frege, Gottlob. 1892. Über Sinn und Bedeutung. *Zeitschrift für Philosophie und Philosophische Kritik* 100:25–50.

Fried, Gregory. 2000. *Heidegger's Polemos. From Being to Politics.* New Haven & London: Yale University Press.

Fu, Charles Wei-hsun. 1978. The trans-onto-theo-logical foundations of language in Heidegger and Taoism. *Journal of Chinese Philosophy* 5:301–333.

Gadamer, H-G. 1984. The hermeneutics of suspicion. In *Hermeneutics: Questions and Prospects,* edited by G. Shapiro and A. Sica, 54–65. Amherst: The University of Massachusetts Press.

Gander, Hans-Helmuth, ed. 1993. *Europa und die Philosophie.* Frankfurt am Main: Vittorio Klostermann.

Gao, Ming. 1996. *The Laozi on the Silk Scrolls* (in Chinese). Beijing: Zhonghua Shuju.

Gosetti-Ferencei, J.A. 2004. *Heidegger, Hölderlin, and the Subject of Poetic Language: Toward a new poetics of Dasein.* New York: Fordham University Press.

Graham, A. C. 1981. *Chuang-Tzu. The Inner Chapters.* Indianapolis: Hackett Publishing Company.

———. 1989. *Disputers of the Tao. Philosophical arguments in ancient China.* Chicago/La Salle, Illinois: Open Court.

———. 1990. *Studies in Chinese Philosophy.* Albany NY: State University of New York Press.

Groth, M. 2004. *Translating Heidegger.* New York: Humanity Books.

Halbfass, Wilhelm. 1988. *India and Europe. An Essay in Understanding.* Albany: State University of New York Press.

Hansen, Chad. 1983a. *Language and Logic in Ancient China.* Ann Arbor: University of Michigan Press.

———. 1983b. A Tao of Tao in Chuang-tzu. In *Experimental Essays on Chuang-tzu,* edited by V. H. Mair, Honolulu: University of Hawai'i Press.

————. 1992. *A Daoist Theory of Chinese Thought. A philosophical interpretation.* New York: Oxford University Press.

Hardy, Julia M. 1998. Influential Western interpretations of the Tao-te-ching. In Kohn and LaFargue (1998) 165–188.

Hart, James G., and John C. Maraldo. 1976. *The Piety of Thinking.* Bloomington: Indiana University Press.

Hartig, Willfred. 1997. *Die Lehre des Buddha und Heidegger. Beiträge zum Ost-West-Dialog des Denkens im 20. Jahrhundert.* Konstanz.

He, Shibin. 2005. A new study of Laozi's dao and its relation with *you* and *wu* (in Chinese). *Research in Philosophy (Beijing)* (7):39–44.

Hecker, Hellmuth. 1986. Als Buddhist im Gespräch mit Heidegger. *Bodhi Baum (Wien):*52–64.

————. 1990. Heidegger und Schopenhauer. *Schopenhauer Jahrbuch* 71:86–96.

Hegel, G.W.F. 1971. *Werke in zwänzig Bände.* 20 vols. Frankfurt am Main: Suhrkamp.

————. 1982. *Lectures on the Philosophy of Religion.* Vol. II. Determinate Religion. Editor Peter C. Hodgson. Berkeley: University of California Press. *Vorlesungen über die Philosophie der Religion.* Teil 2. Die bestimmte Religion. Editor Walter Jaeschke. Hamburg: Felix Meiner.

————. 1990. *Hegel's Science of Logic.* Editor A.V. Miller. Atlantic Highlands: Humanities Press International.

Heine, Steven. 1990. The flower blossoms "without why." Beyond the Heidegger-Kuki dialogue on contemplative language. *Eastern Buddhist* 23:60–86. Also in his *A Dream Within a Dream* (1991) 161–187.

Heisig, James W. 2001. *Philosophers of Nothingness: An essay on the Kyoto School.* Honolulu: University of Hawai'i Press.

Heisig, James W., and John C. Maraldo, eds. 1994. *Rude Awakenings: Zen, the Kyoto School, & the Question of Nationalism.* Honolulu: University of Hawaii Press.

Held, Klaus. 1993. Europa und die interkulturelle Verständigung. In Gander (1993) 87–103.

————. 1995. Intercultural understanding and the role of Europe. *The Monist* 78:5–17.

Henricks, Robert G. 1989. *Lao-Tzu. Te-Tao Ching. A new translation based on the recently discovered Ma-wang-tui texts.* New York: Ballantine Books.

Hirsch, Elisabeth Feist. 1970. Martin Heidegger and the East. *Philosophy East & West* 20 (3):247–264.

Hisamatsu, Shinichi. 1963. *The Vocabulary of Japanese Literary Aesthetics.* Tokyo: Centre for East Asian Cultural Studies.

Hoch, Erna M. 1991. *Sources and Resources. A Western psychiatrist's search for meaning in the ancient Indian scriptures.* Chur/Zürich: Rüegger.

Hölderlin, Friedrich. 1801. Über Urtheil und Seyn. In *Hegel's Development: Toward the Sunlight 1770–1801,* edited by H. S. Harris, 515–516. Oxford: Clarendon Press (1972).

Hsiao, Paul Shih-yi. 1977. Wir trafen uns am Holzmarktplatz. In Neske (1977) 119–129.

———. 1987. Heidegger and our translation of the *Tao Te Ching*. In Parkes (1987) 93–104.

Husserl, E. 1935. Philosophy and the crisis of European humanity. In *Edmund Husserl: The Crisis of European Sciences and Transcendental Phenomenology*, edited by D. Carr, 269–300. Evanston: Northwestern University Press (1970).

Ihde, Don. 1973. Language and two phenomenologies. In *Martin Heidegger: in Europe and America*, edited by E. G. Ballard and C. E. Scott, 147–156. The Hague: Martinus Nijhof.

IJsseling, Samuel. 1992. Speech and writing in Heidegger's philosophy. In *Phenomenology and Indian Philosophy*, edited by D. P. Chattopadhyaya, L. Embree and J. Mohanty, 318–331. New Delhi: Indian Council of Philosophical Research.

Inwood, Michael. 1999. *A Heidegger Dictionary*. Oxford: Blackwell Publishers.

Ivanhoe, Philip J. 2002. *The Daodejing of Laozi*. New York/London: Seven Bridges Press.

Jaspers, Karl. 1986. *Basic Philosophical Writings*. Editors Edith Ehrlich, Leonard H. Ehrlich and George B. Pepper. Athens: Ohio State University Press.

Julien, Stanislas. 1842. *Le livre de la voie et de la vertu*. Paris: L'Imprimerie Royale.

Karatani, Kōjin. 1988. One spirit, two nineteenth centuries. *The South Atlantic Quarterly* 87:615–628.

Kästner, Erhart. 1973. *Aufstand der Dinge. Byzantinische Aufzeichnungen*. Frankfurt am Main: Suhrkamp.

Kisiel, Theodore. 1970. The language of the event: The event of language. In Sallis (1970) 85–104.

———. 2002. *Heidegger's Way of Thought: Critical and interpretative signposts*. Translated by A. Denker and M. Heinz. New York—London: Continuum.

Klostermann, Vittorio, ed. 1970. *Durchblicke. Martin Heidegger zum 80. Geburtstag*. Frankfurt am Main: Vittorio Klostermann.

———, ed. 1977. *Dem Andenken Martin Heideggers. Zum 26. Mai 1976*. Frankfurt am Main: Vittorio Klostermann.

Kockelmans, Joseph J., ed. 1972. *On Heidegger and Language*. Evanston IL: Northwestern University Press.

Kolb, David. 1986. *The Critique of Pure Modernity. Hegel, Heidegger and After*. Chicago and London: Chicago University Press.

Kohn, Livia, and Michael LaFargue, eds. 1998. *Lao-tzu and the Tao-te-ching*. Albany NY: State University of New York Press.

Kuki, Shūzō. 1997. *Reflections on Japanese Taste. The Structure of Iki*. Translated by J. Clark. Sydney: Power Publications.

Kusch, Martin. 1989. *Language as Calculus vs Language as Universal Medium: A Study in Husserl, Heidegger and Gadamer*. Dordrecht: Kluwer.

Lafont, Christina. 2000. *Heidegger, Language, and World-Disclosure*. Cambridge: Cambridge University Press.

Lau, D. C. 1958. The treatment of opposites in Lao Tzu. *Bulletin of the School of Oriental and African Studies* 21 (2):344–360.

———. 1982. *Tao Te Ching.* Hong Kong: The Chinese University Press.

Legge, James L. 1961. *The Chinese Classics.* Hong Kong: Hong Kong University Press.

Liederbach, Hans Peter. 2000. *Martin Heidegger im Denken Watsuji Tetsuro's. Ein japanischer Beitrag zur Philosophie der Lebenswelt.* München: Iudicium.

Light, Stephen. 1987. *Shuzo Kuki and Jean-Paul Sartre: Influence and counter-influence in the early history of existential phenomenology.* Carbondale: Southern Illinois University Press.

Lin, Yutang. 1976. *The Wisdom of Laotse.* New York: Modern Library.

Lopez Jr., Donald S. 1988. *The Heart Sutra Explained: Indian and Tibetan Commentaries.* Albany: State University of New York Press.

Loscerbo, John. 1981. *Being and Technology.* The Hague/Boston/London: Martinus Nijhoff.

Macquarrie, John. 1994. *Heidegger and Christianity.* London: SCM.

Mair, Victor. 1990. *Tao Te Ching. The Classic Book of Integrity and the Way.* Westminster Maryland: Bantam.

Mall, R.A. 2000. *Intercultural Philosophy.* Lanham MD: Rowman and Littlefield.

Marchianò, Grazia. 1997. The flowers of the *Noh* and the aesthetics of *iki.* In *East and West in Aesthetics,* edited by G. Marchianò, 99–106. Pisa: Instituti Editoriali e Poligrafici Internazionali.

Marra, Michael F. 2004. On Japanese things and words: An answer to Heidegger's question. *Philosophy East & West* 54:555–568.

May, Reinhard. 1989. *Ex Oriente Lux: Heideggers Werk unter Ostasiatischem Einfluss.* Wiesbaden: Franz Steiner Verlag.

———. 1996. *Heidegger's Hidden Sources : East Asian Influences on His Work.* Translated by G. Parkes. London: Routledge.

Mayeda, Graham. 2006. *Time, Space and Ethics in the Philosophy of Watsuji Tetsuro, Kuki Shuzo, and Martin Heidegger.* New York & London: Routledge.

Mehta, Jarava Lal. 1970. Heidegger and the comparison of Indian and Western philosophy. *Philosophy East & West* 20:303–318.

———. 1976. *Martin Heidegger: The Way and the Vision.* Honolulu: The University Press of Hawaii.

———. 1987. Heidegger and Vedanta: Reflections on a questionable theme. In Parkes (1987) 15–45.

Mishima, Kenichi. 1992. Über eine vermeintliche Affinität zwischen Heidegger und dem ostasiatischen Denken. Gesehen im politischen Kontext der faschistischen und nachfaschistischen Zeit. In Papenfuß and Pöggeler 3 (1992) 325–341.

Mohanty, Jitendrana Nath. 1992. *Reason and Tradition in Indian Thought.* Oxford: Clarendon Press.

———. 2000. *The Self and Its Other.* New Delhi: Oxford University Press.

Mugerauer, Robert. 1988. *Heidegger's Language and Thinking.* Atlantic Highlands NJ: Humanities Press International.

Naas, Michael B. 1997. Rashomon and the sharing of voices between East and West. In *On Jean-Luc Nancy. The sense of philosophy*, edited by D. Sheppard, S. Sparks and C. Thomas, 63–90. London and New York: Routledge.

Nagley, Winfield E. 1970. Introduction to the symposium and reading of a letter from Martin Heidegger. *Philosophy East & West* 20:221–222.

Nancy, Jean-Luc. 1990. Sharing voices. In *Transforming the Hermeneutic Context. From Nietzsche to Nancy*, edited by G. L. Ormiston and A. D. Schrift, 211–259. Albany: State University of New York Press.

Neske, Günther, ed. 1959. *Martin Heidegger zum siebzigsten Geburtstag*. Pfüllingen: Neske.

———, ed. 1977. *Erinnerungen an Martin Heidegger*. Pfüllingen: Neske.

Neske, Günther, and Emil Kettering, eds. 1990. *Martin Heidegger and National Socialism*. New York: Paragon House. *Antwort: Martin Heidegger im Gespräch*, Pfüllingen: Neske (1988).

Nietzsche, Friedrich. 1962. *Philosophy in the Tragic Age of the Greeks*. Translated by M. Cowan. Washington DC: Gateway Editions.

Nishitani, Keiji. 1966. Reflections on two addresses by Martin Heidegger. In Parkes (1987) 145–168. Vorbereitende Bemerkungen zu zwei Meßkircher Ansprachen von Martin Heidegger. In Buchner (1989) 147–158. Originally published in *The Eastern Buddhist* (New Series), 1 (2) (1966) 48–59.

———. 1976. Ein tiefes Gefühl für die Krise der modernen Zivilisation. Nachruf auf Martin Heidegger. In Buchner (1989) 193–194.

Ogawa, Tadashi. 1992. Heideggers Übersetzbarkeit in ostasiatische Sprachen. In Papenfuß and Pöggeler 3 (1992) 181–196. Also in Tadashi Ogawa, *Grund und Grenze des Bewußtseins: Interkulturelle Phänomenologie aus japanischer Sicht*, Würzburg (2001).

Ōhashi, Ryōsuke. 1989a. Heidegger und die Frage nach der abendländischen Moderne-ausgehend von einem Text Tschuang-Tses. In Buchheim (1989) 129–139.

———. 1989b. Die frühe Heidegger-Rezeption in Japan. In Buchner (1989) 23–38.

———. 1989c. Heidegger und Graf Kuki: Zu Sprache und Kunst in Japan als Problem der Moderne. In *Von Heidegger her: Wirkungen in Philosophie—Kunst—Medicin*, edited by H.-H. Gander, 93–104. Fankfurt am Main: Vittorio Klostermann.

Oshima, Yoshiko. 1985. *Zen- anders denken? Zugleich ein Versuch über Zen und Heidegger*. Heidelberg.

Panikkar, Raimundo. 1977. Eine unvollendete Symphonie. In Neske (1977) 173–178.

Papenfuß, Dietrich, and Otto Pöggeler, eds. 1992. *Zur philosophischen Aktualität Heideggers*. 3 vols. Symposium der Alexander von Humboldt-Stiftung vom 24.-28. April 1989 in Bonn-Bad Godesberg. Frankfurt a/M: Klostermann (1990–1992).

Park, Bradley Douglas. 2005. Differing ways, *Dao* and *Weg:* Comparative, metaphysical, and methodological considerations in Heidegger's "Aus einem Gespräch von der Sprache." *Continental Philosophy Review* 37:309–339.

Parkes, Graham, ed. 1987. *Heidegger and Asian Thought.* Honolulu: University of Hawai'i Press. Editor's introduction pp. 1–14. Editor's afterwords pp. 213–216.

———. 1992. Heidegger and Japanese thought: how much did he know and when did he know it? In *Martin Heidegger: Critical Assessments,* edited by C. Macann, 377–406. London: Routledge.

———. 1996. Translator's preface, translator's notes, and complementary essay: Rising sun over black forest: Heidegger's Japanese connections. In May (1996) vii-xv, 65–71, 79–117.

———. 1997. The putative fascism of the Kyoto School and the political correctness of the modern academy. *Philosophy East & West* 47:305–336.

Pattison, George. 2000. *The Later Heidegger.* London / New York: Routledge.

Petzet, Heinrich Wiegand. 1993. *Encounters and Dialogues with Martin Heidegger 1929–1976.* Translated by P. Emad and K. Maly. Chicago: The University of Chicago Press. Original edition, *Auf Einen Stern Zugehen: Begegnungen mit Martin Heidegger 1929 bis 1975.* Frankfurt: Societäts-Verlag (1983).

Pfau, Thomas, ed. 1988. *Friedrich Hölderlin. Essays and Letters on Theory.* New York: State University of New York Press.

Pincus, Leslie. 1996. *Authenticating Culture in Imperial Japan: Kuki Shuzo and the Rise of National Aesthetics.* Berkeley: University of California.

Pöggeler, Otto. 1987a. West-East Dialogue: Heidegger and Lao-tzu. In Parkes (1987) 47–78. Slightly revised version in Pöggeler (1998).

———. 1987b. *Martin Heidegger's Path of Thinking.* Translated by D. Magurshak and S. Barber. Atlantic Highlands, NJ: Humanities Press International. Original edition, *Der Denkweg Martin Heideggers,* Pfullingen: Neske (1963).

———. 1989. Destruktion und Augenblick. In Buchheim (1989) 9–29.

———. 1998. *The Paths of Heidegger's Life and Thought.* Translated by J. Bailiff. Amherst NY: Humanity Books. Original edition, *Neue Wege mit Heidegger,* Freiburg/München: Alber (1992).

———. 1999. Noch einmal: Heidegger und Laotse. In *Phänomenologie der Natur,* edited by E. W. Orth and K.-H. Lembeck, 105–114. Freiburg/München: Karl Alber.

Polt, Richard. 1999. *Heidegger: An Introduction.* Ithaca/New York: Cornell University Press.

Polt, Richard, and Gregory Fried, eds. 2001. *A Companion to Heidegger's Introduction to Metaphysics.* New Haven and London: Yale University Press.

Prins, A.W. 1996. "Im Westen nur Neues." Martin Heidegger und die interkulturelle Auseinandersetzung. In *Das Multiversum der Kulturen. Beitrage zu einer Vorlesung im Fach 'Interkulturelle Philosophie' an der Erasmus Universität Rotterdam,* edited by H. Kimmerle, 77–101. Amsterdam: Rodopi.

Richardson, Willliam J. 1963. *Heidegger. Through Phenomenology to Thought.* The Hague: Martinus Nijhof.

Rojcewicz, Richard. 2006. *The Gods and Technology. A Reading of Heidegger.* Albany: State University of New York Press.

Rorty, Richard. 1989. Wittgenstein, Heidegger, and the reification of language. In *Essays on Heidegger and Others,* 50–65. Cambridge: Cambridge University Press. Also in *The Cambridge Companion to Heidegger,* ed. Charles. B. Guignon, 337–357. Cambridge: Cambridge University Press (1993).

Safranski, Ruediger. 1998. *Martin Heidegger: Between Good and Evil.* Translated by E. Osters. Cambridge MA: Harvard University Press.

Saito, Yuriko. 1988. Heidegger and Asian Thought—Parkes, G. *Journal of Asian Studies* 47:576–578.

Sakai, Naoki. 1997. *Translation & Subjectivity: On "Japan" and Cultural Nationalism.* London: University of Minnesota Press.

Sallis, John, ed. 1970. *Heidegger and the Path of Thinking.* Pittsburg: Duquesne University Press.

Sandford, Stella. 2003. Going back: Heidegger, East Asia and "the West." *Radical Philosophy* (120):11–22.

Scheiffele, Eberhard. 1991. Questioning one's "own" from the perspective of the foreign. In *Nietzsche and Asian Thought,* edited by G. Parkes, Chicago: University of Chicago Press.

Seeland, Klaus. 1998. *Interkultureller Vergleich: Eine Theorie der Weltaneignung nach Heidegger.* Würzburg: Königshausen & Neumann.

Sheehan, Thomas. 2001a. A paradigm shift in Heidegger research. *Continental Philosophy Review* 34:183–202.

———. 2001b. Kehre and Ereignis: A prolegomenon to *Introduction to Metaphysics.* In Polt and Fried (2001) 3–16.

Siao Sci-yi, Paolo. 1941. *Il Tao-Te-King di Laotse.* Bari: Laterza.

Sonoda, Muneto. 1989. Wohnen die Ostasiaten in einem anderen "Haus des Seins"? Probleme einer Aufnahme Heideggers in japanisches Denken. In Buchheim (1989) 149–160.

Stambaugh, Joan. 1973. Introduction to *The End of Philosophy.* In [1973] vii–xiv.

Stambaugh, Joan. 1984. Heidegger, Taoism, and the question of metaphysics. *Journal of Chinese Philosophy* 11:337–352. Also in Parkes (1987) 79–92.

Strolz, W. 1984. Heideggers Entsprechung zum Tao-te-king und zum Zen-Buddhismus. In *Sein und Nichts in der abendländischen Mystik,* edited by W. Strolz, 83–104. Freiburg i. Br.

Taminiaux, Jacques. 1994. Philosophy of existence I: Heidegger. In *Twentieth-Century Continental Philosophy,* edited by R. Kearney, 38–73. London & New York: Routledge.

Tanabe, Hajime. 1959. Todesdialektik. In Neske (1959) 93–133.

Taylor, Carman. 2002. Was Heidegger a linguistic idealist? *Inquiry* 45 (2):205–215.

Taylor, Charles. 2005. Heidegger on language: In Dreyfus and Wrathall (2005) 433–455.

Tezuka, Tomio. 1968. Kaisetzu "Kotoba ni tsuite no taiwa," Haidegā to no ichi jikan. In *Haidegā zenshū (The Complete Works of Heidegger),* 137–166. Tokyo: Risō.

Thomä, Dieter, ed. 2003. *Heidegger-Handbuch.* Stuttgart: Verlag J.B. Metzler.

Thurnher, Rainer. 1993. Der Rückgang in den Grund des Eigenen als Bedingung für ein Verstehen des Anderen im Denken Heideggers. In Gander (1993) 129–141.

Trawny, Peter. 2004. *Heidegger und Hölderlin oder Der Europäische Morgen.* Würzburg: Königshausen & Neumann.

Tsujimura, Kôichi. 1969. Martin Heideggers Denken und die japanische Philosophie. In Buchner (1989) 159–165.

Ular, Alexander. 1903. *Die Bahn und der rechte Weg.* Leipzig: Insel-Verlag (1912).

Ulenbrook, Jan. 1962. *Lau Dse, Dau Dö Djing. Das Buch vom Rechten Wege und von der Rechten Gesinnung.* Bremen: Carl Schünemann Verlag (1962).

van Buren, John. 2005. The earliest Heidegger: A new field of research. In Dreyfus and Wrathall (2005) 19–31.

Vetsch, Florian. 1992. *Martin Heideggers Anfang der interkulturellen Auseinandersetzung.* Würzburg: Königshausen & Neumann.

von Strauss, Victor. 1870. *Lao-Tse's Tao Te King.* Leipzig: Verlag der "Asia Major" (1924).

Waldenfels, Hans. 1976. *Absolutes Nichts. Zur Grundlegung des Dialogs zwischen Buddhismus und Christentum.* Freiburg: Herder.

Waley, Arthur. 1934. *The Way and its Power. A study of the Tao-te-ching and its place in Chinese thought.* New York: Grove Press.

Wang, Qingjie. 1995. Heidegger and inter-cultural dialogue. In *Analecta Husserliana,* edited by A.-T. Tymieniecka, 287–311. Dordrecht: Kluwer.

Watson, Burton. 1968. *The Complete Works of Chuang Tzu.* New York: Columbia University Press.

Weinmayr, Elmar. 2005. Thinking in transition: Nishida Kitaro and Martin Heidegger. *Philosophy East & West* 55:232–256. Denken im Übergang—Kitarô Nishida und Martin Heidegger. In Buchner (1989) 39–62.

Wilhelm, Richard. 1911. *Laotse Tao Te King: Das Buch des Alten vom Sinn und Leben.* Jena: Eugen Diederichs Verlag (1921).

Wisser, R., ed. 1970. *Martin Heidegger im Gespräch.* Freiburg: Alber.

Wittgenstein, Ludwig. 1953. *Philosophical Investigations.* Translated by G. E. M. Anscombe. Oxford: Blackwell (2001).

Wohlfart, Guenter. 2003. Heidegger and Laozi: *Wu* (Nothing)—on chapter 11 of the *Daodejing. Journal of Chinese Philosophy* 30:39–59.

Wolin, Richard, ed. 1993. *The Heidegger Controversy.* Cambridge MA: MIT Press.

Wolz-Gottwald, Eckard. 1997. Die Wendung nach Asien. Heideggers Ansatz interkultureller Philosophie. *Prima Philosophia* 10:89–107.

Xiong, Wei. 1997. *The Essence of Freedom: Selected Writings* (in Chinese). Beijing: National Translation Publishing Company.

Xiong, Wei [Hsiung Wei]. 1992. Chinesische Heidegger-Rezeption. In Papenfuß and Pöggeler 3 (1992) 292–298.

Yoneda, Michiko. 1989. *Gespräch und Dichtung. Ein Auseinandersetzungsversuch der Sprachauffassung Heideggers mit einem japanischen Sagen.* Frankfurt a/M: Peter Lang.

Yuasa, Yasuo. 1987. The encounter of modern Japanese Philosophy with Heidegger. In Parkes (1987) 155–174.

Zhang, Xianglong. 1998. A Biography of Heidegger (in Chinese), Shijiazhuang: Hebei Renmin Publishing House. Reprinted as *Heidegger: The Most Original Thinker in the Twentieth Century* (in Chinese), Taipei: Kant Publishing House (2005).

———. 2005. Heidegger on the uniqueness of Laozi and Hölderlin's thinking: An analysis of a newly published text (in Chinese). *Social Sciences in China (Zhongguo shehui kexue)* (2):69–83.

Zhu, Qianzhi. 1984. *A Collation and Annotation of the Laozi* (in Chinese). Beijing: Zhonghua Shuju (1996).

Zimmerman, Michael E. 1981. *Eclipse of the Self. The Development of Heidegger's Concept of Authenticity.* Athens—London: Ohio University Press.

———. 1990. *Heidegger's Confrontation with Modernity. Technology, Politics, Art.* Bloomington and Indianapolis: Indiana University Press.

———. 2001. The ontological decline of the West. In Polt and Fried (2001) 185–204.

Index

Lightning Source UK Ltd.
Milton Keynes UK
25 May 2010
154719UK00001B/56/P